The Missing Cryptoqueen has become one of the BBC's most popular podcasts. It's been downloaded millions of times all over the world, generated countless news headlines, sparked heated debate and discussion, and helped turn OneCoin into a household name. A story about cryptocurrency might not seem an obvious podcast hit, then again, it isn't really about cryptocurrency: it is a tale of greed, herd mentality, corruption, 'fake news', regulatory failure and hype. In other words, it is a story about our technology-obsessed world. Wherever there is shiny new tech, you will find the scammers, grifters and con-artists lurking close by, ready to take advantage of the shifting sands. But, as we uncovered, rarely with such audacity, or on such a gigantic scale.

When the two of us first met up to discuss the strange case of OneCoin, in late 2018, neither of us imagined where it would take us. But the more we investigated, the stranger the story became: a world of cartoonish villains, heroic whistle-blowers and financial ruin. Our listeners began to talk online about the compelling new drama series from BBC Sounds – occasionally we'd have to point out that it was, in fact, a true story. We sometimes found ourselves asking each other if we'd made some kind of enormous mistake – did this all really happen? Why don't more people know about it? And above all, was it possible that the Cryptoqueen herself, Ruja Ignatova, had actually pulled this off?

This book was born out of the podcast and, thanks to the extra time and space afforded by the written word, it delves far deeper into the story. Based on countless new interviews, hundreds more leaked documents, and months of detailed investigation and analysis, it reveals how exactly the scam of the century came about, collapsed, and, for the first time, what really happened to the genius behind it all, Dr Ruja Ignatova.

The story will doubtless change again. And when it does, we'll be back there with it.

Jamie Bartlett and Georgia Catt
Presenter and producer of *The Missing Cryptoqueen* podcast

For all the citizen journalists and armchair investigators who tried to warn the world about OneCoin when no-one else would.

The Missing Cryptoqueen

The Crypto Con That Fooled the World

JAMIE
BARTLETT

WH
ALLEN

1

WH Allen, an imprint of Ebury Publishing,
20 Vauxhall Bridge Road,
London SW1V 2SA

WH Allen is part of the Penguin Random House group of companies
whose addresses can be found at global.penguinrandomhouse.com

First published by WH Allen in 2022
This edition published in 2023

www.penguin.co.uk

A CIP catalogue record for this book is available from the British Library

ISBN 9780753559598

Printed and bound in Great Britain by Clays Ltd, Elcograf S.p.A.

The authorised representative in the EEA is Penguin Random House Ireland,
Morrison Chambers, 32 Nassau Street, Dublin D02 YH68

Penguin Random House is committed to a
sustainable future for our business, our readers
and our planet. This book is made from Forest
Stewardship Council® certified paper.

CONTENTS

Part 7 – The Missing Cryptoqueen

CHARACTERS (SELECTED)

Dr Ruja Ignatova: visionary founder and boss of the crypto-currency OneCoin and its sister company OneLife. Born May 1980 in Ruse, Bulgaria. She holds three degrees and speaks five languages fluently. AKA: the Cryptoqueen.

Sebastian Greenwood: Ruja's Swedish business partner who co-founded OneCoin and OneLife with her in April 2014.

Irina Dilkinska: OneCoin's head of 'legal and compliance'.

Juha Parhiala: the first MLM (multi-level marketing) seller for OneCoin, who was recruited by Sebastian in early 2014.

Igor Alberts: one of the world's top-earning MLM promoters, and disciple of the legendary American salesman Zig Ziglar.

Gary Gilford: a trained solicitor who became co-director of Ruja's private 'family office' called RavenR. His job was to find ways to invest Ruja's personal fortune.

Konstantin Ignatov: Ruja's younger brother (by six years) who became Ruja's personal assistant in summer 2016.

Mark Scott: a corporate lawyer from Florida who was a partner of the respected firm Locke Lord. He set up and ran the Fenero Funds.

Gilbert Armenta: a Floridian financier who became Ruja's lover.

Bjørn Bjercke: a Norwegian IT specialist and Bitcoin enthusiast in his early forties who was approached in 2016 with a surprising job offer from OneCoin.

BehindMLM: a website that critiques MLM companies, with a talent for exposing pyramid and Ponzi schemes. Created in 2010 by a man called 'Oz'.

Duncan Arthur: head of OneCoin's e-commerce platform, 'Dealshaker', opened in 2017 with aspirations to become 'the next eBay'.

Frank Schneider: a former Luxembourg spy chief and close confidant of Ruja's, who ran her security and risk management from mid-2015.

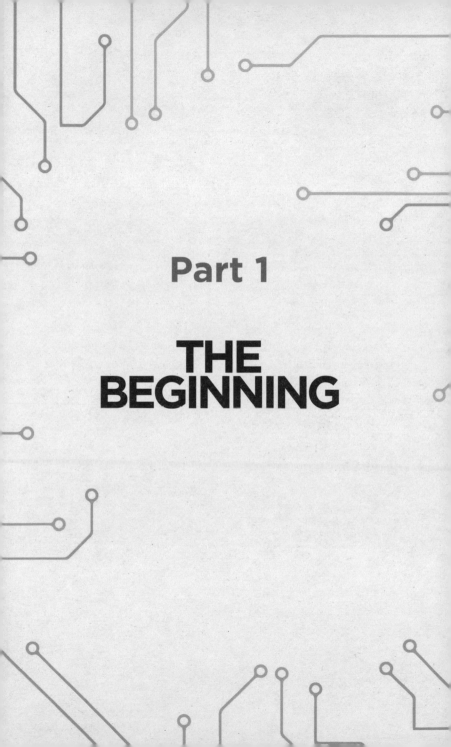

Part 1

THE BEGINNING

CHAPTER 1

THE CRYPTOQUEEN

London, 11 June 2016

Backstage at London's Wembley Arena, Dr Ruja Ignatova was nervously pacing up and down, dressed, as usual, in a full-length ball gown. *I will double your coins, I will double your coins.* She could hear the whoops and cheers of thousands of adoring fans in the background. Ruja wasn't usually nervous before events, but today she was announcing something that went against every rule of financial investment – even the idea of money itself. If she couldn't convince the crowd, who'd already invested a fortune in her promise of a global 'financial revolution', the whole thing would be over. Up to a billion dollars were at stake.

Her second-in-command, Sebastian Greenwood, was on stage warming them up. 'I'm proud to be here today!' he shouted. 'All of you are extraordinary!' The pair had founded the company just two years earlier. And, of the two, Sebastian had always been the better salesperson. But 3,000 people hadn't travelled from 70 countries to see *him*. They'd come for her: the genius behind the most exciting new cryptocurrency in the world.

Sebastian introduced Ruja in his typically over-the-top manner: 'The reason we are all here . . . please give a warm welcome to our creator, our founder . . .'

'This Girl is on Fire' by Alicia Keys blasted over Wembley Arena's sound system and pyrotechnics lit up the stage. Every small detail, right down to the wording on the invitations, had been carefully planned. Ruja knew that appearance was everything, that people will believe anything if you look the part. She strode out confidently, her long black hair, the deep-red lipstick, the embellished red gown glittering under the spotlights, the diamond earrings – everything exhibited success and glamour. Behind her a giant logo was engulfed in flames: 'OneCoin'.

The investors in the audience – the well-dressed Ugandan businessman, the devout Muslim from east London, the Scandinavian door-to-door vitamin seller – could recite Ruja's backstory already. It was the reason most of them entrusted her with their money. Star student at Oxford University. A glittering spell in international finance with a top-end consulting firm. Only 36 years old but already two-time Bulgarian Businesswoman of the Year and *Forbes* cover star. Fluent in Bulgarian, German, English, French and Russian. Some of the crowd whispered that she had an IQ of 200+. Others wore badges with her face on.

It was only two and a half years since she'd had the idea that had changed everyone's life. When Ruja first heard about something called 'Bitcoin' in 2011, she was sceptical. She was from the world of finance and traditional banking, where things were done a certain way; money was backed by governments and run by central banks, as sure as night follows day. But the more she looked into this strange new virtual money, which operated online and outside banks or governments, the more fascinated she became. The inventor was a brilliant but mysterious computer coder who worked under the pseudonym 'Satoshi Nakamoto'. Satoshi created Bitcoin in 2009 and subsequently vanished, but he left behind a blueprint for a whole new type of money that seemed tailor-made for the internet age. Money without banks or borders. A 'cryptocurrency' that no single person controls, which can be sent around the world as easily as sending an email. Where most people saw a weird experiment, Ruja saw world-changing technology. She decided that instead of trying to make money buying and selling these peculiar new coins, she would go one better and make her own cryptocurrency.

In the tech world, she sometimes told the sceptics, it's never the person who has the idea first who gets rich – it's the person who makes that idea work for the man and woman on the street. Jeff Bezos didn't invent e-commerce; he simply made it accessible to everyone. MySpace came before Facebook, but it was Mark Zuckerberg who changed the world. Steve Jobs, Bill Gates, Elon Musk, even Thomas Edison took ideas that were already out there and turned them into something ordinary people could use. That was OneCoin – cryptocurrency for the masses. It might have been smaller than its better-known rival Bitcoin, but not for long. Ruja promised that it was faster, smoother and easier to use. She predicted that, one day, workers would get their wages in OneCoin. Buy their shopping in OneCoin. Anyone who invested now, before the price skyrocketed, would make a killing.

But OneCoin was about much more than getting rich. Bankers and governments had been ripping people off for decades, all because they control money: they print it; set the interest rates to lend it; speculate with it; charge extortionate fees to borrow it. The 2008–9 financial crisis had proved that. Cryptocurrencies like Bitcoin and OneCoin were the solution, thanks to a revolutionary idea hidden within the tech: fixed supply. Satoshi Nakamoto created Bitcoin because he was angry about the way governments bailed out the failing banks in 2008 by printing more money, which in the end made poor people poorer. So he'd placed a cap on the total number of bitcoin that could ever be produced at 21 million, which would be released at a pre-programmed, tamper-resistant rate. A fixed-supply currency that governments couldn't mess with.

Ruja had designed OneCoin to be bigger than Bitcoin, although it followed the same principle. Rather than 21 million coins, there would only ever be 2.1 billion OneCoin in circulation. That number – 2.1 billion – was everything. It was built into the technology itself, set in stone. No one could ever print more OneCoin, not even Ruja herself. No wonder the powers-that-be were so scared of cryptocurrencies like OneCoin. They couldn't control it.

'Now I think it's time,' Ruja told the crowd in her unusual Bulgarian-German accent, adding carefully controlled pauses for applause; 'do or do not. We want to be the *number one* cryptocurrency out there.'

There was barely a soul inside Wembley Arena who doubted her. Everything else Ruja had told them had come true. In the space of 18 months, two billion euros had been invested into OneCoin, pushing the value of a single coin from zero to €5.95 – exactly as she'd predicted. Hundreds of people in the Arena had already become millionaires thanks to her.

But now, she told them, we have a problem. Apparently, OneCoin had got so big so fast that she was running out of coins.

'Can we become the biggest cryptocurrency in the world with what we have now?' Ruja asked rhetorically.

'Yes!' someone shouted from row Z. It was so loud and so certain that Ruja heard it all the way up on the stage.

'No. We cannot,' said Ruja. This was the moment she was dreading. '[We will] create a bigger coin than anyone . . . we will go up to 120 billion coins.'

She slowed down to emphasise the spoonful of sugar that would obscure this dramatic – and, in theory, impossible – increase in OneCoin's supply. 'For you, as existing members, people who supported us in phase one . . . we as a company will *double* the coins in your account.'

The crowd went ballistic. The frenzied atmosphere was more like a religious celebration than a sales conference. Anyone who wasn't cheering was stunned into silence. On 1 October 2016 – just over three months away – everyone's OneCoin would be doubled. And, better still, Ruja promised the value of the coin wouldn't change. Each OneCoin will still be worth €5.95.

'We love you, Ruja,' someone shouted.

'Thank you,' she replied. 'In two years, nobody will talk about Bitcoin any more.'

With a click of her fingers, Dr Ruja doubled the wealth of every single person in the crowd. Not to mention the hundreds of thousands of investors who hadn't made it to London. It didn't seem to matter that she was breaking rule 101 of economics: that when the supply of something goes up, the price goes down. Nor did it matter that she was breaking her own promise: that there would only ever be 2.1 billion OneCoin in circulation, and that 'fixed supply' was the whole point of cryptocurrency. So how was it possible to increase the number of coins by a factor of 50? And without affecting the price?

But if anyone could mint millionaires overnight, it was Dr Ruja.

Los Angeles International Airport, 6 March 2019

'Would Konstantin Ignatov and Duncan Arthur please report to the counter?' announced a voice over the airport speaker system.

Konstantin's flight was already over two hours delayed, which was the last thing he needed. It had been a tiring few days. For three straight days, he'd been stuck in a hotel conference room with his colleague Duncan Arthur, a heavy-set IT guy from South Africa, planning a US expansion of the e-commerce arm of the OneCoin business. At least he'd soon be sitting comfortably in business class, reading his new Stephen King novel and heading back home to Bulgaria.

He had been warned several times that going to the US was an unnecessary risk. But his security adviser Frank, who had mysterious high-up 'sources', had assured Konstantin that he wasn't on any Interpol arrest lists. Konstantin was a little surprised he'd made it into the United States in the first place. On arrival two weeks earlier, he told the inquisitive border officers that he'd come to train with a mixed martial arts fighter. With his muscular frame and all-over tattoos, the 33 year old certainly looked the part. Maybe that was why they let him in.

'Is business class boarding now?' Konstantin asked the Turkish Airlines flight attendant when he reached the departure gate. He was feeling upbeat again. Boarding first was one of the perks of his job.

'Through that door please, Mr Ignatov,' she replied calmly, gesturing towards a door.

The moment he walked through the door Konstantin knew he wouldn't be flying anywhere. Five large men in suits were waiting for him. In a sudden blur of action, two of them twisted his arms behind his back, and a third cuffed him and bundled him through a side door. Before he could splutter out a word, Konstantin was sitting in an interrogation room that resembled the set of a 1990s TV detective series. The sort of room where scruffy detectives from the LAPD play good cop, bad cop. Duncan, meanwhile, was sat in a similar room down the hall.

'Where is your sister?' they asked.

For two years, the FBI had been asking that question.

They'd almost got her 18 months earlier – they practically had her. They'd even sent the Bulgarian prosecutors an indictment request. But Ruja Ignatova was too smart for the FBI. Too quick. Too well-connected. The officers knew Konstantin was just a lackey. He'd only started working for his sister the week of the big London event where she'd doubled everyone's coins. But he was one of the few people who might know where she was.

'Where is Dr Ruja Ignatova?'

Konstantin knew all the rumours and well-rehearsed excuses. She was on maternity leave. She was in London, living in Buckingham Palace. In Russia with Vladimir Putin. On her private yacht in the Black Sea with all the money and a new plastic face. Holed up in a private compound in Dubai. She was dead – captured and murdered by Albanian gangsters in Greece who wanted their money back. He'd even repeated some of them.

'I don't know,' he replied. 'I've not seen Ruja for eighteen months.'

CHAPTER 2

RUJA AND SEBASTIAN

Sofia, 2008

Sitting in front of two large monitors filled with updating charts and numbers as she sipped on a Diet Coke, 28-year-old Ruja Ignatova was frustrated. There was nothing wrong with her job *per se* – quite the opposite, in fact. She loved that the whole world was there on her screen: share prices; currency exchange rates; investment portfolios. It was these numbers that most accurately, most *precisely*, reflected what was going on out there. Being a consultant for the prestigious McKinsey & Company was about the best job available in Sofia in 2008, and her clients were a checklist of the top banks in the world: Sberbank, UniCredit, Allianz. She got to travel too. Like many Bulgarians, Ruja spoke fluent Russian, which meant she was often flown to Moscow or St Petersburg to help Russian banks tap into the European markets. Everyone at McKinsey was ambitious, but Ruja stood out. She was one of those people you could email any time of day or night and receive a reply within minutes. 'I don't want children,' she used to tell co-workers in her slightly cold and matter-of-fact way. 'I'm far too busy trying to change the world for anything like *that*!' Colleagues in the ten-person office sometimes found her a little distant, mistaking her work ethic and obsession to detail for rudeness. Clients, on the contrary, found her charming as well as effective – one major Bulgarian bank had even tried to poach her. No, it wasn't the job that was the problem. It was her.

Working as a consultant for McKinsey was a million miles from the Bulgarian port town Ruse, when, under the never-ending rule of the Soviet loyalist Todor Zhivkov, Ruja was born to Veska and Plamen Ignatov on 30 May 1980. Her parents might as well have been born in another century. They were the post-war Eastern Bloc generation: stoic, hard-working people (Plamen had trained as a mechanical engineer, Veska was a teacher at a nursery) and their daughter's work in financial services was a mystery to them both. Occasionally Ruja would try, without success, to explain to Veska what she did on her monitors all day. Ruja was only where she was because of Plamen and Veska's decision to leave Bulgaria in search of a better life in Germany when the Iron Curtain was drawn open in 1990. The young family (which by then included Ruja's four-year-old brother Konstantin) finally settled in the poor quarter of the small south-western town of Schramberg. Plamen found work fitting tyres and all four Ignatovs lived in a small apartment above a butcher's at number 11 Marketstrasse. Leaving Bulgaria as a child explained Ruja's unusual accent, which flitted between harsh German consonants and rhythmic Bulgarian. In later years, she sometimes told people it encapsulated the two sides of her personality: the impulsive Bulgarian and the rational German.

Like the children of many immigrant families, academic success was non-negotiable. But even by the standards of demanding parents, Ruja was exceptional. In school she was top of every class, brilliant in every subject. One teacher in Schramberg said she was the smartest student he'd ever taught.[1] In a fifth-grade homework assignment, the class were told to learn the first stanza of a Goethe poem. Ruja had only been in Germany for two years, yet the following morning recited all 13 stanzas perfectly. A little later she skipped a year because she was so far ahead. But it wasn't easy being the brightest kid in school. Fellow students found her aloof and arrogant. While her little brother 'Konsti' skated with friends, 16-year-old Ruja strutted around the corridors in high heels and bright-red lipstick like she was too good for the place. 'Nobody got really close to her,' one schoolmate later recalled. Unlike most teenagers, Ruja rarely went to friends' houses after school, preferring the company of her parents, playing chess, or studying. In her end-of-year school-book, 18-year-old Ruja described herself as 'always well behaved and cheerful ... *faultless*', before adding: 'Stop! Maybe we should stick to the truth? OK, fine. Maybe I did take pleasure in tormenting some students. I was always look-ing for the chance to spread new amusing stories about them.'

Everyone agreed she was destined for greatness. At 18, she won a prestigious scholarship to Konstanz University, one of Germany's elite 'Universities of Excellence', where she completed a PhD in Law, during which she also completed a distance learning course in economics from the university of Hagen. And, just like in high school, she had interests beyond her years. She toyed with politics, briefly becoming a student representative of the centre-right Christian Democratic Union party. While most students attended lectures in track-suits and joggers, Ruja turned up smartly dressed and perfectly groomed. While studying, she met, fell in love with, and eventually married, Björn Strehl, a fellow law student who was ambitious and intelligent. 'It was love at first sight,' Ruja said in a later interview. 'I immediately knew, this guy I will marry.'[2] Academia was a breeze too: after Konstanz, she was accepted into Oxford University for a master's degree in

Comparative European Law. It was always the same story: she stood out as painfully clever yet aloof. Always distant, always top.

No – working for McKinsey wasn't the problem. The problem was her ambition. From a young age, Ruja told friends she would be a millionaire by 30. She desperately wanted to be rich – even devouring books in the early hours about how to make money. But she was already 28 and, with a financial crisis brewing, in danger of becoming just another successful person. That wasn't enough for the woman who was always the smartest in the room.

Stockholm, June 2010

Sebastian Greenwood looked around the quay in front of Stockholm's grand Royal Palace, feeling pleased with himself. The wedding of Crown Princess Victoria and Daniel Westling was Sweden's biggest event of the decade. It was so important that the Swedish government had declared a 13-day national holiday called *Love Stockholm 2010*. TV companies from all over the world clustered and jostled for the perfect shot of the royal steamship SS *Orion*, which had been restored for the occasion. There had been a bun fight over the sponsorship slots – Volvo, Ericsson and IKEA were all desperate to get their famous logos associated with *Love Stockholm*.

Somehow Sebastian had managed to finagle his company, SiteTalk, a sponsorship slot alongside these household names.[3] For the fresh-faced 33-year-old PR guy, who'd only been working for SiteTalk for a few months, it was a huge coup. Career defining? Sebastian would say so. Then again, Sebastian would say anything for effect. He was a born publicist. Although naturally shy, even as a pupil at the exclusive

Östra Real secondary school, he was supremely confident in his own abilities and understood the power of showmanship.[4] His dream was to become a successful entrepreneur, and, by his late twenties, he'd set up several websites dedicated to himself and filled with brazen self-promotion: 'Much can be said about Sebastian Greenwood,' read one. 'However, the best way to talk about Sebastian Greenwood may just be that he is the most well-rounded person you will ever meet.' In other words, Sebastian possessed the perfect mix of charm and bullshit for PR.

That combination had obviously worked on the organisers of *Love Stockholm*, because if they had known anything about SiteTalk, they would have probably returned his sponsorship money. Fortunately for Sebastian, most people had never heard of it, because it came from a strange parallel universe called 'multi-level marketing'.

MLM was invented by accident. In the 1940s, a handful of inventive door-to-door vitamin sellers in California realised they were inadvertently generating sales for their company each time they recruited a friend to become a salesperson, but they never got paid for it. They had an idea: why not pay salesmen a small commission from any sales made by people they'd recruited? *Voilà*! A whole new business model was born. By the turn of the century, MLM had metastasised in a hundred directions, becoming a multi-billion-dollar industry comprising firms like Amway, Avon, Herbalife and Tupperware. Promoters buy products – vitamins, health shakes, coffee, anything – and try to sell them directly to consumers, taking a cut for each sale they make. But the real money is in recruiting a 'downline' of new sellers and accumulating commissions from *their* sales. The year of *Love Stockholm*, roughly 100 million people worked in MLM around the world. While not illegal, MLM is controversial, because those near the top become richer than kings but most people make hardly anything at all. As a result, MLM companies aren't usually invited to sponsor high-profile events like *Love Stockholm*.

Then again, SiteTalk wasn't like other MLM companies. It was special.

The year before *Love Stockholm*, a Norwegian man in his forties called Jarle Thorsen had convened some of the region's top MLM sellers with a promise to revolutionise the whole industry.[5] In a typical MLM business, promoters purchase vitamins or make-up or energy drinks, which they try to sell on. But too many MLM employees were ending up with garages stacked with boxes of immovable product. Everything is going digital, Jarle told the small group in a meeting just outside Stockholm. Facebook and Google don't have physical products, so why should MLM? Jarle created an MLM firm called Enigro (later renamed Unaico). And its main product wasn't vitamin tablets, but virtual shares in a new social media platform: SiteTalk. MLM was going digital.

Over in the US, MLM promoters were still selling Tupperware in the same way they always had: home parties and tedious lunchtime seminars. But SiteTalk transformed the Scandinavians into technologists who talked about 'digital transformation' and 'social networks'. In truth, what exactly investors were buying was vague and unclear – there were few details beyond it becoming a rival to Facebook one day – but, propelled by social media's growing popularity, within a couple of years SiteTalk quickly became one of the biggest MLM products in the region with over 100,000 investors in its virtual shares. A specialised comms firm run by Sebastian's parents was put in charge of the PR, which was how Sebastian ended up on the quay by the Royal Palace in June 2010 doing interviews with journalists about SiteTalk and *Love Stockholm*.

The bosses at SiteTalk quickly spotted that Sebastian was

more than a PR guy – he was a gifted salesman too. He could confidently recite word-for-word an entire sales pitch he'd heard only ten minutes earlier. (And, by virtue of having a British father, Sebastian spoke near flawless English.) He was soon on stage himself, enthusiastically selling SiteTalk directly to investors all over Europe. 'Our growth is amazing,' he roared at an event in Slovenia in early 2011. 'That is thanks to all of you guys!'[6] Sebastian loved the work and was soon spending most of his life promoting what he called the 'next Facebook'.

When the company decided to target the fast-growing Far East market, Sebastian made a life-changing decision. He left his wife Helen, two young children and pleasant suburban house in Stockholm, and headed for Singapore, determined to make his fortune in MLM.

Sofia, 2011–13

Big firms like McKinsey were mostly sheltered from the worst of the financial crash, but not entirely. In 2009, the Sofia office was closed. Economic crises produce victims and losses, but, for the fleet of foot, the fissures are opportunities. Ruja considered returning to Germany, and had recently bought a property just outside Frankfurt.[7] But Bulgaria had changed a lot since the Ignatovs left in 1990. The highly educated children of the post-Cold War immigrants had been flooding back to the country since Bulgaria joined the EU in 2007 and Ruja was impressed by her countrymen's business acumen and excited by Bulgaria's strategic location between European and Russian markets. She also felt more connected to the country of her birth than she'd expected, later telling a journalist she'd been 'missing something the whole time I was living in Germany'.[8]

Deciding to stay was a smart choice and Ruja quickly fell in with all the right people. Before too long she was seen around town with senior politicians – contacts from the Mc-Kinsey or Oxford days. For a spell she even worked at Bulgaria's biggest investment firm, which was run by Tsvetelina Borislavova, the long-term partner of the president Boyko Borisov. Borislavova was a highly successful business-woman in her own right, who was rated by *Forbes* magazine as the 'most influential woman in Bulgaria' in 2012.[9] Ruja looked up to the attractive and successful older woman, even studying carefully how she behaved and dressed.

The one thing Ruja liked as much as money was fashion. She was obsessed with style and image. Her Facebook profile picture at this time was a montage of Marilyn Monroe and Jackie Kennedy: 'My thesis is that most women are either a Jackie or a Marilyn,' she wrote underneath. 'Just for myself, I cannot decide.' These interests opened up less conventional circles. She started hanging around with a celebrity hair stylist called Borislav Sapundjiev, and even set up her own hair salon called 'Funky Hair'. 'Vanity will always need service,' she said at the time. She attended parties with Sofia's most famous PR man Evgeni Minchev (who later appeared on Bulgaria's *Celebrity Big Brother* TV series), and became best friends with Asdis Ran, a fast-talking Icelandic Playboy model known as 'the Ice Queen', even investing in Ran's fashion business. For a while, Ruja planned to launch a line of cosmetic products called 'RujaNoir', although nothing came of it.[10] 'She was very ambitious,' recalls one friend from that period. When she wasn't working or networking Ruja read, studied languages, or went clothes shopping: 'She was always working on trying to improve herself one way or another.'

All in all, by early 2013, Ruja's efforts were paying off.

She was becoming a recognisable face within the city's fashion, business and politics scene. And yet she still wasn't *rich*. That same niggling fear of unrealised potential still stalked her. Although she now had a few business interests of her own, they weren't making change-your-life money. Around this time, Ruja started researching Bitcoin.

Singapore, 2012–13

SiteTalk didn't become the next Facebook. Like the majority of 'the next –' companies, it struggled to transition from hype to serious business. Almost as soon as he arrived in Singapore, the bosses changed the name of Unaico to 'The Opportunity Network' and SiteTalk shrank almost as quickly as it had grown, leaving many investors out of pocket. Although it limped on for another few years, Sebastian left some time in early 2013 after an uneventful and largely unsuccessful spell trying to promote the product (according to one former colleague, Sebastian was fired). But the experience had persuaded him there was money to be made in MLM. The serial entrepreneur in him must have noticed how complicated it was for SiteTalk to pay its salespeople, a common problem in an industry where commissions change weekly and promoters live all over the world, because together with a former SiteTalk colleague called Björn Thomas, Sebastian created a new company called Towah Group Cyprus, which promised to be a kind of PayPal for MLM firms that would take care of processing commission payments.[11] When that didn't work out, he tried again, this time calling it Loopium.[12] Sebastian had a genius for seizing opportunities and getting people excited, but he lacked the application and patience required to turn ideas into successful businesses and it wasn't long before

Loopium was struggling for clients too. He'd left Sweden with a dream of making it big in MLM, but by the middle of 2013, Sebastian found himself travelling between Singapore and Cyprus, and running out of money.

He might have returned home and re-joined his parents' communications firm, but, one day, a former SiteTalk colleague from Hong Kong called John Ng got in touch. John had been involved in SiteTalk's Far East expansion and had noticed MLM's rapid growth in China and Hong Kong. SiteTalk's early success was thanks to the clever way it combined MLM with the latest technology. John had found something that was even more exciting than 'the next Facebook'. It was 'the next money'. It was called Bitcoin.

CHAPTER 3

BITCOIN AND BIGCOIN

Somewhere on the internet, 2008

No one knew who Satoshi was or exactly why he did it, but the roots of his thinking were clear to anyone who paid attention: Bitcoin was a political project to weaken not just one government, but *governments* – plural.

It all started with the Crypto Wars of the 1990s, when a group of early computerists gathered in a niche online forum to discuss how to prevent emerging digital technologies creating a *1984*-style surveillance nightmare. This eclectic band of hackers, anarchists and libertarians called themselves the 'cypherpunks'. For several years, they discussed and designed encrypted web browsers and anonymous emailing systems, looking for ways to enhance online privacy and weaken overbearing governments in the process. But the one technology that really excited the cypherpunks was money. Governments had an iron grip on money – they printed it, they monitored it, they taxed it. They set the interest rates that valued it and made the rules about who could have it. As far as the cypherpunks saw it, politicians had used this power to further their own interests rather than help citizens.

For years, the cypherpunks tried to come up with a form of virtual currency that governments couldn't control, but they always got stuck in the same place. The trouble with creating a new form of digital money was that each unit was just a string of numbers, which could be easily copied. This problem (known as the 'double-spend' flaw) meant digital currency had no scarcity and subsequently no value. A brilliant mathematician called David Chaum solved the double-spend flaw in 1990 with a project called 'DigiCash', thanks to a cleverly designed database that recorded who owned what amount, but that simply created another problem: what if whoever was in charge of the database decided to keep all the money for themselves? For years that was the Gordian knot of digital money: how to create an online currency that was secure and valuable without relying on someone in charge. It seemed insoluble until October 2008 when a mysterious person calling themselves Satoshi Nakamoto posted in an obscure cryptography email list claiming to have cracked it. He called it 'Bitcoin'.[1] 'I've been working on a new electronic cash system that's fully peer-to-peer, with no trusted third party,' he wrote. 'It's very attractive to the libertarian viewpoint if we can explain it properly. I'm better with code than with words though.'

Satoshi received a sceptical reception at first. But scepticism turned to curiosity and then amazement once the cypherpunks understood how it worked. A quantity of bitcoin, Satoshi explained, is just a string of numbers that can be sent to anyone who downloads the specialised software, just like sending an email. The magic lay in what follows. Every time someone sends a bitcoin, it is listed on something called a 'blockchain', which keeps a perfect record of every single transaction made in precise chronological order. But, unlike DigiCash, no one is in charge: instead an identical copy of this blockchain is maintained and verified by thousands of different computers and updates every few minutes, making it impossible for anyone to tamper or edit the entries once they are added. The smartest part was the way new bitcoin were created. In order to stop governments meddling in his invention, Satoshi programmed that only 21 million bitcoin would ever be produced, released at a pre-programmed rate until the year 2140. Every ten minutes a new batch of coins is created (or 'mined'), and to receive those new coins, computers compete to crack a mathematical puzzle. As a final flourish, he made it encrypted and quasi-anonymous, which made linking a bitcoin transaction to a real-world person tricky. Even though the blockchain records the transactions, it doesn't reveal who is behind them.

Even for the technically minded cypherpunks, it took a bit of getting used to, but pretty soon they realised Bitcoin was something special: fixed supply digital money without banks, borders or governments. Satoshi had invented cryptocurrency.

Although it's taken for granted, money is a phenomenally strange thing. Most people think of notes or coins, but money can be almost anything if enough people believe in it. Shells, rare metals, clay tablets and even cigarettes have all been used as currency at one time or another. Until the last century, the Micronesian island of Yap used enormous doughnut stones called Rai. They were far too big to move so the Yapese maintained an oral record of who owned what, even down to small fractions of each stone. The physical location of the Rai didn't matter: one of the stones was at the bottom of the ocean, but it continued to be used in transactions because the Yapese collectively agreed who owned it. In a way, the Rai isn't so dissimilar to the US dollar. For several decades, every dollar could be exchanged for its equivalent value in gold, but ever since the Gold Standard was abandoned in 1971, even the mighty greenback has no inherent value beyond society's collective belief that it is valuable and will continue to be so. Ultimately people accept dollars because they know that other people will also accept dollars.

At first, very few outside the cypherpunks paid much attention to this latest iteration of money. But, like the dollar or the Rai, a growing number of people started to collectively agree that Bitcoin might be worth something after all. In 2011, it became the currency of choice for innovative drug dealers on the dark net who appreciated its anonymity. The whistle-blower site WikiLeaks accepted it as payment when PayPal and Mastercard cut off their supply following pressure from the US authorities. Libertarians and anarcho-capitalists joined too, fascinated by the idea of a currency with a fixed supply that governments couldn't meddle with. Pretty soon 'exchange sites' turned up, where bitcoin could be bought and sold for dollars or Euros, just like foreign exchange markets. The 'price' wasn't set by Satoshi or anyone else but rather what people were willing to pay for it. In February 2011, it reached parity with the US dollar, and by July it topped $31.

Despite Bitcoin's growing success, Satoshi never revealed his true identity. In April 2011, he sent a message to a fellow cypherpunk saying he had 'moved onto other things' and was never seen or heard from again. The elusiveness of its founder merely added to Bitcoin's mystique. Well-known stores started accepting bitcoin, the police started seizing it and news outlets started writing about it. Before long, rival cryptocurrencies were created, all based on Satoshi's original recipe. In 2011, 'Litecoin' was launched with more coins and faster mining. A couple of years later, 'Dash' turned up with added privacy features. By 2014, hundreds of these 'altcoins' had appeared, each promising tweaks and improvements to Satoshi's design.

It wasn't a smooth adoption curve. Dark net drug dealers gave Bitcoin a bad reputation. Although the blockchain itself was impossible to hack, some users stored their bitcoin on specialised exchange sites, which would periodically disappear along with all the coins (850,000 bitcoin was stolen from the world's largest cryptocurrency exchange Mt Gox around this time). Governments might not have been able to control Bitcoin, but they could make life difficult. In 2012, the FBI published an internal document entitled *Bitcoin Virtual Currency: Unique Features Present Distinct Challenges for Deterring Illicit Activity*.[2] 'Bitcoin might logically attract money launderers, human traffickers, terrorists, and other criminals,' it read, 'who avoid traditional financial systems by using the Internet to conduct global monetary transfers.'

These difficulties might have killed off the experiment entirely, but political turmoil in Europe provided a timely proof-of-concept. In March 2013, the government of Cyprus announced a controversial bank bailout, paid for by forcibly lopping ordinary savers' deposits. Suddenly a currency ruled by unchangeable maths and code looked reliable in comparison to money controlled by politicians. The Cypriot 'haircut' transformed Bitcoin from a cypherpunk fantasy into the hottest investment in Wall Street. By April 2013, a single bitcoin was worth $250. And when it was reported in the news that a Norwegian man had bought $27 worth of bitcoin in 2009 and was now almost a millionaire, there was an investment stampede not seen since 'tulip mania' in the seventeenth century.

Nowhere was Bitcoin mad like China. The expanding cash-rich Chinese middle class saw it as an exciting investment, while Communist Party oligarchs jumped at the chance to circumnavigate the country's strict capital controls. The Chinese search engine Baidu accepted it as payment for certain services and almost overnight dozens of warehouses full of computers mining Bitcoin were set up all over the country.

John Ng saw the Bitcoin craze grip the region and,

realising that crypto was the next big thing, designed his own Bitcoin spinoff called BigCoin. But rather than buying and selling this new coin on currency exchange websites, BigCoin would follow the MLM model: people join, buy coins, and then recruit promoters to sell the coin to other people, with commission accumulating up the levels. He started calling around to see who was interested in joining. One of the people he contacted was his former SiteTalk colleague, Sebastian Greenwood.

Sebastian was everything John Ng was not. John, who was a little older, was hard-working and organised. But he needed someone who could whip up a crowd. At a loose end and always interested in new technology, in August 2013, Sebastian flew from Cyprus to Hong Kong's upmarket Kowloon Shangri-La hotel to attend the BigCoin launch party.[3] Three hundred people listened to John talk about the future of money and explain how BigCoin was a 'game changer'. Every new vitamin or energy drink is described as a 'game changer' in MLM, but BigCoin had tapped into something. According to someone present that day, people from mainland China – farmers, teachers, accountants – turned up to the Kowloon Shangri-La hotel begging to invest. Some brought plastic bags full of cash, praying they'd found the next Bitcoin.

Although he continued to work on his payments start-up Loopium which was based in Cyprus (in late 2013 he joined a hearing remotely from there, where his wife Helen was granted full custody of the children), Sebastian soon moved to Thailand. From there he started travelling regularly to Hong Kong where he was often seen flanking John Ng, discussing sales techniques and payment systems. At events he appeared on stage and wooed potential investors. Whereas John prepped his lines and rehearsed his slides, Sebastian would stroll on stage without notes and talk fluently for 30 minutes about 'financial revolution' and 'the future of payments'. In the previous three years, Sebastian had gone from PR expert to social media expert to payments expert. Now he was a crypto-expert too. With Sebastian's help hundreds of thousands of dollars was pouring into BigCoin.

At some point in November 2013, as the price of a single bitcoin surged past $500, Sebastian attended a small cryptocurrency seminar in Singapore. One of the speakers at the seminar was a Bulgarian-German woman who was rumoured to be a financial wunderkind.

Ruja Ignatova's idea itself – a crypto-based pension plan – wasn't especially memorable and she wasn't a brilliant speaker either. But she clearly understood finance and banking.[4] Around this time, a crack within the crypto world was starting to appear between those who saw it as a cypherpunk project and those who thought it should be integrated within the existing banking system. Ruja was definitely the latter – she saw crypto as a money spinner and fascinating innovation, not some anti-establishment fantasy. With her McKinsey and Oxford CV, Ruja *was* the establishment.

Once she'd finished her pitch, Sebastian walked over and introduced himself. Ruja had first heard about Bitcoin a couple of years earlier but had dismissed it. Yet, the more she read, the more interested she became. And a few months earlier, as Bitcoin's price started to take off, she realised that, with her banking and finance experience, she could create her own, less anarchic, version. She was in Singapore looking to raise money to get the new idea off the ground. 'Have you considered multi-level marketing'? Sebastian suggested. It was working well for him, after all. Ruja hadn't heard of it. 'I don't know what it is,' she replied. 'It doesn't sound very good.' After Sebastian explained how it worked, she still didn't like it. But the top-end businesswoman and the MLM grifter got on, which was unusual because Ruja didn't usually like new people. But the pair shared a love of technology, money and fashion (Sebastian's nickname in school was 'Flash' because he was obsessed with clothes, just like Ruja).[5] Years later, people close to the pair could never work their relationship out. It was rumoured that they started an affair shortly after this first meeting, but no one knew for sure. Even Ruja's brother Konstantin later admitted: 'they had something strange going on. They called themselves once brother and sister. Then you see them hugging. Then you see them holding hands . . . It's just a strange relationship.' But in November 2013, all that mattered was that Ruja and Sebastian had arrived in the same place at the same time with roughly the same idea. Out in the Far East, trying to figure out how to capitalise on the cryptocurrency craze sweeping the world.

CHAPTER 4

MLM MEETS THE 'BITCH OF WALL STREET'

Before the end of 2013, Sebastian persuaded John Ng to hire Ruja as BigCoin's legal adviser, someone who could sort out the boring corporate stuff that Sebastian hated. John found her distant and guarded but he could see she was competent and valued the younger man's advice. By early 2014, Ruja was spending several days a month in Hong Kong, co-ordinating her visits with Sebastian's as the trio promoted BigCoin. While John took care of the overall strategy and direction of the new company, Sebastian focused on market-ing and payments (he even created a new payments system called BigPay) and Ruja chipped in with legal, banking and corporate advice.

BigCoin was going so well that Sebastian was soon neglecting his other company, Loopium. Invoices started going unpaid. While he carried on promoting Loopium in public, Sebastian confided to a colleague that it was strug-gling. Despite a decent salary, one former friend recalls Sebastian travelling with a tatty old suitcase with broken wheels, and barely able to afford a replacement. Things got so bad that Sebastian even accused Loopium investors of trying to steal the company from him.[1] He asked Ruja to help him formally wind Loopium up, which she did in April 2014.[2] As far as John Ng was concerned, this was good news because it freed up more of Sebastian's time to push BigCoin,[3] but Sebastian and Ruja had different ideas.

It's not clear at what point exactly Sebastian and Ruja decided they would steal John Ng's idea, but the more they promoted BigCoin, the more they realised they could do a better job of it. From early spring 2014, the pair worked all day on BigCoin with John, and then secretly met each evening in the business lounge of the Harbour Plaza Metropolis hotel. Overlooking Hong Kong's skyscraper skyline, they started to design their own, improved, version of BigCoin.[4] There was a natural division of labour. With her perfect CV and banking know-how, Ruja could take care of the technology and be the respectable face of the new company, while Sebastian could build the MLM teams and drive sales. 'You as the magic sales machine – and me as someone who really can work with numbers, legal, and back you up in a good and professional way,' Ruja told him via email. 'We could really make it big – like MLM meets bitch of wall street ;-)'[5]

Privately, though, Ruja was nervous about MLM. The promoters she'd met at BigCoin were more like car dealers and budget motivational speakers than the business consultants and Harvard MBA grads she knew in Sofia. Nevertheless, people were arriving every day at the BigCoin office with their plastic bags full of cash. By spring 2014 Ruja and Sebastian didn't have the tech to create a cryptocurrency, or even a network of sellers, but they did have an idea, and a name to match their growing ambition: OneCoin.

For all his gusto, Sebastian didn't know how to create an MLM company from scratch, and most new firms collapse within a year unless they tempt established promoters to join. He told Ruja he needed an industry veteran to help him and already had someone in mind who was perfect: a balding, overweight, middle-aged, medallion-wearing motormouth from Sweden called Juha Parhiala.[6]

Juha wasn't a natural salesman like Sebastian. When he was introduced to MLM by a friend in the 1990s, it took several attempts before he made enough money to call it a career. For a while he'd worked at the MLM coffee company Organo Gold, drumming up mediocre sales with his catchphrase 'monkey see, monkey do'. But he was an enthusiastic showman who would bound on stage carrying a diamond-laced silver skull cane and roar passionately about whatever life-changing product he was selling that year. More importantly, Juha had moved to Thailand years earlier and had established a large network of MLM promoters in Asia who he could potentially bring into OneCoin to kick-start the new company. Almost as soon as he started plotting with Ruja in Hong Kong, Sebastian asked Juha if he'd like to get involved.

Juha Skyped Ruja, and she spent 40 minutes explaining the technology as simply as she could. All cryptocurrencies, she told him, run on a specialised piece of software called a blockchain, an immutable database that is updated every few minutes. It's a diary of the coin, which publishes every transaction made by anyone anywhere using the cryptocurrency. And, thanks to some clever mathematics, no previous entry can ever be deleted from this diary. Cryptocurrencies are the future of money, she told him, which means anyone investing now will make a fortune.

Juha nodded along. And after he hung up turned to Sebastian with a confused look on his face.

'What's she talking about?' he said. '*Cryptocurrency*? I don't understand shit!!'

'Don't worry,' Sebastian replied, laughing. 'I'm going to teach you.'

'*You're* going to teach me?!' said Juha. It was the blind leading the blind.

But Juha's job wasn't to understand OneCoin, it was to sell it. Sebastian promised him that, as the first recruit, Juha would be the top promoter in the whole pyramid, which meant he would make a tiny commission from almost everyone who invested after him. Sebastian's promise did the trick – and Juha agreed to become OneCoin's first formal recruit. He didn't understand anything about OneCoin, and it didn't matter either. MLM promoters don't truly care what they're selling, because their product isn't really coffee or vitamins or cryptocurrency but the dream of a better life. In fact, the most important ingredient in a good MLM company is not the product, but the 'compensation plan', which determines how promoters will earn commission. Sebastian and Juha spent the summer in Thailand thrashing out the OneCoin comp plan, phoning Ruja as often as ten times a week. Juha sat at his grand wooden desk with a painting of a large white horse looming over him, trying to figure out what mix of incentives and bonuses would work best for a challenger firm selling a novel product. 'With a new company,' Juha told Sebastian, 'simplicity is everything.' They agreed on two main ways to make money. First, anyone who sold OneCoin should receive a 10 per cent 'direct sales' commission. Second, promoters should also get a 10 per cent 'business volume' commission based on all sales from anyone they recruit to join. It was simple but lucrative. Imagine that in week one Joey sells Stefan and Aisha €5,000 worth of OneCoin each. That's €10,000 in total, and Joey gets 10 per cent: €1,000 commission. Now let's say that in week two Stefan and Aisha also both sell €10,000 worth of OneCoin. Stefan and Aisha each receive €1,000 sales commission. But here's the magic: Joey, who recruited Aisha and Stefan, now has €20,000 worth of sales in his so-called 'downline', and gets 10 per cent of that business volume: €2,000.[7]

Ruja quickly grasped the potential of exponential pyramidal growth. If the pattern above repeated itself ten times – two recruit two who recruit two who recruit two, then 2,000 people would invest €10 million and Joey at the top would make €1 million just by virtue of being there first. Juha and Sebastian threw in some other sweeteners, such as dispensing with the usual monthly fees or minimum product purchases that some MLM companies insist on.[8] They also agreed that all commissions would be paid out 60 per cent in real money and 40 per cent in OneCoin.

There was a third way to make money too, of course, and that was the most important of all. At some point in the very near future, OneCoin would be listed on a cryptocurrency exchange site where it could be sold for real money, just like Bitcoin. And like Bitcoin, Ruja said, the value of OneCoin would quickly rise. That set OneCoin apart from every other MLM company. None of them – not Amway, Tupperware or Herbalife – sold products that *increased* in value.

By the end of summer 2014, the trio had agreed on the basic business model and sales pitch. OneCoin was the 'next Bitcoin', sold via MLM. Ten per cent direct sales commission, 10 per cent 'business volume' commission, of which 40 per cent would be paid in OneCoin. Investors could make commissions selling and recruiting, or simply by waiting for the value of OneCoin to increase. Ideally both.

There were lots of new cryptocurrencies. But, by combining MLM and crypto, OneCoin was targeting a new market: a non-technical audience that didn't know anything about 'mining' or 'blockchains', but knew about MLM and wanted to get rich. It probably helped that none of the founders were techies or computer geeks. OneCoin was a middle-aged MLM promoter, a smooth-talking PR guy, and a genius businesswoman with a background in banking. Ruja started confidently telling friends that OneCoin could become one of the biggest cryptocurrencies in the world. Maybe bigger even than Bitcoin.

While Sebastian and Juha finalised the comp plan, Ruja got to work creating the corporate structure for the new firm: websites, staffing, company registration, branding. She set up OneCoin Ltd in Gibraltar, which was owned by OneCoin Ltd in Dubai.[9] She renamed some of her old Bulgarian companies and handed a couple over to her mother Veska. She incorporated a second Dubai-based company called RISG (probably an acronym of the founders' names: Ruja Ignatova, Sebastian Greenwood), which would hold her personal wealth.[10] She arranged for her book about investment, *Learning for Profit* – which had been written in 2013 just before she met Sebastian in Singapore – to be translated into four languages and reformatted to feature OneCoin branding. She also opened a modest HQ on Sofia's famous Tsar Osvoboditel Boulevard and hired a few key staffers. The most significant were a pair of Bulgarians in their mid-thirties. An IT specialist called Momchil Nikov, with deep-set eyes and constant five o'clock shadow, was appointed Chief Operating Officer. His scruffy suits and loose neck ties disguised a sharp mind and professional work ethic, traits which were essential as he was tasked with building the company's IT systems in double-quick time. Soon after, Ruja employed Irina Dilkinska, a quietly competent and discreet married mother of two. Irina held a degree in law from the Russian State University of Oil and Gas, and was made OneCoin's Head of Legal and Compliance, in charge of ensuring the firm followed the various laws and regulations relating to cryptocurrency and MLM.

As well as launching OneCoin, Ruja also needed to launch 'Dr Ruja'. She was ambitious and painfully clever but unaccustomed to the spotlight and not disposed to charming people that didn't impress her. She was awkward on stage and lacked Sebastian's easy charisma. But, as the face of a new cryptocurrency in a crowded market, Ruja needed to become the 'Bitch of Wall Street', as she had put it. She hung copies of her multiple university degrees in her office, and incorporated photos of them into corporate PowerPoint slides. 'Dr Ruja' started turning up to meetings dressed in over-the-top clothes and deep-red lipstick. According to the OneCoin promotional material published at this time, 'Dr Ruja' had done 'consulting for cryptocurrency companies' and was 'an expert in the new financial era – cryptocurrency'.[11] In June 2014, she registered the domain name www.onecoin.eu. The landing page read: 'OneCoin, the next Bitcoin. OneCoin is aiming for the sky.'[12]

'I am in,' Ruja wrote to Sebastian. 'No going back now!'

With the corporate structure and comp plan in place, it was time for Ruja and Sebastian to extricate themselves from Big-Coin. The same month that Ruja registered the OneCoin website, she and Sebastian flew to Hong Kong for a large BigCoin sales conference at the Kowloon Shangri-La hotel where she presented a smart idea for BigCoin investors to exchange their coins for shares in an investment fund she'd created called 'CryptoReal Investment Trust'. But that was likely just a decoy to distract John Ng from the truth: that Sebastian and Ruja were on the verge of launching their own, rival, project.

As soon as Ruja returned to Sofia, she had one, final, job to do: building the all-important blockchain that would power the coin. Neither Sebastian nor Ruja (and certainly not Juha) knew how to do it. Not even Momchil Nikov, One-Coin's IT expert, fully understood this mysterious new tech. Ruja instead contracted a Bulgarian IT firm, who in turn outsourced some of the work to some Indian developers, who 'forked' the original Bitcoin blockchain (in other words, copied it and added a few tweaks to make it their own).[13] Just as Satoshi Nakamoto decided at the very start there would only ever be 21 million bitcoin in circulation, Ruja had to decide how big OneCoin should be. Once that was programmed in, it would be set in stone forever. Ruja told her developers she wanted 2.1 billion coins. One hundred times more than Bitcoin.

In July, Sebastian was due to speak at a BigCoin event in South Korea. There was no phone call, no apology – nothing. He just didn't turn up. A former colleague remembers that a few hours later, Sebastian sent John a photo of himself lying in a hospital bed covered in intravenous tubes. 'I'm very sick,' he said. Before long Sebastian was back in Thailand working the phones with Juha, trying to persuade established MLM sellers to stop whatever they were selling and join his exciting new company, OneCoin.

CHAPTER 5

WE SELL EDUCATION!

Bangkok, August 2014

Ruja decided that the OneCoin blockchain would be officially launched in January 2015, but she wanted to start selling right away. All summer, Sebastian and Juha worked the phones – 'I'm going to make history!' Juha told old contacts and former colleagues – but signing up new sellers to push OneCoin was hard work. None of them had ever heard of cryptocurrencies and they were quite happy selling vitamins and energy drinks. The only recognisable name Juha landed was a British promoter in his fifties called Nigel Allan. Nigel had been in the industry since the 1980s and had done stints at several top MLM companies, including Herbalife.[1] Nigel was at a loose end after the collapse of his company 'Brilliant Carbon', which sold carbon offsetting via MLM, and he agreed to become OneCoin's first president.

Pehr Karlsson and Petri Välilä – two Scandinavian MLM sellers in their thirties that were contacts of Juha – also liked the idea.[2] Sensing the chance to get her sales team moving, Ruja flew the pair business class from Helsinki to Bangkok to persuade them to join the fledgling company.[3] But when they arrived to learn about this exciting new digital money, it would have been apparent they weren't technically selling cryptocurrency after all.

Everyone knew 'the rules'. They were stamped into the brain of every MLM promoter. The rules were what distinguished legitimate MLM companies like Amway or Tupperware from illegal pyramid schemes like Business in Motion or Speedball. Pyramid schemes are the evil cousin of MLM – an investment scam where promoters sell a non-existent product, and make commission through an endless cycle of recruitment. Speedball, for example, sold an 'opportunity' to invest in some clever-sounding tax minimisation scheme, which turned out to be non-existent.[4] But thousands of people signed up, recruited others and banked commissions. MLM critics argue there are more similarities than differences, but ever since a landmark 1979 ruling by the Federal Trade Commission, MLMs have stayed on the right side of the law by (broadly) selling real products to real consumers. Amway's products, for example, include high-quality cleaning products and wildly popular nutrition supplements, while Tupperware is so successful that the brand is synonymous with the plastic containers it sells. Both companies also make sure that the majority of promoter earnings come from direct sales rather than recruiting new promoters.

OneCoin's problem in 2014 was that cryptocurrency was so novel that no one knew whether it would count as a 'real product' or not. It was also rumoured that the American and Chinese authorities were considering classifying cryptocurrencies as 'regulated assets', which would make selling them akin to trading stocks and shares, which was a legal minefield.

Juha and Sebastian's plan was to sell education instead. Sebastian explained to Pehr and Petri that OneCoin's product, the thing the promoters would technically sell, was five education 'packages', which consisted of training videos and a lengthy PDF full of advice and information about finance, investment and crypto. The coins were *free* with each package. (To be precise, investors received free 'tokens' with packages, which could then be turned into coins via another of Satoshi's ideas, called 'mining'.* 'This concept of converting tokens into OneCoin is an important phase for validity and truth,' Sebastian told Ruja in August 2014. 'Mining of coins is a concept that is very familiar in the industry.' OneCoin tokens also doubled every few weeks, which was designed to incentivise investors to keep tokens inside the company rather than trying to turn them into coins and sell them immediately.)

The cheapest package was the 'Starter Pack', which cost €100. With that came one education PDF and 1,000 tokens, which could be turned into approximately 200 coins (although, thanks to the doubling of tokens, known as 'splits', that could increase over time to as many as 600). Each package was more expensive than the last – Trader, Pro Trader, Executive Trader and finally Tycoon Trader, which cost €5,000 and came with all five educational PDFs. The Tycoon Trader came with as many as 48,000 OneCoin.[5] Although the website claimed the education packages were 'for those who want to bring their trading skills to the top level', the PDFs were poor quality and contained barely any

---

* One of Satoshi's innovations with Bitcoin was the way new coins were created. Anyone who dedicated his or her computing power to verifying the transactions in the blockchain would compete to earn a very small amount of new Bitcoin. They did this by cracking a maths puzzle, and the winner would be rewarded with a few new coins. Over time, the puzzles would get harder to maintain a steady and predictable supply of coins. OneCoin had a similar system: each investor received tokens, which would then be used to generate the new coins, and the number of tokens it took to 'mine' new OneCoin gradually increased. While Satoshi's mining system was in order to keep supply constant, OneCoin appears to have been designed to incentivise sales.

useful or original information. ('We all know that life has its own ups and downs and that we eventually have to face them,' read one. 'If there are no ups and downs in your life, then you are probably dead.')[6] What investors were *really* buying was the 'free' coins that came with them.[7] True, 48,000 coins were worth precisely zero at that time. (In fact they wouldn't even technically exist at all until the blockchain was launched.) But the hope was to follow Bitcoin's trajectory. The Scandinavian pair didn't know much about crypto but they did know about MLM. OneCoin's comp plan was generous and simple and the tech was exciting. It sounded like something they could sell.

Although there was still no public blockchain, by late August 2014, Nigel Allan, Juha and the two Scandinavians were marketing OneCoin packages. Petri had returned to Finland and created a small team, who set up a website and ran some online ads. Nigel Allan called some contacts and hosted online seminars while Juha posted in Thai expat Facebook groups. They were working like dogs, but most people had no interest in sending €5,000 to a Bulgarian cryptocurrency in exchange for coins that didn't exist yet. Only €20,000 was invested in August, which barely covered the cost of running the Sofia HQ. Some staff weren't getting paid and according to one early investor, Juha started offering free packages to anyone who agreed to join.

The very first OneCoin event took place on 27 September 2014 in Helsinki. By that time, OneCoin had only sold 27 packages, mostly to investors in Finland or Sweden.[8] Ruja – who was starting to worry that she'd been right all along about MLM – promised Pehr that if he could convince 50 people to attend an event, she'd fly over from Bulgaria to speak. Somehow he managed it and, in a very ordinary conference room at the Marina Congress Centre, Ruja confidently described for the first time how OneCoin would become one of the top three cryptocurrencies in the world. Although the attendees weren't sure what to make of this crazy-sounding billion-dollar promise, they were excited by the vision and unshakeable self-belief of 'Dr Ruja'. Pehr must have spotted something in the crowd's reaction. After the event, he bet Ruja that OneCoin would have 10,000 members before the official launch in January 2015.

The single most important word in MLM is *momentum*. It happens when a team is big enough to start growing by itself, just like when a virus reaches an unstoppable tipping point. Most new MLM companies never reach that moment and peter out within a year or two. Everyone, including Ruja and Sebastian, feared that OneCoin might collapse before it even started.

After the Helsinki event, something strange started to happen. There was no single defining moment, no sudden change of wind or dramatic news story. But word started to spread just like Pehr and Sebastian had predicted. Friends heard from friends that there was an exciting new crypto from Bulgaria. The handful of OneCoin promoters noticed that their evening sales pitches were getting a warmer reception, and their cold calls, which had previously been met with silence, now elicited cautious curiosity: *Is it like Bitcoin? Do you really think it's legit? Am I definitely going to make money?* Pehr and Petri picked up steam, some of Nigel's old colleagues signed up, as did a handful of BigCoin defectors. One day in early October 2014, Ruja logged on to see that someone in American Samoa had bought the €5,000 Tycoon Trader package. The next day it was some Starter Packs in Finland and a Pro Trader package in Estonia. Then Malaysia, then Spain, then Singapore, then Germany, then . . . she didn't know how they'd heard about her coin. Word of mouth? An online seminar? A Facebook message between family? That was the genius of MLM: she didn't need to know. It was growing itself.

Within weeks, Ruja and Sebastian were getting contacted by OneCoin promoters all over the world, desperate to have the founders visit their city and hype the coin. In early November, Sebastian and Ruja organised a one-week tour to a corner of the world where OneCoin was taking root more than anywhere else: Malaysia (including Kuala Lumpur), Singapore and Hong Kong.

'I cannot sleep. I can-not sleep!' Sebastian said to 150 potential investors who'd packed into the second floor of the grand Merdeka Hotel in Kuching, Malaysia, on 7 November 2014. He patrolled up and down the large room holding a microphone in one hand and slideshow clicker in the other. 'OneCoin is a once-in-a-lifetime opportunity, just like Bitcoin was a once-in-a-lifetime opportunity!'[9]

The crowd nodded along. They were as excited as Sebastian.

Although it would be tweaked slightly in the coming months to fit circumstance and audience, the basic sales pitch Ruja tested on this first tour hardly changed for the next three years. It pivoted on a single powerful argument: Bitcoin was good but OneCoin was better. Ruja had taken all Bitcoin's problems and fixed them.

Bitcoin was complicated – users needed, for example, to create their own 'wallets' and manage their own 'private key' to make it work. OneCoin was simple: all you needed to do was sign up on the website – and by signing up you could learn about this strange new world too. In Malaysia, Ruja called it 'the people's coin'.

Bitcoin was about speculation and high-powered traders. It was slow and inefficient. But OneCoin was about everyday use: in the future shops would accept it. One day there would be OneCoin credit cards and an exchange site where investors will buy and sell OneCoin easily for real money.

Bitcoin was decentralised and anonymous, which was why criminals and anarchists liked it. But OneCoin was centralised and monitored. Sofia HQ knew exactly who signed up, ran anti-fraud 'Know Your Customer' checks, and controlled the blockchain to make sure it wasn't misused. OneCoin was Bitcoin minus the crime.

Bitcoin's founder was the faceless alias Satoshi Nakamoto who had vanished without a trace. OneCoin's founder was in plain sight with a degree from Oxford. 'It's not every day you meet a person like this . . . especially not in this [MLM] industry,' Sebastian said to the increasingly enthusiastic audience. He had a knack for spotting doubts and seeing them off at the pass. Ruja smiled meekly.

It was true, too. Ruja wasn't like other MLM sellers. There was no brashness or bravado, just cold logic and common sense. That made her argument even more powerful: in every way, OneCoin was superior to Bitcoin.

While Ruja explained the tech and the vision, Sebastian was left to close the deal. Although the coin didn't technically exist yet, Sebastian told the room that when the OneCoin blockchain launched in January 2015, the company would also set up an internal currency exchange site called 'OneExchange' where investors would be able to trade their coins for Euros. The price, he said, would be €0.5 per coin. OneExchange was an internal market, designed for OneCoin users to sell to each other. But, one day, Ruja and Sebastian promised, the coin would 'go public'. In other words, get listed on a large, public exchange for anyone in the world to buy or sell.

No one asked Sebastian how he knew in advance what

the price would be. Ruja had already said something about 'demand and supply' but the audience were already busy doing the maths in their heads. A Tycoon Trader package, which cost €5,000, came with 48,000 coins, each one soon worth €0.5.

'Invest €5,000 now,' said Sebastian excitedly, 'and you are pretty much guaranteed €24,000 within three months.' And that was just the starting price. 'Can you imagine how quick the price of this coin can go up because of the amount of people we have?' Sebastian asked, rhetorically. Of course they could! It was impossible to think of anything else. Ruja had spent the last hour explaining why OneCoin was superior to Bitcoin. If OneCoin reached the same price as Bitcoin, a €5,000 Tycoon Trader package would be . . . well, it would be worth millions of Euros.

Was it so ridiculous? People in the audience had read articles by the *New York Times* and the *Guardian* about how crypto could be the future of money. They thought about that Norwegian guy who bought $27 of Bitcoin in 2009, which was worth almost $900,000 four years later. They'd missed out on Bitcoin and didn't want to miss out a second time. Almost 700 people signed up to OneCoin from Malaysia the month Sebastian and Ruja visited. The pair repeated the same schtick in Hong Kong and Singapore. Each time they were greeted at the airport by a small band of enthusiastic new followers desperate for selfies, before being driven to a conference room full of restless 'prospects'. When Ruja returned to the European winter, and Sebastian headed back to Bangkok, they left behind a cohort of converts who were both investors and promoters, thrilled to be part of Ruja's financial revolution, and getting rich in the process.

Having seen the energy and enthusiasm that her new coin was generating, Ruja installed a member counter in the

Sofia HQ. Each time a local promoter put on an event – a seminar in Germany, a meet-up in Tokyo – staff would notice an uptick, as people bought a Tycoon Trader one week and started selling Tycoon Traders to friends the next. In November 2014 alone, nearly 2,000 people invested over €1 million in Australia, China, Estonia, Laos, Malaysia, Singapore, Pakistan, Norway, Romania, the United States . . . and the stories starting trickling in. People were selling their cars, going without food, taking out bank loans. All to buy more OneCoin.

As the coin grew, so did the Sofia HQ. It transformed from a temporary work space to a fully gassed tech start-up, with staff in their twenties and thirties buzzing around laptops and coffee machines. 'It was an exciting place to be,' one employee later recalled. And unlike most technology firms, the place was run by women: in addition to Ruja, there was Irina Dilkinska, the head of legal; Veneta Peeva, head of finance; Jacqueline Gotcheva ran marketing; and Ruja's old friend Maya Antonova was on accounts. And wandering around the office muttering under her breath in Bulgarian was Ruja's mother Veska, who became an unofficial PA.

It wasn't only OneCoin on the move: 'Dr Ruja', the carefully constructed cryptocurrency guru, was also becoming a minor celebrity. Even for a short meeting with staff, she dressed like she was attending an evening ball. In late November 2014, she won the Bulgarian Businesswoman of the Year Award at a glitzy event in central Sofia and flew a couple of the Finns over to celebrate, as well as her husband Björn Strehl. 'In two months we've done over €2.5 million,' she said in her acceptance speech, which switched seamlessly between English and Bulgarian. 'We are amazing and we're here to stay.' Her parting words paraphrased one of her heroines, Marilyn Monroe: 'It's a man's world but I love being a woman in it.'

It wasn't all smooth sailing, however. Ruja was less well received the morning after when she attended a meeting of Sofia's small but serious Bitcoin community. Ruja listened as developers discussed the problems Bitcoin was facing at that time: drug dealers on the dark net were giving the coin a bad rep; hackers were stealing people's coins; and the press seemed determined to criticise everything about this nascent currency. Ruja confidently told these technical specialists that she was a former McKinsey employee who had built 'a better Bitcoin'. But no one was interested in her ideas about a new cryptocurrency. 'She was very cocky through the whole two days,' recalled one unimpressed attendee, who thought she was 'talking bullshit'. But Ruja left the event more convinced than ever that OneCoin would eventually topple its better-known rival.[10] In fact, shortly afterwards, she lost her bet to Pehr Karlsson. As the OneCoin ticker clocked past its 10,000th member a few days before Christmas, there was a loud cheer in the office and Ruja threw a party to celebrate. They'd hit momentum.

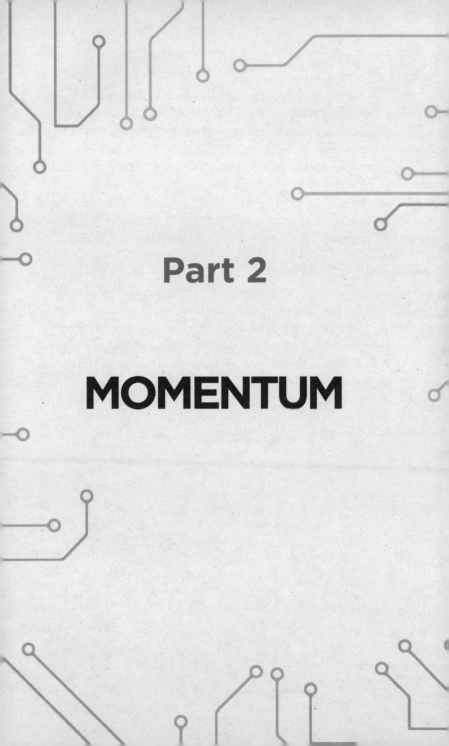

Part 2

MOMENTUM

CHAPTER 6

THE GENESIS BLOCK

Hong Kong, 20 January 2015

Most successful companies have a foundational story – a chance idea while climbing a mountain, a fortuitous meeting, a Eureka! moment. But, in truth, they all begin life in the same way: incorporation documents are filed in an airless company registrar. The birth of a cryptocurrency, by contrast, starts when the blockchain creates its first set of coins, known as the 'genesis block'.

When he created Bitcoin, Satoshi invented a whole new way to record information. He did this using some simple but brilliant mathematics that tied every Bitcoin transaction together in a single unbreakable chain. The Bitcoin genesis block contained a record of any coins that were sent between users, plus a few other technical details. Satoshi programmed an algorithm to reduce its entire contents into a unique 256-digit string – a car crusher for numbers. That unique 256-digit string became the first line of the second block of transactions. Block 2 – which included the 256-digit string of block 1 – was in turn crunched to form the opening line of block 3. Every ten minutes or so, another block of transaction records is crunched into 256 digits, and opens a new block. That's why it's called a blockchain: it is a chain of interlinked blocks of transaction records. By weaving all the blocks into the entries around them, previous entries can't be deleted or tampered with. Bitcoin now has over 700,000 blocks in its chain, each of which represents ten minutes' worth of activity and has a reference to the preceding block. All except genesis – the first block of all.

Satoshi understood the theatre of the genesis block. He slipped a secret message in there, a headline from that day's newspaper: *The Times 03/Jan/2009 Chancellor on brink of second bailout for banks.* Every single Bitcoin contains a homeopathic trace of that headline. Banks – always too big to fail. Governments – always bailing them out.

Hong Kong's 1,026-room high-rise Panda Hotel was a perfect location for OneCoin to launch its blockchain. It was close to the airport, which was handy, given all the investors and promoters jetting in, and its events room – popular for large, expensive Chinese weddings – could accommodate the 500 plus guests expected. 'An unforgettable night,' read one official flier. Sofia was the more obvious choice, but, ever since Ruja and Sebastian's November tour, growth in South Asia had been supersonic. OneCoin even opened a new 'hub' office at the Admiralty Centre on Hong Kong Island in December. It wasn't cheap to rent the Panda Hotel's Grand Ballroom, and Ruja also offered free tickets and subsidised flights for top promoters, but money was no longer an issue. There had been a sales frenzy in the preceding weeks: at least €15 million was invested in January 2015 alone.[1] Momentum was a powerful force.

Sebastian Greenwood and Juha Parhiala were in attendance, of course, as were OneCoin's president Nigel Allan and COO Momchil Nikov. The industrious Finns and Swedes made the list and Ruja's best friend from Sofia – the 'ice queen' Asdis Ran – flew in to co-host. Everyone was excited to witness the moment OneCoin would be transformed from salesman's promise to mathematically clad reality. Ruja, wearing a long blue satin dress, meeted-and-greeted nervously in front of the raised stage. Demand for tickets had been enormous: it seemed like half of mainland China had turned up and some attendees were forced to watch from an overflow room. There was an electric thrill in the air, a sense that something momentous was about to happen.

'*Nǐ hǎo*,' shouted Sebastian, wearing a black tuxedo and bow tie. He only knew two Mandarin words and used them whenever he could. (The other was *xièxiè* – *thank you*.) 'This is an amazing opportunity!' he declared, in front of the 500 attendees and their raised camera phones. 'There is no limit to how many people we can put into the system!'[2] Fernando Rhys, the newly appointed Hong Kong office manager, translated enthusiastically, even adding his own flourishes. Ruja watched and chuckled at her excitable co-founder; Sebastian was nearly 40 years old but had the energy and face of a 25 year old. 'Everybody in this room will become very rich!' he shouted. Unlike in Helsinki, four months earlier, it no longer seemed impossible.

As Ruja took to the stage the crowd stood and cheered. She placed her hand on a large translucent ball, which looked like a Van der Graaf machine. Five, four, three, two . . . when the number hit zero, the ball span and whirled and burst into colour. Gold confetti fell from the ceiling and the room erupted with cheers, champagne corks and photographs as Ruja was almost crushed by enthusiastic selfie hunters.

The genesis block was now launched and the first set of new coins was being 'mined'. People in the room must have wondered what that phrase actually meant. Oh, they all repeated the words – genesis block, mining, algorithms – but few had any idea about the technology behind it all. What *exactly* was happening? Bitcoin's mining was transparent and distributed – anyone could join, and thousands did. But One-Coin's mining process was mysterious and secretive. Some in the crowd had heard rumours that two 'supercomputers' at hidden locations were cracking puzzles and getting the newly generated coins, which would then be sent to investor accounts, depending on how many packages they'd bought. Most people didn't care about the finer details though. They'd just heard it was the next Bitcoin.

It took 11 minutes for the genesis block to appear on the OneCoin blockchain. 'The longest eleven minutes of my life,' Ruja said a few weeks later. But, at last, OneCoin were being generated and hit investor accounts within a day or two. Even better, the 'OneExchange' was ready to start trading too. Each coin was priced at €0.5, just as Sebastian had promised back in November in Malaysia, and could now be exchanged for real money. Fearing an immediate run on the coin, Ruja wisely placed a temporary limit on how much people could withdraw each week, but, even so, some started selling immediately. 'I know two people who have no reason at all to lie who told me they have taken money out already,' wrote one early Swedish investor.[3] But most preferred to sit and wait. Remember that Norwegian guy who invested $27 in Bitcoin in 2009 and . . .

Until this point, Ruja had said she wanted OneCoin to be one of the 'top three' cryptocurrencies in the world. After the successful launch in Hong Kong, she set her sights on becoming number one. Juha, Pehr and Petri were good sellers – they'd generated the momentum that got the coin this far. But there were others who were even better. And Ruja was determined to get them.

CHAPTER 7

SELLING THE DREAM

When Igor Alberts gets dressed each morning, every outfit is meticulously co-ordinated. One day it's black-and-gold shoes, black-and-gold pleated suit, black-and-gold shirt, black-and-gold sunglasses, and a thick black-and-gold ring (all Dolce & Gabbana, except the ring). 'When you look at my clothes, they are *dis-ci-plined*,' he says. If Igor Alberts puts on pink underwear, he walks up and down one of his walk-in wardrobes until he finds a pink shirt and pink trousers to match.

Igor didn't always have walk-in wardrobes full of matching designer gear. He was brought up in an unremarkable Amsterdam suburb where his parents ran a garden centre. Selling his mother's flower arrangements was his first taste of sales, and, after finishing school in the mid-1980s, he stayed with the family business. By his early twenties, Igor was ready to start out on his own, and one day a friend told him about an MLM company called Amway.

All MLM firms are an offshoot of Amway: its origins go back to that original 1940s Californian vitamin company that started the whole industry. Amway pioneered most of the recruitment techniques and compensation plans all MLMs now use. When Igor joined the company in 1987, it was already a billion-dollar operation with over one million distributors selling its health, beauty and cleaning products all over the world.[1] The eighties were a golden era for the company: most cities in America had a healthy-sized Amway network, and some of the top promoters were respected businessmen, philanthropists and even politicians. But even for a talented seller like Igor, his first taste of MLM was disappointing. That wasn't unusual: studies have consistently found that most newcomers to MLM only last a few months before they realise that constantly selling to people – and trying to encourage them to sell for you – is much harder than it looks. Although Igor struggled to get any momentum at Amway, he wasn't discouraged. He loved being his own boss (in MLM parlance, every promoter is a 'unique business') and admired Amway legends like Dexter Yager, the multi-millionaire 'father of MLM', who was rumoured to own 50 cars. And Igor's outgoing personality and boundless ambition were well suited to an industry that thrived on positivity. Even his unconventional appearance helped: no one who met Igor ever forgot his cartoonish face and garish suits. He had the raw materials, but not yet the craft to make it in MLM.

When Igor was 27 years old – that age when you first realise you won't be young forever after all – he saved up and travelled to America to attend a seminar series by one of the MLM superstars of the time, Zig Ziglar. Zig was a proto-Tony Robbins: part salesman, part motivational speaker. People travelled from all over the world to attend Zig's seminars, all hoping to learn 'how to develop excellence in yourself and others'. Igor was blown away as Zig explained how he'd become the top seller in several organisations due to his philosophy. 'Your attitude, not aptitude, will determine your altitude,' he used to say. As far as Zig saw it, selling was a spiritual endeavour and MLM demanded a life of endless self-improvement. It was the American dream boiled down and distilled, the one place where you could achieve anything with sufficient effort and self-belief. For a brief spell, Igor became Zig's unpaid personal assistant, doing dogsbody work in exchange for a free spot at one of his packed business classes. The experience changed Igor's entire approach. What you're selling, Zig explained, is not the product. It's a lifestyle. A philosophy. A dream. The product is irrelevant. Zig's stock phrase ('You can get everything you wish for out of life when you first help other people with what they wish for') became Igor's stock phrase too.

Igor returned to Amsterdam in the late 1990s with his head full of Zig's you-can-do-it-if-you-believe philosophy and his prospects started to change. The secret to MLM was not selling vitamins or Tupperware; it was getting other people motived by the dream so they would sell it for you. That's what the Zig mantra meant – help other people first, and you'll make commission too. By 2012, Igor was a leading seller at the coffee MLM Organo Gold and had built a large and loyal downline of sellers. All big-time MLM sellers are showmen, but Igor was a pantomime act, and people loved it. On stage he bought people free products and on one occasion proposed to his girlfriend. He created his own catchphrases, including 'be the one you're destined to be', and told crowds they could become as rich as him if they followed his advice: don't sell the product, sell the dream! MLM is about personal development and changing your life! You can do it if you really want! He never told potential recruits that unless they were near the top of the pyramid they would almost certainly make no money. It just wouldn't have been *helping other people get what they wish for* to direct them to the study of 350 MLM companies which found that 99 per cent of people who join MLMs will most likely make nothing at all.[2]

In 2014, Igor's personal life slowed his ascent. While pushing Organo Gold in Italy, he met an ambitious young promoter in her twenties with movie-star good looks called Andreea

Cimbala who was running a small Organo Gold recruitment party – a 'coffee club' – at her house. Igor 'fell in love immediately' and told her as much. 'I was direct – extremely Dutch,' he said later. He divorced his (fourth) wife Maria and moved in with Andreea. (Igor and Andreea were later married in a castle in the Netherlands, dressed up like a medieval king and queen.) Intra-team relationships were forbidden at Organo Gold, because it was thought to complicate loyalties and downlines, and, in mid-2014, the pair were forced to leave.

That summer, just as Igor was looking for a new product to push, an old colleague from Organo Gold called Juha Parhiala phoned him with a proposition. 'We are going to build a cryptocurrency,' Juha explained, and asked Igor if he'd be willing to help him write the compensation plan. Igor knew nothing about cryptocurrency, and politely declined.

He tried an e-cigarette company, which didn't really work out. Another venture involving perfume sales also didn't take off.

Word gets around when a successful seller like Igor is free. A few months later, another former Organo Gold colleague called Aron Steinkeller phoned him. Aron was one of three brothers, who were all rising young stars in the MLM world. He'd joined a new company too, and it turned out to be the same one Juha had pitched.[3] Aron invited Igor and Andreea to the next big OneCoin event called 'Gold Rush' in Dubai on 15 May 2015. Still looking for the next opportunity, they agreed.

Dubai, May 2015

There are two types of MLM events. There are the small-scale sales pitches that take place every day – a gruelling cycle of local meet-ups, coffee clubs, online seminars and Tupperware parties that are put on by promoters in order to sell products and recruit new people. (Books on the subject advise new sellers to use a mixture of flattery and promise to get people to attend. Eric Worre's bestseller *Go Pro – 7 Ways to Becoming a Network Marketing Professional* explains, 'When you start with urgency and a compliment, it becomes very difficult for a person to react negatively to your invitation . . . This simple step will literally double your invitation results.'[4]) But there are also lavish set-piece corporate events, which are organised by the company itself. They drive sales too, but the purpose is to bring the company's promoters together, gee them up, and send them back out into the world with renewed hunger. Corporates are the fun part of the job. They are champagne, loud music, bright lights, on-your-feet-cheering events, a cross between an AGM and a rock concert.

When Igor and Andreea arrived at the luxurious Madinat Jumeirah resort in Dubai, they struggled to force their way through the stampede at the entrance. However, when he listened to the boilerplate bumf from Sebastian about 'changing your life' and a 'the rise of an empire', Igor wondered what the fuss was about: he'd heard the same lines a thousand times about coffee and cleaning products. But then Igor saw Ruja.

It wasn't like the MLM talks Igor was used to. As Ruja calmly patrolled the enormous stage in a gold dress and red earrings, lecturing the hall about growth, payments and blockchains, it was more like a lecture than a sales pitch. And yet the crowd were bewitched. When she announced that OneExchange was going to be replaced with an independent exchange site called xcoinx, which had agreed to buy and sell OneCoin on its platform alongside Bitcoin with a starting price of €1 per coin, the hall erupted. Once xcoinx is open, she explained, they would be able to 'cash out' their coins on an open, independent marketplace. And the company's growth was incredible. They already had 100,000 members, who between them had invested €16.7 million in January 2015 when the blockchain was switched on; then €65 million in March; then €80 million in April. Something big was happening.

All corporate events finish with the 'recognitions'. If a seller hits a certain monthly sales target, they receive a title and a gift. Every MLM company has their own ranking system to incentivise this way. (Amway's is based on precious metals and stones. There are 22 ranks from the lowly Silver Producer up to the mighty Crown Ambassador.) The bigger the downline, the higher the rank and commission, and the better the freebies. When Igor first topped $50,000 monthly sales at Organo Gold in 2012, he was made an 'Organo Gold Knight' in front of thousands of screaming promoters and ceremoniously handed a sword. If a OneCoin promoter made €7,000 worth of sales a month in their downline, they became a 'Sapphire'. €40,000 worth of sales – no mean feat – made Ruby. Diamonds were the big league, responsible for a downline that sold at least €200,000 worth of OneCoin packages a month. The Black Diamonds had downlines generating €1.5 million a month, and for that they received a free Rolex on top of several hundred thousand Euros in commission. The top of the pile, the Crown Diamonds, the Cristiano Ronaldos of the company, were earning close to a million Euros a month, with downlines pulling in at least €8 million. The Dubai recognitions seemed to last for ever. The company was only a few months old and there were already 6,633 Rubies; over a hundred Diamonds, who could barely fit on the stage when they were invited up; seven Black Diamonds each received a gold Rolex; three Crown Diamonds . . . OneCoin spent €800,000 at this event just on the recognition gifts.

Three Crown Diamonds already?! Organo Gold, even Amway, couldn't match this kind of momentum.

Before he left for Amsterdam, Igor met up with Juha. Igor had always been the more successful of the pair in the MLM world. But this was a different Juha – he was top of the OneCoin sales network, a Crown Diamond. And each time one of the tens of thousands of promoters below him made a sale, he received a small cut. There were so many cuts coming his way that Juha was becoming extremely rich. As a goodwill gesture, and a tempter to join, Juha gave Igor a load of free OneCoin – coins that he could soon turn into real money on the xcoinx exchange site. (Although Igor insisted on paying for them.) Igor could sell anything to anyone, but blockchains and mining and genesis blocks were from a world he didn't understand, and it made him uncharacteristically nervous. Igor thanked Juha, but didn't join OneCoin. It wasn't long before he regretted that decision.

Igor, equally impressed and baffled by what he had witnessed in Dubai, was a dead end, but Ruja pressed ahead with her plan to recruit the best MLM sellers she could find, especially after the president Nigel Allan quit over a pay dispute. Kari Wahlroos agreed to join ('after a ten-minute conversation with Ruja,' Kari later said). Kari was a former contestant on Finland's *Gladiators* programme and professional hype-man who would run on stage with his own theme music shouting, 'Do you know why I wear shades? It's because the future looks so bright!' Kari was installed as European ambassador.[5] Ed Ludbrook, a more measured pro from New Zealand, also signed up along with some other former Amway and Organo Gold promoters.

The arrival of people like Ed Ludbrook and Kari Wahlroos, who were now armed with a blockchain and exchange site, helped drive sales through the roof. By the summer of 2015, the €5,000 Tycoon Trader package wasn't enough to meet the growing demand. In July, OneCoin introduced the €12,500 'Premium Trader' package. The press release declared it 'a serious must-have package for all members, realising where the coin is heading in the future and who want as many coins as possible'. The Premium Trader package came with all five levels of education and roughly 40,000 OneCoin, each worth €1.

Warren Buffett, the world's most famous and successful investor, has managed 20 per cent return a year. In comparison, the Premium Trader package offered an almost immediate return of *300 per cent*: invest €12,500 and get €40,000 back. Was it too good to be true? At that point, a single bitcoin was selling on the cryptocurrency exchange sites for around $600. Three years earlier it was $9. Everything seemed possible. There were teething problems of course: some investors found that they couldn't always cash out on xcoinx as Ruja had promised because there were daily withdrawal limits and glitches on the newly built site. But OneCoin was booming.

With the Premium Trader package, OneCoin smashed MLM monthly earning records and quickly reached 175 countries. In August 2015, income was over €150 million and rising. When Igor went to see Ruja again at the next corporate event in Macau in September 2015, the Dubai Gold Rush just four months earlier seemed tame by comparison. There must have been 5,000 attendees, all gripped by a sales fever whose symptoms included making a OneCoin hand gesture (a '0' with the thumb and index finger) and talking feverishly about 'the future of money'. Lamborghinis were parked out front. A handful of hardcore fans even paid $10,000 each to meet Ruja backstage in person.

OneCoin was transforming from an exciting start-up to global powerhouse and Ruja was changing with it. The slightly awkward, standoffish consultant was now gone, replaced by Dr Ruja, the crypto-genius visionary behind a multi-million-dollar business: a Steve Jobs, a Mark Zuckerberg. Her clothes were now designed by top London tailors and she was tracked everywhere by a personal make-up artist and camera crew. She hired a security team, who lingered quietly in the background scanning the room for any sign of trouble or over-excited fans. In her home city of Sofia, word about the home-grown tech pioneer was spreading too: between the Dubai and Macau events, Ruja hosted the famous Russian ball in Sofia and her 35th birthday party made the local papers.

The dramatic growth of the company – and her own profile – forced Ruja to bring in outside help. She hired a blockchain auditor to publish monthly reports about their tech and a 'search engine optimisation' team to improve her PR. Her new-found wealth also made her think carefully about her reputation and security. When OneCoin hit serious numbers in mid-2015, Ruja contacted a man called Frank Schneider and hired him to run a 'security and reputational risk audit'. Frank was a former Director of Operations at the Luxembourg intelligence agency, SREL, where he investigated financial fraud. When he left in 2008, Frank set up a private intelligence firm called Sandstone.[6] With his contacts and experience, Frank was a useful man for rich and powerful people. A buttoned-up, thoughtful and well-spoken spook, he was a refreshing change from Ruja's bombastic MLM promoters. Over time, he would become one of her most trusted advisers.

Igor had been watching OneCoin's growth, wondering if he'd made a terrible mistake. Former colleagues who'd been struggling were suddenly swimming in OneCoin money. He decided to travel to Macau for the big event, to take a second look. He spotted Ruja in the middle of a large crowd of fans, wearing a green designer dress and a diamond necklace that was rumoured to have cost a million dollars. 'She looked like a queen,' Igor said later. 'She was dominant.' The pair spoke briefly in the VIP room, where she gave an impromptu lecture about the problems with banking, payments, interest rates and asked again whether he would join OneCoin. The offer was still open.

Later, as he sat through more talks and announcements, all Igor could think was how much better he was than the speakers up on stage. For example, good MLM sellers know the optimum room temperature for sales is 18 degrees – any hotter and potential buyers tend to switch off. You check and double-check! Igor sometimes talked to the building maintenance people beforehand, just to be sure. In Macau, it was 27 degrees at least. Igor looked at Andreea and said: 'We are not too late. We can [sur]pass everyone.'

When he got back to Amsterdam, Igor's head was spinning. True, there was some uncertainty about how exactly OneCoin's 'price' – which was by now €2.45 per coin – was set. Originally Ruja had said it was a market rate. But now she said it was based on a complex algorithm that factored in how many coins were bought, the mining difficulty, electricity costs and the transaction volume. (Later OneCoin would claim it was based on trading activity on their e-commerce site, Dealshaker.) Then there were the online critics, who appeared as the company hit momentum. One specialist website in particular, called BehindMLM, infuriated Ruja. It was run by a mysterious MLM critic known only as 'Oz'. Within weeks of OneCoin's formal launch in Helsinki, Oz had posted a lengthy article describing the company as a get-rich-quick scam that 'functions no differently to any other Ponzi points-based scheme, only they pretend to be involved in crypto-currencies'.[7] Everyone who worked in MLM knew about Oz. Ever since he'd set up BehindMLM in 2010 as a one-stop-shop guide to the latest opportunities, his ruthless dissection of MLM products and comp plans was a constant irritant.

Most promoters thought Oz was just another internet 'hater' who labelled legitimate MLM firms as 'scams' too. After all, Amway was sometimes described as a pyramid scheme by internet critics, and that was listed on the New York Stock Exchange. Excited by the company's obvious momentum but still uncertain, Igor had an idea. He logged into the OneCoin website and found the coins Juha had given him back in Dubai. The value of those coins had increased from €1,000 to €2,500 just as Juha had predicted. He then logged on to xcoinx.com, which looked like other forex trading sites he'd used before. Because of the platform's daily trading limits, Igor could only sell a few per cent of his total holdings each day but, over the next few weeks, he traded some of his coins for real, physical money. Money he could spend in the shops, use to pay his staff, buy more clothes. That was proof enough.

OneCoin made sense to him at last. Cryptocurrency plus MLM created synergy. Use the network to drive up the price of the coin, and use the price of the coin to help grow the network – a virtuous cycle of growth and sales, sales and growth. He called the senior members of his downline, the people he'd worked with at Organo Gold and elsewhere and told them: we're now promoting OneCoin.

CHAPTER 8

MONEY TROUBLES

The myth that MLM sells to the world is that it's easy. The Facebook ads and YouTube infomercials that promote 'earning a few extra dollars on the side' and 'writing the story of your future in the present tense' rarely mention the cold calls, the endless no-thank-yous, the subtle transformation of every lunch into a business pitch. Every few years, one of the big MLM companies is bundled into a lawsuit and – despite their lawyers' best efforts – forced to reveal earnings data. That's how the world knows that 87 per cent of Herbalife (*we give people a chance to have success and change their life*) vitamin sellers earn a median annual income of just $637, and that the overwhelming majority of MLM participants make little to nothing at all.[1] The bosses prefer to emphasise the tiny number of success stories: the one percenters like Igor or Juha.

The possibility that *you* might be the next Igor (if you just believe!) has lured 120 million people around the world into the industry, most of them women. (OneCoin was unusual among MLMs in that it was run by a woman but populated by men, the opposite of the norm.)[2] Even those lucky few who make it to the top require a Stakhanovite work ethic. Igor had always been a 15-hours-a-day guy but after he returned from Macau (and a quick trip to Sofia, where he saw Ruja speak impressively at an event hosted by *The Economist* magazine), he started working harder than he'd ever worked before.

Although Igor was a pantomime act on stage, offstage he was diligent and calculated. He studied the different OneCoin packages, the token system, the mining. He analysed the compensation plan and worked out the most profitable way to create a downline of sellers.[3] (Igor never bought and then sold products – he built teams of sellers below him who signed up directly with whatever company he was promoting.) He designed PowerPoint slides that favourably compared OneCoin to Apple and Google, and started to believe he was part of a financial revolution. Some of this came naturally, because Igor described MLM itself as a form of 'financial freedom' long before Bitcoin arrived. Each week, Igor taught new sellers in his downline the liturgy and craft of MLM: don't firehose people with information; check they are free *before* telling them about the opportunity; remember you are not selling a product but a lifestyle; don't promote on your Facebook page – display your successful life instead.

OneCoin was the perfect MLM product. It had Juha's simple comp plan, a non-physical product that grew in value, and a boss with a PhD in law. Better still, the Sofia HQ put out a never-ending stream of one-time-only special offers, which ensured a constant pressure to buy more. Periodically, the tokens people had purchased would double (the 'split') and, as the moment approached, there was always a sales rush. Another innovation was called 'CoinSafe', where coins were given as a 'gift' rather than as interest, which was an important consideration for the company's growing number of Muslim investors. The company even had a cleric from Pakistan issue a certificate, which said that CoinSafe made OneCoin compliant with Islamic Sharia law.

The only downside, at least as far as Igor was concerned, was America. A long-prepared 4 July 2015 'Independence

Day' US launch was postponed because Ruja was wary of the Securities and Exchange Commission (the 'SEC') who were rumoured to be planning a crackdown on cryptocurrencies. Nevertheless, there were still OneCoin promo events in the US that summer, even if they weren't on the scale originally planned. But after the SEC announced in September that Bitcoin needed more regulation, Ruja decided the risk was too great and the company formally suspended all registrations from the US. (Some promoters continued to sell the coin anyway, telling investors to write down 'US Virgin Islands' on their registration form.)[4]

Even without the US, there were plenty of other markets to conquer. In his first month, November 2015, Igor made €90,000. That was more than his best-ever month at Organo Gold. In December, it was €230,000. Even that was still some way behind Juha, who earned €1.5 million that month, which made him the number one MLM seller in the world. Fairly soon, Igor was earning €1,000,000 a month and he moved to an eight-storey mansion in an affluent neighbourhood on the outskirts of Amsterdam, which used to be owned by John de Mol Jr, the billionaire creator of the reality TV show *Big Brother*. (Igor sometimes showed visitors the room where De Mol Jr apparently had the idea for the programme.) He purchased an Aston Martin and a Maserati, filled his garden with fibreglass life-size animals and installed a ten-foot-high wrought-iron entrance gate with the slogan 'What Dreams May Come'.[5] When groups of promoters turned up to train Igor would always give a small tour of the indoor swimming pool, the sauna, the billiards room, the Swarovski crystals, his 200 plus shoe collection, his expensive watches-in-boxes, his hand-painted Dolce & Gabbana bags. It was a virtuous cycle – the more money he made, the more expensive stuff he bought; and the more expensive stuff he bought, the more people wanted to join his team.

It was the same story in Latin America, in Asia, in Africa. Top leaders were training teams of new sellers and making crazy commissions. Sebastian bought motorbikes, cars and a dozen luxury condominiums in Panama. Juha bought a private resort in Thailand. Kari, OneCoin's sunglass-wearing 'European Ambassador', splashed out on cars, notably a yellow Ferrari 488, Bentley and Lamborghini Huracán.

But the real engine of the company was ten miles below Igor or Juha: it was the hungry promoters they trained and sent out into the world. By late 2015, there were roughly 20,000 active Diamonds, Rubies and Sapphires, between them responsible for tens of millions in sales a month. Some were professional sellers with a dozen years' MLM experience who'd jumped companies, but many were enjoying their first taste of the industry, trying anything they could think of to drive sales. It wasn't five-star hotels and private jets at the bottom – it was hard work day in day out, as promoters sold Ruja's promise in every corner on earth.

In the United States, a trio of Christian promoters ran twice-weekly webinars in which they claimed OneCoin was a 'divine intervention' that had come to them directly from God. Despite Ruja's ban on American sales, all over the United States people were hearing from friends and relatives about a new 'opportunity': a former winner of the Eurovision Song Contest for Israel from New Jersey called Estére Tzabar invested her late husband's fortune; a well-respected oncologist from Montana called Donald Berdeaux invested almost a quarter of a million Euros in 2015 alone.[6] Many American investors wound up in webinars hearing about Ruja's CV and the $27 Bitcoin story. In August 2015, one of those prospects was Christine Grablis, a single mother in her fifties from Tennessee who'd saved up over €100,000, which she planned to spend buying a house. Christine, a devout Christian, quickly invested €25,000. Within a year, she'd invested every last dollar of her savings.

Over in the UK, Layla Begum, a youth worker at a local council in London, attended a large OneCoin conference in Aldgate, not too far from her home. She'd been invited by a family friend and colleague from the council called Saleh Ahmed. Layla didn't know anything about cryptocurrencies – she was only there because Saleh was a friend. But she noticed how well dressed and successful everyone appeared, and how most of the participants were Muslims, like her. She saw a persuasive Dutch guy called Igor Alberts on stage talking about financial independence and freedom; another speaker explained how he'd gone from dishwasher to millionaire. A third proudly showed the crowd OneCoin's Sharia-compliant certificate. Layla jotted in her diary: 'likable, professional yet humble, dress sharp, the rise of the financial revolution'.[7] Shortly after the event, Saleh phoned her. 'You've been working so hard,' he said. 'I want you to be successful. I don't want you living in a council house.' He told her an investment of €40,000 Euros would, within just a few months, be transformed into somewhere between €300–400,000. Enough for Layla to buy the house she'd been saving for. She wired €7,500 over to Saleh's bank account. 'You're making the best decision of your life,' he told her. Soon after the first investment, Layla bought another two Tycoon Trader packages and a Premium Trader. After a few weeks, the coins in her account had doubled in value. Her mother and brother quickly put in another €15,000.

It was the same everywhere. But nowhere symbolised the OneCoin craze better than Uganda. For years, MLM companies like AMGlobal and GNLD had been building a presence across the country. The products would often change – one month it was vitamins, then bed sheets, then vouchers – but the promise remained constant: there is opportunity open to anyone willing to work for it. In the big cities, everyone knew at least one person who ran an MLM side hustle. If an uncle or cousin called out of the blue, there was always a chance it was to convince you to buy the latest anti-ageing cream or face scrubber. And even though there were always reports of people getting scammed, they were drowned out by the handful of testimonies of the lucky few that had become Shilling millionaires.

Dr Saturday David gave up training to be a dentist and joined an MLM company selling vitamins. But, with all the local competition, Saturday found it difficult to generate sales. As soon as he heard about OneCoin – despite being clueless about technology – he made the switch.[8] He'd been sold the same message as everyone else, but with an added African angle: OneCoin was a way to avoid extortionate remittance fees and untrustworthy banks (a quarter of Ugandan adults don't have a bank account because they don't trust them).[9] David became the very first person in Uganda to promote OneCoin and started recruiting sellers. It was slow-going at first but, pretty soon, doctors, health workers, teachers and farmers were quitting their day jobs and joining Dr David's downline. Within months, he had Rubies and Emeralds knocking on doors, armed with photos of Ruja. 'This genius woman,' they would say. 'She will make you rich.' By 2016, 50,000 people in Uganda had invested in OneCoin. Offices – and rival downlines – sprung up all over the country.

The pyramid went down and down, burrowing into small villages via friends and family. One of the new recruits in Uganda's pyramid was Prudence, a pharmacist in her early thirties who ran a small and poorly stocked pharmacy in a Kampala slum where 60 per cent of the residents don't have access to drinking water. Like so many others, she put her day job on hold when someone told her she could become a 'future billionaire' by selling OneCoin. Promoters above her gave her a fancy car and smart phone and told her to dress sharp and hit the villages. 'Try to catch the farmers just after the harvest,' they said. 'That's when they have money.' Prudence found people were so desperate to join OneCoin that they were selling their homes, their land, their cattle, to put every last penny into the scheme.[10] Prudence recruited Daniel, a smart and ambitious 22 year old who lived nearby. Daniel sold his goats to buy OneCoin and then took the six-hour drive west from Kampala to his small village near Mbarara on the Uganda–Rwanda border. There, in his mother's small concrete home in a village of no more than ten families, Daniel recruited *his* mother into OneCoin too. She was a plantain farmer, who'd worked every day for 20 years on her small holding. Over the years, daily physical labour had taken its toll but she'd saved €4,000 to buy a maize store. Daniel told her all about Dr Ruja's vision: how money was changing, how crypto was the future. How they could soon buy *ten* maize stores if they invested now. Daniel's mother didn't really understand it. She couldn't speak English and didn't have a phone or computer. But in the end she bought a Tycoon Trader package and started to dream, too.

For investors, the fun part was planning how to spend the money when OneCoin went *public*. That was the phrase: to *go public*. It referred to the moment OneCoin would be listed on one of the major cryptocurrency exchange sites where it could be bought and sold for traditional money. Xcoinx was just a teaser – a boutique and unreliable website where investors could turn a few coins back into dollars or Euros. The moment OneCoin was listed on a big exchange, like Kraken or Binance, investors would be able to sell all their coins to members of the public at a huge profit.

From the beginning of 2015, Ruja promised this *going public* moment would be very soon. For those lower down the network who'd bought just one or two €5,000 Tycoon Trader packages, *going public* meant a holiday, college funds, cars, houses, clothes. For Daniel's mother in Uganda, it was retirement. Layla Begum planned to buy a house and pay for a wedding. For Christine Grablis in Tennessee, it was a luxurious holiday, buying a house and setting up a charity for mothers whose children had been abused. Sapphires and Rubies – the lower-ranked promoters who were usually struggling to get by in the real world – would meet at OneCoin events and be transformed into prospective on-paper millionaires, discussing what colour Bentley they'd buy when OneCoin went public. And those near the top started to dream big. Igor Alberts thought he'd one day be 'richer than Bill Gates', having bought or earned millions of OneCoin. Dr Saturday David, Uganda's top seller, quickly accumulated €200 million worth of OneCoin and told friends he planned to build his own city called 'CryptoCity', which would run on OneCoin.

Greed or desperation alone don't explain why OneCoin hit momentum so fast, because those emotions are present in every MLM company, including the ones that fail. Something more powerful was at play: the fear of missing out . . . *FOMO*. Most OneCoin investors who put money in around this time said the same thing: they didn't understand the technology but they'd heard of Bitcoin and regretted having not invested. When Bitcoin went stratospheric in 2013, stories proliferated of ordinary people making life-changing money not because of any particular skill or specialised knowledge, but because they got in early. The majority of these early investors weren't destitute, but they were often just getting by. OneCoin felt like, for once in their life, they'd finally got a break.

The collective efforts of 20,000 'ranked' sellers – and tens of thousands more who had sold just one or two packages a month – drove sales to yet another level. The month Igor joined, November 2015, OneCoin passed €1 billion in revenue. What took Facebook six years, OneCoin had managed in 15 months. It raised almost €300 million in December alone. It was madness: investors were turning up at the Sofia office with plastic bags full of cash to buy OneCoin in person. Someone from the finance team used to dash down to the reception and hand over a password for a pre-loaded account in exchange for the money, which was then put in a fridge-sized safe inside a secure room on the third floor. Soon the oversized safe wasn't enough. Ruja even bought a flat in Hong Kong just to store cash. One room was stacked floor to ceiling with notes.

But the momentum driving OneCoin's stratospheric rise was also becoming a problem. The company was growing too big, too quickly. It was felt most acutely at precisely 4pm GMT every Monday. Promoters called it 'Happy Monday': the day commissions were paid. If a Ruby had persuaded a brother or cousin to buy a €5,000 Tycoon Trader package, they would find €500 (their 10 per cent direct commission bonus) in their OneCoin account. (As per the comp plan, 60 per cent was paid in Euros and 40 per cent in OneCoin. Only the former could be immediately withdrawn.) If they'd followed Igor's advice and managed to create a network of sellers below them, it could be five, ten, twenty times more. Sometimes promoters from a city all met up to celebrate the moment together.

Paying 20,000 OneCoin promoters spread over a hundred countries was a logistical nightmare. Roughly one third of all revenue went back out in commissions, and, on busy weeks, that meant moving tens of millions of Euros. In theory, it was simple: when someone bought a OneCoin package, they were given bank account details (often a OneCoin business bank account in Dubai) and told to transfer the money there. They were also given a code which ensured they, and their payment, were registered in the downline of whoever recruited them. Commissions were calculated and then transferred from a OneCoin-controlled bank account into the promoter's personal account.

The bigger OneCoin became the harder it was to keep on top of this. At least once a month there would be a scramble as one of Ruja's banks grew suspicious of the implausible volumes of money being moved, and froze transactions, which led to a mushrooming of new accounts. 'We no longer accept payments in [Dubai] Mashreq bank account,' read one typical press release on 8 September 2015. 'Please use the new bank details: OneCoin Limited, Noor Bank, DMCC Branch, Dubai.' Ruja was frequently in the office shouting down the phone at bank managers who'd refused a transfer or closed down one of the company accounts. 'Money was her biggest headache,' one close associate later recalled. Too much was coming in. One Germany-based company called 'IMS', which processed payments for OneCoin, was receiving thousands of deposits from excited investors – its IMS bank account at Kreissparkasse Steinfurt took in €2.5 million in just two days, which caused the bank to file a suspicious money laundering report to the authorities in North Rhine-Westphalia. (This resulted in an IMS bank freeze in August 2016, although this was subsequently overturned.)

For a period, Ruja may have experimented with the shadowy world of Maltese gambling websites. Malta was a well-known 'gateway' location to move money in and out of the European Union, and the tiny island nation had a thriving online gambling industry. Using a Bulgarian formation agent, Ruja or people close to her set up or purchased multiple companies in Malta all based at the same address: 1, Birds of Paradise, Mosta.[11] These in turn were mostly owned by trust companies based on the tiny Caribbean island of Curaçao. She also enlisted a Vanuatuan foreign exchange platform – where different currencies are traded – called SmartHubFX, run by a peripatetic money man from Mauritius. But most ingenious of all was how she fixed her money troubles in Dubai.

Ruja had several personal and corporate accounts in the Emirate. But as OneCoin's growth went stratospheric in mid-2015, some of the banks there grew nervous. Her OneCoin corporate accounts at al-Mashreq Bank were suddenly receiving millions in unexplained payments each month from oddly named companies like 'Swift Electronics Limited' and 'World Creation Electronics Limited'. And money was going out almost as quickly: Sebastian Greenwood was paid €9.5 million in May 2015 alone, and another €5 million went to a company called Royal Yachts and Boats. By late autumn, trouble was brewing. In September, Mashreq Bank filed a 'suspicious transaction report' to the UAE Central Bank, followed a few weeks later by Commercial Bank Dubai. On 14 September 2015, Ruja told Sebastian that she had '€50 million stuck in space' in Dubai. Frozen.

But Ruja had a brilliant solution. Around this time Ruja flew to Dubai to meet with a well-connected member of the Sharjah royal family called Sheikh Saud bin Faisal al Qassimi. Al Qassimi was in his mid-thirties, and was the son of one of the wealthiest men in the UAE. The younger man was a well-known technophile. Shortly after the meeting, Ruja and Sheikh al Qassimi are believed to have agreed an audacious deal. Although disputed by representatives of al Qassimi, court filings in Dubai suggest that Ruja sold OneCoin Limited to al Qassimi, and handed over three cheques from Mashreq Bank totalling around 210 million Emirati dirham (roughly €50 million).[12]

In exchange, al Qassimi handed Ruja four USB memory sticks. On them were approximately €48.5 million worth of Bitcoin.[13] A little later al Qassimi also appointed Ruja as

'Special Adviser' to his New York-based charity, which may even have granted her some form of diplomatic status.[14]

Perhaps the Sheikh had a particular liking for this strange new cryptocurrency and hoped to get in early. Another possibility (which is challenged by lawyers acting for al Qassimi) is that the well-connected Sheikh could take over and unfreeze Ruja's assets for himself; while she would have access to digital money she could use immediately. Indeed, some months later, al Qassimi wrote to the attorney general of Dubai, explaining that Ruja's bank accounts had been frozen without good reason, that he had a power of attorney over them, and that the whole affair is 'an affront' to Ruja.[15]

Bitcoin swaps in Dubai, Vanuatuan foreign exchange platforms, Maltese casinos owned by Curaçaoan trust companies: Ruja's financial affairs were starting to look like a checklist of dodgy money deals.* She wanted something more legitimate. Fortunately, one of her banks, JSC Capital in Tbilisi Georgia had just been bought by a Florida-based financier in his fifties called Gilbert Armenta. Bringing Gilbert Armenta into OneCoin would end up being the biggest mistake she ever made. But at the time he was exactly what she needed.

---

* Maltese gaming sites in particular had a well-deserved reputation as a being used by organised criminals to launder money: the journalist Daphne Caruana Galizia was murdered as a result of her reporting (among other things) on the link between gambling and organised crime on the island.

Part 3

THE MONEY

CHAPTER 9

THE FENERO FUNDS

Had he not got into banking and tech, Gilbert Armenta would have been a first-rate MLM seller. He was convivial, intelligent and flash. A cocaine and alcohol addiction prevented him finishing his degree in civil engineering at Fresno College, California. But once he got clean aged 24, Gilbert developed a work ethic that few could match. He loved money and appearance as much as Ruja did, turning up to meetings in his home city of Fort Lauderdale, Florida, in Salvatore Ferragamo shirts, statement watches and luxury cars. He wore his black hair jelled back in the old-school way. His background was also in emerging technology – in the early 2010s, he ran a large telecommunications firm in the Caribbean island of Curaçao called 'Curanet', and later bought telecoms companies in Latin America. Although generally charming, Gilbert had no trouble playing the alpha male if he thought it would help him. 'He's a big bastard and a liar,' recalled one former colleague from this period. 'He has more talk than depth.'

By the mid 2010s, Gilbert dealt in the grey zone of finance, including providing prepaid credit cards for pay-day loan companies, and payments solutions for online casinos based in the Caribbean. At some point in 2015, he started providing banking services for Ruja too. As the OneCoin money flowed in, Gilbert set up business accounts in his name, which received payments from OneCoin investors and used his own bank, JSC Capital, to provide prepaid Mastercards to promoters, in order to pay commissions.[1] In September 2015 $85 million was wired from one of Ruja's Dubai banks to Gilbert's Zala Group account at Comerica Bank.[2]

Things didn't stay professional between them for long. Even though they were similar and pig-headed, Ruja and Gilbert were drawn to each other, and, at some point – likely 2015 – started an affair, which soon developed into an intense romance. He started attending OneCoin events and sat at the top table with Ruja and Sebastian at the corporate event in Macau (the same event that impressed Igor). Ruja loved Gilbert's drive: he was one of the few men she knew who seemed as confident and ambitious as she was. And Gilbert was dazzled by Ruja's star power and intelligence – she used to joke she was so much smarter than him. But he also liked the side of Ruja that few ever saw: her cutting sense of humour and generosity to the people close to her. Despite Ruja's punishing schedule, the pair started seeing each other regularly, catching precious moments together between events and travelling. Ruja asked Gilbert to find someone to help manage her rapidly growing personal wealth. Gilbert knew just the guy.

Mark Scott wasn't an especially warm or likeable man. Fortunately, charm wasn't advantageous in corporate law and he worked damn hard structuring deals for his clients. He was good at it too, and for a while represented the former tennis star Boris Becker. Mark had worked on Gilbert's big telecommunications deals a few years earlier and the pair got on well.[3] Mark had recently become a partner at the highly respected legal firm Locke Lord, and was planning children with his girlfriend Lidia Kolesnikova. He was also looking for ways to make some decent money for himself.

When Gilbert told Mark about Ruja, she probably didn't seem so dissimilar to many of the clients he'd worked for during his 25-year career. They very often wanted the same thing: to use whatever combination of offshore companies, corporate structures and low-tax jurisdictions that would legally protect their hard-earned money. New millionaires often get worried that if something goes wrong – a divorce, a lawsuit, whatever – their new-found wealth will go up in smoke. 'She is a friend and client,' Gilbert told Mark in September 2015. 'Please support her as family.' Mark and Ruja arranged a Skype call and he typed a highly unusual reminder into his calendar: 'T[elephone] Call to discuss money transfer / laundering issues'.

'Asset protection,' Ruja told him. 'The business is profitable and I have some personal assets that I want to protect from several risks.'[4] She wanted her money turned into assets: company shares, funds, properties. Not just sitting in bank accounts like it had been in Dubai. Mark could help, but his fee was 10 per cent of whatever he looked after. A big sum – but worth every bit if he could keep her money safe.

The phrase 'investment fund' is commonplace in business, but most people don't know what it means. Let's say you suddenly find yourself with millions of Euros. There's no point putting it in the bank, since interest rates barely cover inflation. Instead, you might put it in a fund run by a professional who uses their know-how to invest your money in well-performing stocks, under-valued property, and exciting start-ups. Some investment funds are generic and bring in hundreds of millions of Euros from investors all over the world. Others are restricted to specific sectors, like energy or technology. A high net-worth individual might commit a few million to a fund, which the investment manager will draw from whenever he or she spots a good opportunity. According to the Standard & Poor Index, America's 500 largest publicly listed companies have averaged 8 per cent annual growth since the 1950s. A good investment manager like Mark would hope to beat that.

That was Mark's idea: to set up four $100 million investment funds. That meant a lot of paperwork, and Ruja had made it clear she was in a rush. 'Time is ticking,' she told him in January 2016. 'How can we move please?' For added security, Ruja sent him an encrypted phone that was practically un-hackable, even for the FBI.

Mark's firm Locke Lord also took on additional work for Ruja, managing some planned property deals in London. Between January and April 2016, Locke Lord billed Ruja $85,687 for their work on her property deals, but Mark's investment fund plan wasn't included: it was Mark's personal project which he kept hidden from the firm. (Lawyers for Locke Lord emphasise that OneCoin had never been among its clients. They say Mark Scott's work for OneCoin was not done on behalf of Locke Lord and that the company had not been aware of it until almost two years after he had left the company.)

The firm's crypto specialist consultant Robert Courtneidge was privately hired by OneCoin to design a 'roadmap' to help the company to become recognised by the crypto sector. The roadmap boiled down to getting OneCoin accepted on open crypto exchanges and by merchants. Courtneidge recommended OneCoin be split into two distinct entities: 'OneCoin' the cryptocurrency continued to be technically based in Dubai, but the MLM network – the promoters who actually sold the coin – became 'OneLife' on 11 June

2016 and was incorporated in Belize. (According to Court-neidge the reason for this change was that separating the coin from the MLM sales would help it become a competitor to Bitcoin – but in any case as implemented by Ruja it made very little difference to the running of the business.)[5]

On 31 January 2016, Mark sent Ruja the first invoice of $425,000, an advance payment for 'our new project', he said, that would cover 'all attorneys and CPAs [certified public accountants] I would require in different jurisdictions, plus travel and entity formation and dissolution expenses'. He also asked Ruja to stop using his Locke Lord email address.[6] The four investment funds 'would protect all your assets', he assured her.

The invoice was paid in full within 24 hours.

A few days after she'd given Mark the green light, Ruja flew to London and set up camp at the penthouse suite in the Four Seasons Hotel on the exclusive Park Lane. Ruja loved the Four Seasons. The £1,000-a-night price tag was worth it for the black marble lobby and old-worldly elegance. She stayed for two weeks, only leaving in the hotel's rental Rolls-Royce for the occasional meeting or dinner. (She did find time to arrange a PR photoshoot though. The photographer noticed a bodyguard outside her door, which was strange. He'd done shoots with Hollywood stars before. Even Will Smith didn't have bodyguards at hotels.)

When Mark flew to London on 9 February 2016 to meet Ruja at the Four Seasons, the pair spoke in person for the first time. The 'Fenero Funds', as he called them, would comprise four $100 million funds – three registered to the British Virgin Islands and one to the Caymans.[7] They would invest in struggling technology companies in the EU, mostly in the

UK and Ireland. Although it would still be her money, Ruja's name would not appear on the companies' documents. Instead, the Fenero Funds would be owned on paper by a British Virgin Islands investment management firm that Mark was setting up called 'MSSI International Consulting BVI', which would in turn be owned by 'MSS International Consulting', a company in Florida that Mark had owned for years. Some purchases made with the funds would be held by companies he would set up in Ireland, which would also be owned by MSSI International Consulting BVI.[8] Each fund, and each Irish company, would have their own bank account, all controlled by Mark.[9]

The tricky bit was actually getting the money in. The simplest way was to send the money in large chunks, of €5 or €10 million at a time – and Ruja had companies ready to help do it. Between February and March 2016, Ruja – via a Dubai formation agent – signed three service agreements with a set of companies collectively called International Marketing Services ('IMS'). IMS was owned by Frank Ricketts, a Ugandan-born white man in his late fifties who knew more about MLM rules and loopholes than anyone alive. He'd already been working with OneCoin – in fact, it was one of his German IMS bank accounts that had been reported to the German authorities in December 2015. Years before One-Coin he'd also worked with Sebastian at SiteTalk. According to these service agreements, IMS agreed to provide 'implementation, logistics and establishment of new corporate structures and banking in worldwide juristictions . . .' (According to Ricketts, Ruja took control of IMS 'behind our back'.)[10]

One of Gilbert Armenta's companies, called Fates, which already held significant amounts of her money, could also send some over. And Ruja asked Irina Dilkinska, her head of legal and compliance, to create a company called 'B&N

Consult' to move the rest.[11] Once the money was transferred to a Fenero Fund, Mark would be able to invest it however Ruja wanted.

Ruja must have been pleased with Mark's plan. She'd finally entered the world of the super-rich: a place where money never sits still, and clever people work 24/7 turning your cash into assets and shares to make you even richer. Mark headed to back to Florida (and then on to the British Virgin Islands and the Caymans) to finalise the paperwork and start opening the bank accounts. But Ruja didn't leave the Four Seasons after she finalised the Fenero Funds plan. She had other, even more important, business to attend to in London.

CHAPTER 10

LONDON CALLING

Ever since Ruja left university her work came first. Every moment relaxing was time that could be more productively used. And for the first two years at OneCoin she embraced workaholism, just as she had at McKinsey: her life was a punishing routine of meetings, late-night phone calls, endless long-haul flights, and high-profile presentations and speeches. She lived and breathed OneCoin. She had adoring fans on every continent, more money than she could possibly spend, and absolute control over a company that promised to revolutionise money itself. Finally, she was realising her potential.

But fulfilling one's dreams rarely satisfies ambitious people for long. She'd been working flat out for over a decade, and was now well into her mid-thirties. According to close friends, soon after OneCoin took off, Ruja decided she wanted to become a mother and by early 2016 there were rumours among staff and top promoters that Ruja was planning a surrogacy pregnancy. At no point in her extensive public speaking – right until the days before the birth – is there evidence that Ruja was visibly pregnant. The information during this period is limited but shortly before her two-week spell in London, Ruja found out that she would be due a baby in late Autumn 2016.

Ruja was thrilled by the news but realised that it would

mean a lot of changes in her life. Her trip to London was intended not just to meet with Mark Scott, but also to start planning her new life as a mother. Ruja thought that London would be a better place to raise a child than Frankfurt, Sofia or Dubai. So, after Mark left for Florida to deal with Fenero, she turned her attention to opening a 'family office' in the heart of the city.

A family office is like a private investment fund, except it looks after the wealth of a single person. As the owner, Ruja would be able to send some of her money to the family office and handpick a team to advise on how to best invest it. Family offices can also be a good way to pass large sums of money between family members – something that was now more pressing.

Ruja spent several days in her penthouse suite at the Four Seasons interviewing candidates to work for her new family office, which she named 'RavenR Capital'. (Because of her raven-black hair and initial 'R'. In fact, there were two RavenR companies: one in Dubai, created in 2015 to hold some of Ruja's personal wealth there; and RavenR Capital in London.) Gary Gilford, a qualified solicitor in his late forties who'd done a stint at Citibank, agreed to join as director after she promised him it would be well resourced and professionally run. Ruja also hired some sharp financial brains, including a pair of Russians called Anton Zherebtsov and Anatoly Gorlov, and Max von Arnim, a specialist in private equity who supported RavenR Capital as a part-time external consultant.

London was slowly becoming her city of choice. On 23 March 2016, her offer of £13.6 million was accepted for a luxurious four-bedroom Kensington penthouse, complete with swimming pool.[1] Soon afterwards, she also purchased a second flat in the same block, which was used mostly for storage, bodyguards and guests. A few days later, she took out a

36-month lease for office space for her family office RavenR Capital in one of the UK's most prestigious addresses: 1, Knightsbridge.

But before she could focus fully on her future, Ruja had to fix something from her past – a secret she'd been hiding from her investors and the network. It threatened to destroy OneCoin, RavenR Capital and everything else Ruja had worked so hard to build. Shortly after opening the new RavenR Capital office, Ruja quietly headed back to Germany to face justice for a crime she'd committed five years earlier.

CHAPTER 11

WALTENHOFEN GUSSWERKS

Waltenhofen, Southern Germany, 2009

Carlos Gil was worried. Thirty plus years as a tough union guy, a real 'Schwabe' (which is to say too organised, too *German*), he knew when a factory was struggling. Waltenhofen Gusswerks was definitely in trouble and his priority was to save the workers. All 140 of them if he could. It had been floundering for months in administration and had already lost 60 good men, but it had a solid reputation in Bavaria, where it was known for making high-quality casts for machinery.

Securing a buyer was the easy part. Less simple was making sure any deal was good for the workers. Union reps in Germany are powerful enough to nix a deal, and Carlos had done it before. He wouldn't agree to any buyer who didn't care about his guys – full stop. Every saved job meant a lot to him, but the Gusswerks were special. Many of the workers there came from generations of men who had worked in the same factory doing the same hot and heavy work at the blast furnace.

By the time the well-dressed Ruja Ignatova walked into his office in early 2010, Carlos was starting to doubt whether he'd ever find the right person. He'd already said no to three potential buyers because they wanted to slash wages. Almost immediately Carlos knew he'd hit gold. Ruja was business-like, cool and professional. She had spreadsheets, projections and an impeccable CV. If anything, she was *too* qualified. But the best part was that Ruja was proposing to buy the factory jointly with her father Plamen, who had worked in steel foundries in Bulgaria for years. A business consultant and a steel worker, brains and brawn, were the perfect combination. All that was missing was a pretty bow on top.

'Listen,' said Carlos firmly. 'We have only eighty of the one hundred and forty workers left. We have to raise their wages – and get the sixty lost workers back.' He wasn't prepared to negotiate on this.

'No problem,' Ruja replied with a nod. 'We won't dismantle the unions and we'll try to re-employ as many of the lost workers as we can.'

That was all Carlos needed. She offered €2.2 million for the factory and secured a loan with a German bank. (Unusually, as collateral on the loan, Ruja and Plamen used two blast furnaces that they owned in Bulgaria, worth almost €1 million, which they agreed to transport over and install in the factory.) Carlos wasn't interested in the small print – that was for the bankers and the business people to worry about. He was just happy that he'd saved more jobs.

In spring 2010, almost five years before OneCoin mined its first coin, Ruja and her father became co-owners of a steel metal works in southern Germany.

For the first few months, everything was fine. Production ticked along and the workers were paid on time. Ruja sat each day in her on-site corner office, and her mother Veska served as her assistant. Plamen was usually found on the factory floor, overseeing production and talking shop with the workers. The only member of the Ignatov clan not around was Konstantin, who was studying journalism and politics at Tübingen

University, and busy playing bass guitar in a metal band. Carlos forgot about the Gusswerks. He had other workers in other factories to represent. That's how it went with Carlos – he only got involved in a factory when things were going wrong.

One morning, about a year after Ruja bought the factory, an unhappy employee phoned him up.

'Carlos! Miss Ignatova has a consulting company, which she owns, called RilaCap. And she has hired her own company, and she's paying herself out of the factory money.'[1]

'To do what?' asked Carlos. It was the first he'd heard of it.

'I'm not sure,' the employee replied. No one in the factory knew anything.

When Carlos spoke to Ruja, she told him it was just some minor rebranding work – nothing to worry about and the workers were still getting paid. But, slowly, the working conditions started to deteriorate. Staff were asked to work extra hours unpaid. Invoices were ignored. Holiday money was reduced. The mood wasn't helped when Ruja turned up for work one day saying her company car – a Porsche Cayenne – had been stolen during a recent trip to Bulgaria. Something was clearly wrong.

The blast furnaces that Ruja and Plamen had promised to bring across from Bulgaria hadn't turned up either. The factory was struggling with out-of-date equipment and the new furnaces were desperately needed to keep output up. But weeks of waiting turned to months and there was always some new excuse as to why it would be next week, next month.

'We need the blast furnaces now,' Carlos said, over and over.

'Why are you getting involved?' Ruja replied coolly. Ruja hardly ever lost her temper – it was bad for business. 'I am paying the workers' wages – so what's the problem?'

Carlos – who by this point doubted whether these furnaces even existed at all – started turning up at the factory unannounced demanding to see her, but Ruja would simply walk out of the room as if she were too important to be dealing with a union boss. No one had ever treated him like this before.

One morning, Carlos had a phone call from one of the workers.

'Carlos, Ruja has sold the factory,' he said, panicking.

'*What*? What do you mean sold the factory?!'

'Ruja has sold the factory to a man for one Euro,' he replied. The workers had all come to work as normal that morning, only to find the place had been abandoned. Pandemonium was breaking loose. No one knew what to do.

'Where is she?' asked Carlos.

'She's gone.'

Carlos dropped everything and rushed down to the factory. It was like a movie scene. The place had clearly been abandoned in a rush: there were missing papers, burnt documents, broken laptops. Carlos called and called, but Ruja didn't answer her phone. He drove to her home, but no one was there. And when he started investigating the paperwork, Carlos was staggered to find out it was true: Ruja had sold the Waltenhofen Gusswerks to a German businessman for a grand total of one Euro. For 30 years Carlos had dealt with his fair share of slippery bosses and money grubs but he'd never seen anything like this. The factory was dead – that much was obvious. There would be no new buyers. Within weeks Waltenhofen Gusswerks was shuttered for good, along with the livelihood of 140 workers.

For years afterwards, Carlos thought about the strange businesswoman who'd bankrupted one of the factories he represented. Some days, he imagined that Ruja had started with good intentions, but things spiralled out of control.

Other days, he was convinced she planned it all along. And the workers! He still found it difficult to talk about them. He bumped into some of them on the streets every once in a while; most of them were still unemployed.

One day in 2015, someone from the local paper sent him an article via Facebook. 'Carlos,' he wrote. 'Have you seen this?'

For a moment his heart almost stopped. It was *her*. The same confidence, the same clothes, the same red lipstick. But Ruja Ignatova wasn't a disgraced executive who'd bankrupted a business, destroyed 140 lives and vanished: she was a celebrity, a business guru, a 'Cryptoqueen'.

'How is it possible?' he said to himself. 'How could anyone trust this woman?' Didn't they know what she'd done? He wondered if she might disappear again – just like she had done in Waltenhofen.

On Tuesday 12 April 2016, Ruja stood in the dock at Augsburg District Court, a small town about 70 kilometres from the Gusswerks. Her authorised defence attorney was Martin Breidenbach, her increasingly trusted lawyer who'd worked previously with Sebastian and also helped her set up the One-Coin companies. She showed no emotion as she pleaded guilty to intentional breach of duty in the event of insolvency, to fraud, to withholding and embezzlement of employee's wages and violation of accounting duties.[2]

After seeing the Facebook article, Carlos's union had hounded Ruja and her father Plamen and pressed charges. His union calculated that she'd made off with roughly a million Euros – including €120,000 from suppliers who never received their orders. Prison time would have been a disaster for Ruja. Not only would it annihilate her credibility, she had a major corporate event coming up in London in two months.

The judge gave her a 14-month suspended sentence and an €18,000 fine. Plamen, who wasn't present, had to pay €12,000. Carlos thought it was a light punishment for having destroyed the lives of so many people, but the judge concluded that Ruja was a 'smart young woman' who had a 'socially positive future'.

She slipped out of the court room and returned to Bulgaria as if nothing had happened. Less than two weeks later, Ruja (wearing her trademark red lipstick, professional make-up and a black and red lace dinner dress, although it was only early afternoon) cut the red-ribbon for the brand-new OneCoin headquarters at 6A Petko R. Slaveykov Square, Sofia. Confused commuters wandered past as Ruja gave an impromptu speech in front of dozens of excited staff. The grand-fronted six-storey building, which overlooked the tramline that ran through the tree-lined pedestrian street, was a sign of the company's growing stature: a large portrait of Ruja hung in the main meeting room, and Ruja built a 'Crypto Centre' next to the reception, which was a shrine to her vision. It had a gold black counter and a large acrostics on the main wall, which spelt OneCoin: grOwth, sustaiNability, SafEty, BloCkchain, lOyalty, stabIlity, ceNtralised. She had a life-sized cardboard cut-out of herself installed, which admiring fans would touch on entry. (In later months, promoters who were in her graces would be greeted at the Crypto Centre and taken up to Ruja's fourth-floor office; while those out of favour would be left in the Crypto Centre for hours, and sometimes sent home without seeing anyone.) Visitors to the Crypto Centre could buy merchandise, pens, hoodies and learn all about Ruja's achievements. Waltenhofen wasn't mentioned anywhere.

CHAPTER 12

HAPPY BIRTHDAY, CRYPTOQUEEN

London, May 2016

Early evening on 30 May 2016, dozens of immaculately dressed people were gathered outside the Victoria and Albert Museum on South Kensington's famous Exhibition Road. The grand old building, whose foundation stone was laid by Queen Victoria, traced its roots back to the Great Exhibition of 1851, which celebrated the nation's world-beating industry and design. The Great Exhibition was more exciting and dramatic than a thousand Microsoft or Apple launch events. Six million people, including Charles Darwin, Charles Dickens, Michael Faraday and Karl Marx, marvelled at the wonders of the age: microscopes, barometers and electric telegraphs.

Tonight the museum was rented out to celebrate a modern champion of industry. It was Dr Ruja's 36th birthday.

Dr Ruja's parties – Christmas and summer every year – were the most sought-after invite for anyone involved in OneCoin. They were always sparkling affairs (this one cost roughly €1 million) and an invite meant recognition. Their location was symbolic too. Over the preceding months, Ruja had been spending more and more time in London. The RavenR Capital family office team had quickly grown to ten staff who were researching potential investments for Ruja – foreign exchange, property, tech companies. When they weren't researching clever ways to spend Ruja's personal fortune (Gary Gilford has said that at no point did RavenR London invest on behalf of OneCoin), they were trying to talk her down. Periodically she would arrive in the office, fresh off the flight from Bulgaria, holding a Pret a Manger sandwich and Diet Coke she'd picked up en route and declare that she was considering investing in a sex toy manufacturer or buying a toothpaste factory in China. It would take hours for the director Gary Gilford or others to dissuade her. Holding her party in London was a sign that the balance of gravity was moving slowly away from Sofia and the MLM network, and towards the UK and more serious finance.

Although the network now numbered hundreds of thousands of people, only 150 were lucky enough to receive the gold-on-black art deco invitation:

> *Please join us as we celebrate this incredible woman's*
> *special day! You are invited to the exclusive Birthday*
> *Party of Dr Ruja Ignatova. Dress code: Dress to impress /*
> *black tie.*

Everyone who got the gilded invite RSVP'd 'yes' immediately. Those lucky few, some of whom had flown halfway across the world for this, made their way into the V&A and were greeted with complimentary pink champagne, oysters, cigars and sushi. Unusually, for a CEO, Ruja often got involved in the planning of the big events, choosing the appetisers, the posters, the free drinks. As far as she was concerned, it was exactly those small details that mattered – they were the things people remembered, the things that created the desired impression.

The guest list was a who's who of Ruja's life. The Sofia office and London RavenR Capital staff were there, despite a growing rivalry between them. Sebastian, of course. Old friends from before OneCoin caught up. Asdis Ran, the 'Ice Queen'. Ruja's husband Björn Strehl. Krassimir Katev, a former Bulgarian government minister, puffed on a Cuban cigar. Her most valuable promoters, like Juha and Kari Wahlroos, mingled and smiled for photos. Not to be outdone, Ruja turned up in the Rolls-Royce Phantom that she'd rented from the Four Seasons Hotel.

Her younger brother Konstantin was wandering round the V&A in a bit of a daze, mostly talking to his parents Veska and Plamen about Ruja's transformation and refusing the free booze. (Konstantin had been teetotal for some years.) It was all so surreal. He followed Ruja's life from afar and told friends about his increasingly famous big sister, but he hadn't seen Ruja since her last party in Sofia. He noticed how much richer she'd become in such a short space of time, how expensive her clothes were now, and how all the MLM people were in awe of her. Ruja flirted and flattered the men and complimented the women as she worked the room introducing her sibling. She'd finally learned how to charm people.

Despite their ostentatious conviviality, Konstantin noticed there was an emptiness to the MLM people he was introduced to. All they talked about was money: their cars, their new recruits, their Dolce & Gabbanas, their rank. Conversations revolved around the new downline they'd just opened or their weekly business volumes. Normal human interactions had been hijacked by a commissions parasite that turned everything meaningful into plastic talk disguised by self-help mantras about 'first helping others'. They talked about the books they had read, not for enjoyment but to learn how to win friends and influence people. They met relatives for coffee, not to catch up but to propose an exciting new opportunity. Years in MLM does that to people. Only newcomers could ever notice it – after a few months it got inside you. One day it would infect Konstantin too.

Halfway through the night, a five-storey crown-topped golden birthday cake was wheeled out, with the words 'Happy

Birthday Cryptoqueen' iced on top. The singer Tom Jones arrived on stage to perform a private gig, for which he was paid a small fortune. Sebastian and Ruja shared a slow dance, while Juha Parhiala, silver-topped cane in hand, stood at the front and sang to the crowd as Tom Jones looked on. Konstantin took a video of himself dancing and singing along to 'Kiss' and posted it on Instagram. Ruja told him off for that. But who knew if something like this would ever happen again?

A few days after the party, Konstantin was at home in Stuttgart when Ruja phoned him. She'd just found out that Sebastian was having an affair with one of her personal assistants. The pair were even considering marriage. When she learned about it, Ruja flew into an irrational rage. Some of her colleagues wondered if jealousy was behind it. There had always been rumours that Sebastian and Ruja were lovers, although no one ever knew for certain. Ruja had meltdowns over innocuous things all the time, and she usually recovered quickly. But, on this occasion, she fired her PA. 'I need someone who won't betray me,' she told Konstantin. 'Will you come over and become my personal assistant?'

Konstantin was quite happy where he was. Earning €2,800 a month operating a forklift truck in the nearby Porsche factory wasn't perfect, but he had friends and a life in Stuttgart. In many ways, he was the polar opposite of his sister. He went to his local gym at least four times a week and volunteered at the dog sanctuary, where he would sometimes take home rescued dogs. He also didn't understand her business. Downlines and blockchains were ancient Greek to him. But he trusted Ruja and she told him not to worry because his work would mostly involve sorting out travel, arranging meetings, dealing with invoices and picking up her shopping.

Even from a very young age, Ruja used to lecture Konstantin about the importance of loyalty. If his big sister, who Konstantin had idolised since childhood, needed him, then of course he would leave Germany. It was also a chance to spend more time with his parents, who'd returned to Sofia as Ruja's star rose. She promised to pay him more money too.[1] Ruja asked Konstantin to quit his job immediately and fly to London for the corporate event taking place in a few days' time. She wanted him there to hear her big announcement, about 'a new blockchain'.

CHAPTER 13

MONEY IN

By 2016, the British Virgin Islands had shed its soft-touch image. After years of light regulation and a long-standing reputation as one of the world's most secretive tax havens, it had finally introduced strict rules about big investment funds like Fenero. For one thing, all British Virgin Island (BVI) funds needed to appoint an independent 'administrator' to ensure they were professionally run and investors' interests were protected.[1] Administrators serve as an investment fund's back office. They set up the bank accounts, pay investors dividends, value the assets, make the money transfers, and even write up minutes. A decent administrator makes a fund run smoothly by taking care of the boring stuff. But, if they suspect anything illegal is taking place, such as money laundering, they can also stop payments going through.[2] Fund managers like Mark Scott sometimes fall out with their fund administrators because their job is to keep the fund honest.

That was Paul Spendiff's job. His company Apex administered thousands of investment funds all over the world. Paul's London branch alone administered over a hundred. From 10 May 2016, one of them was Fenero Equity Investments LP.[3] When Paul and his team looked at the paperwork Mark had sent them the previous month, it all seemed typical enough. Mark had recently become a BVI 'approved fund manager', which meant he could conduct business without going through lengthy approval procedures. Mark told Paul that the investors in this new fund were 'wealthy European families' that he'd worked with before. The mission statement was fairly standard too: 'Fenero has been created at the request of a select group of European-based families and companies that want to take advantage of potential business synergies.' To the untrained eye, the corporate spider web might look suspicious (Fenero was owned by MSSI International Consultants BVI, which was owned by MSSI International Consultants, Florida, which was owned by Mark).[4] But, over the years, Paul had seen company structures that went on for pages. Apex's background checks on Mark came back clean. And, according to Paul, Mark never mentioned Ruja Ignatova or OneCoin.

As soon as Apex opened bank accounts at DMS Bank in the Cayman Islands for Fenero Equity Investments LP, Mark told Ruja and Irina the news. Background checks were passed and they could start sending money to one of the Fenero Fund bank accounts.[5]

'Hi Mark,' wrote Maya Antonova, OneCoin's chief accountant. 'What payment reference should we use for the transfer?'

'Write: partial payment for subscription,' he replied.[6]

Almost immediately a stupendous amount of money flooded in.

On 2 June, three separate payments of €5 million went from the IMS Germany Commerzbank account to Fenero Equity Investments LP's DMS Cayman account.

On 3 June, another €5 million from the IMS Germany Commerzbank account.

On 6 June, another €5 million from the IMS Germany Commerzbank account.

On 7 June, another €5 million from the IMS Germany Commerzbank account.

On 8 June, €5 million from the B&N Consult DSK account.

On 15 June, €5 million from the IMS Germany Deutsche Bank account.

On 20 June, €5 million from the IMS Singapore OCBC account.

It went on like this all summer. Tens, then hundreds, of millions of Euros were making their way into Mark's Fenero accounts.[7] For two years, OneCoin investors had been buying packages for between €100 and €12,500 and diligently sending their money to various bank accounts all over the world. That money was now being kneaded into €5 million lumps and sent into an investment fund in the Caribbean. None of the thousands of ordinary people – not Daniel from Uganda, who'd sold everything, not Christine Grablis from Tennessee, not the Indian village that had all chipped in together – had any idea their money was ending up in a far-away bank account controlled by a man called Mark Scott.

In June 2016, Mark told Apex that he'd identified the first investment opportunity for his Fenero Fund. He wanted Apex to authorise a €7 million payment for a stake in a London-based payments company called 'Payment Card Technology'. Ruja's advisers at the RavenR office looked at the numbers and thought it was a smart purchase, and, as far as Apex were concerned, it was in line with the mission statement: Payment Card Technology was a legitimate London company in good standing with sound accounts. Apex transferred the money in five wires, and the Fenero Funds had its first purchase.

That was small fry. The next purchase was the big one: a multi-million-dollar purchase of an oil field involving Hong Kong's second richest man and the brother of a former president of the United States.

CHAPTER 14

I WILL DOUBLE
YOUR COINS

London, 11 June 2016

Ruja was pacing up and down backstage. *I will double your coins, I will double your coins.*

Three thousand people were waiting for her. Most of them were investors like Christine Grablis or Layla Begum: ordinary people who'd gradually become more involved in OneCoin and wanted to hear the top leaders and meet fellow 'coiners'. Wembley Arena, London's premiere indoor venue, was better known for hosting world-famous bands. But demand for the 'CoinRush' event had been off the charts, even at €200 a ticket. Several Chinese members were supposed to be attending the event but they had their visas rejected by the UK's Home Office. It cost OneCoin at least half a million Euros to put this corporate event on, but they'd make the money back in new sales. Ruja and some of the other top people stayed in London between her birthday party and the London event, mostly working from the RavenR Capital office in Knightsbridge. As usual, the night before the event there was an expensive dinner for the top promoters in central London, most of whom stayed at the Hilton in Kensington.

The purpose of CoinRush was the same as the Dubai and Macao corporates: re-energise the network and send promoters back out with fresh determination. From midday, the stars of the network went on stage to share their stories or give motivational speeches. Hype-man Kari Wahlroos charged around the stage like a madman, screaming that everyone could get rich. The New Zealand MLM expert Ed Ludbrook, who prided himself on being more buttoned up than the average MLMer, said he'd 'never seen anything like this'. Chris Principe from *Financial IT Magazine* opened with a little in-joke: Last year there was a thirty-seven per cent decrease in people robbing banks . . . but a one hundred per cent increase in the banks robbing people. Many OneCoin investors had become keen students of finance, reading up on how the banks could print money and then make interest on it, and so this joke went down well. Kari Wahlroos, dressed in a sharp blue suit, announced that OneCoin had created 320 millionaires via sales commissions and a further 2,500 via the OneCoin they owned. There was the same quasi-religious feel as in Macau: the faithful walked around wearing One-Coin medallions and making the special OneCoin hand gesture at each other.

Online critics, especially from the ever-vigilant website BehindMLM, were watching closely. Following the first article about OneCoin back in 2014, Oz, the founder of BehindMLM, had continued to monitor the company, often publishing several critical articles each month about the firm's unusually fast growth and hyped-up promises. His work had picked up a following and by 2016 an informal community of armchair detectives had coalesced around the site, where they started to share insights or titbits they'd dug up online. Some of this crew had even managed to get a couple of OneCoin events closed down in the US in 2015 by contacting the venues where meetings were scheduled to take place – alleging that the education 'products' were just a cover, and that no one knew how the price of the coin was really set. They tried to alert Wembley Arena staff about the big London corporate event too in the hope that might get cancelled: 'Please do what you can to stop the event!' begged one on the forum. Several BehindMLM contributors even phoned the venue to ask about it – but the staff were tight-lipped. 'I hope no one's expecting British Bobbies to turn up and start arresting people,' said one disappointed contributor just hours before the event was due to start. 'This is twenty-first-century laissez-faire Britain, not the movies.'

He was right – there were no bobbies and no arrests. In fact, the mood backstage was jubilant. The recently added 'Infinity Trader' package – at €25,000 the largest the company sold, along with fresh educational materials – was doing a fine trade. A 10 per cent price hike in April had lifted profits without hurting growth, and the value of a single OneCoin had just increased again to €5.95. But Ruja was unusually nervous because of the controversial announcement she was about to make. She was going to launch a brand new blockchain.

Changing blockchains went against everything Ruja had said about the importance of having a fixed-supply currency. For three years, she'd evangelised about the power of a fixed-supply money that couldn't be tampered with – back in Malaysia with Sebastian in 2014 she even said, 'I cannot print more . . . even if I think, oh this network is growing so fast let's make five billion now . . . it's impossible.' No other cryptocurrency company had ever tried anything like this before. And now she had to tell the audience she was ripping it all up and starting again.

In truth, she had little choice. OneCoin's popularity had taken everyone by surprise, including Ruja. When she'd designed the technology back in July 2014, she assumed that

2.1 billion coins would last a lifetime. But growth had been so fast that, even though OneCoin was barely 18 months old, they were running out of coins. And because OneCoin was sold via MLM, no more coins meant no more packages for promoters like Igor to sell, and everything would grind to a halt.

Ruja's solution to this coin shortage was to move everything on to a bigger and faster blockchain. The new blockchain would comprise 120 billion coins – 50 times more than the original. And it would create them much faster too, increasing from 10,000 new coins per ten minutes to 50,000 a minute.

Any investor with an ounce of financial acumen could spot the problem. Economics 101 states that an increase in supply results in a reduction in value. Increasing the supply of OneCoin by a factor of 50 overnight should, all else being equal, result in a catastrophic collapse in the value of investors' coins. That was why Ruja planned to make an audacious promise too: when the new blockchain is launched on 1 October 2016, the price would remain exactly the same and everyone's coins would be immediately doubled. The whole plan strained credibility.

Sebastian called Ruja on stage: 'Please give a warm welcome for our creator, our founder . . .'

'This Girl is on Fire' by Alicia Keys blasted over Wembley Arena's sound system and pyrotechnics lit up the stage. Wearing a flowing red gown and deep-red lipstick, Ruja strode out confidently in front of the giant logo which said, 'OneCoin: The Bitcoin Killer'. She bowed, paused, smiled, looked out at the vast audience and milked the applause. If she was nervous, she didn't show it. From Hong Kong to Helsinki, to Singapore with Sebastian on the first ever tour, to Dubai, to Macau and now London, Dr Ruja had finally become a good performer.

After praising the OneCoin network as 'global citizens wanting to make a change', and promising that the coin would soon *go public* on a currency exchange, it was time to make the announcement. She had speech prompts on the stage floor monitor, but she barely looked at them. She had practised this moment for six months.

'Now I think it's time,' Ruja told the crowd, with carefully controlled gaps between each sentence, timed for applause; 'do or do not. We want to be the *number one* cryptocurrency out there . . .' There was no doubt, no hesitation. As for Bitcoin? It was far too slow, far too technical.

'Can we become the biggest cryptocurrency in the world with what we have now . . . ?'

'Yes!' shouted a promoter from row Z.

'No. We cannot.' She explained that OneCoin had run out of coins. There wasn't enough to go around, which left only one option: '[We will] create a bigger coin than anyone . . . we will go up to one hundred and twenty billion coins.' There was only one snag of course. That needed a new blockchain. 'We will launch a new blockchain on the first of October.'

Ruja now slowed down. She needed to ensure the crowd was on side. 'For you, as existing members, people who supported us in phase one . . . we as a company will *double* the coins in your account.'

The crowd roared. They were still cheering as Ruja hastened to add, 'This will only happen only once in OneCoin history. Never again.'

'We love you, Ruja,' someone shouted.

'Thank you,' she replied. 'In two years, nobody will talk about Bitcoin any more.'

Within minutes, Oz and the BehindMLM investigators found a video of Ruja's speech on YouTube and watched it with horror. 'A OneCoin pumper I follow on Facebook proclaimed today that he just became a millionaire. He said he was trembling with excitement,' wrote one. Tim Tayshun, a regular contributor, couldn't believe what he'd just seen. 'Ruja is so amazing she bends entire mathematical principles,' he wrote. He was being facetious, of course. But most people in the London audience believed exactly that.

CHAPTER 15

PROJECT X

Hong Kong, summer 2016

No one knows exactly how the meeting came to pass. Maybe it was via Ruja's long-standing contacts in finance. Perhaps Dr Hui's fascination with cryptocurrency allowed him to be bewitched by the crypto businesswoman with a new office in Hong Kong. However it happened, a few days after the London event, Ruja found herself sitting at a meeting room table in Hong Kong with Sebastian, Hong Kong's second richest man Dr Hui Chi Ming and, reportedly, Neil Bush, the brother of one former US president, and son of another. They were discussing a deal to buy an African oil field.

Dr Hui was one of Hong Kong's most powerful men, a billionaire Beijing loyalist with a glittering career. Born into a poor family in Guangdong province in 1964, Hui epitomised the ambition and drive of Deng Xiaoping's 'new entrepreneurs'. He was the youngest ever recipient of the Order of the Bauhinia Star – a civilian honour equivalent to a British CBE, something he'd earned for his work on poverty reduction in the country. His loyalty and drive helped him build a fortune in property and then energy, where he became the boss of one of the country's largest energy companies, Hoifu. At the turn of the century, Hui purchased – in a deal that upset some of the locals – 9,000 square miles of oil-rich land in Madagascar, called 'Area 3112'.[1] There was approximately $4 billion worth of untapped oil under Area 3112, all owned by one of his companies, called Barta Holdings.

Dr Hui was also a technophile with a keen interest in cryptocurrency and, given its popularity in both Hong Kong and mainland China, it is hardly surprising he knew of Dr Ruja. And he was prepared to sell Barta Holdings – and its oil field – to Ruja for $560 million. Dr Hui was keen on the deal. According to later court testimony Neil Bush – who had a long-standing relationship with Dr Hui and sat on the board of some of his companies – reportedly flew over to attend too. Ruja loved being surrounded by rich, smart people talking about big deals. She proposed paying $60 million cash up front and the remaining $500 million in OneCoin at the-then price of €7 a coin. She told Dr Hui that as he exchanged his coins back into real money Ruja would own an ever-increasing portion of the land. 'I think this is a very innovative idea,' Dr Hui said at the time. According to someone close to the deal, Ruja called it 'Project X'.

When Ruja sent the details about Barta Holdings and Area 3112 to her RavenR Capital advisers, Gary Gilford later recalled that staff there tried to talk her out of the deal entirely. But Ruja, for reasons no one fully understood, had her heart set on Area 3112. On 7 July 2016, Dr Hui and Ruja signed a 'term sheet for future cooperation', which outlined the prospective deal. It revealed that, for Ruja at least, there may have been more to this transaction than simply a purchase of land.

Ever since OneCoin hit momentum in late 2014, the company had been growing in almost every country on earth. But nowhere was quite like China. The country fell in love with Dr Ruja in the same way it had fallen in love with Bitcoin two years earlier. Network marketing and cryptocurrencies were both enormously popular with the opportunity-hungry middle class and OneCoin's promise of a 'centralised' blockchain was more in tune with the politics of the nation than Bitcoin's libertarian origins. By the time Dr Hui and Ruja met, roughly €1.5 billion had been invested from Chinese investors alone. One man who'd spent 23 years wrongly imprisoned even spent all one million yuan of his compensation money on OneCoin.

Notwithstanding the country's importance, however, Ruja had never managed to acquire an official network selling licence for mainland China. She had tried in 2015 and 2016 but her applications always got ground down in China's confusing licencing systems – and neither cryptocurrency nor education were 'approved products' permitted under MLM rules. (In fact, at some point in mid-2016, the Ministry of Public Security in China opened an investigation into OneCoin.)[2] As OneCoin continued to grow and grow, Ruja grew increasingly worried that the Chinese authorities might move against her.

The deal with Dr Hui appears to have been, for Ruja's part at least, a hedge against the risk of her Chinese market collapsing. The 'term sheet' stated that Dr Hui would 'support OneCoin in becoming a recognised and as official a currency as possible and strive towards granting it a banking licence making the work easier in China'.[3] In addition to the $560 million, Dr Hui would be given his own downline of OneCoin promoters, and could take a small cut of their sales. (Dr Hui later explained that he understood the true meaning of this statement of support was to ensure the payment of $560 million made in OneCoin could ultimately be redeemed as official currency, and was not an indication that he personally supported the project, in which he had no stake.)

Shortly after signing the term sheet with Dr Hui, Ruja told Mark Scott she wanted this strange deal run through the Fenero Funds.

The problem was that the Fenero mission statement stated that the fund invests in 'struggling EU technology companies', not oil fields in Africa. It was therefore unlikely Apex would sign off an investment so far outside the fund's stated objectives. But Ruja, as usual, had a solution. She already owned a European technology firm, which she'd set up years earlier. The 'CryptoReal Investment Trust', which was registered in Zurich, was an aborted effort to create her own investment fund in 2012, but she'd never disbanded the company. (It was the company she'd pitched at her final Big-Coin event with Sebastian in July 2014.) Ruja's German lawyer Martin Breidenbach was appointed director and owner. A power of attorney was drafted around this time, which gave Ruja control over the company. (It is not known whether this was ever signed.)[4]

Mark informed Apex that he had found a second investment opportunity for Fenero: a $30 million loan to a technology company called 'CryptoReal Investment Trust' that was owned by a German lawyer called Martin Breidenbach. He explained that CryptoReal was planning to buy an oil field in Madagascar, and the Fenero Funds wanted to lend money toward the deal and earn interest from the loan. On 12 July, Mark wrote to Apex formally requesting the payment of $30 million be processed. 'Purpose: Loan to CryptoReal Investment Trust Ltd (BVI) Martin Breidenbach for acquisition of Madagascar oil field'.[5]

Loans to German lawyers for oil fields in Madagascar weren't a standard deal, even in the complex world of private equity. Paul Spendiff thought it was on the 'very edge' of what was in the mission statement. But Apex received a reassuring letter from Martin Breidenbach, signed off on the loan and wired $30 million over.

That was when things started to come apart.[6]

Dr Hui wanted his second $30 million by 4 August

2016. By now, over €100 million had been sent to Fenero Equity Investments LP. But there were other deals and commitments (including a transaction Ruja had lined up for buying 29 industrial extraction and haulage vehicles in Venezuela). It's possible the fund needed more money in order to make the second payment.[7] Not only that, IMS Germany – which had been the most active investor – was now being seriously investigated by the German authorities, following that tip off months earlier. (The Münster public prosecutor ended up freezing an IMS bank account in mid-August 2016.)[8]

At short notice, Ruja told Mark to fly to Sofia to talk in person.[9] He left Florida on 19 July and was met in Sofia the following day by Ruja's armed bodyguards. 'Even police is polite. LOL', Mark texted his partner Lidia, who was back in Florida. When he arrived at OneCoin HQ, he was greeted by Konstantin, now settled into his new role as Ruja's PA, who gave him a drink and took him up to Ruja's office on the fourth floor.

According to Konstantin, Ruja sent everyone on the fourth floor home. Exactly what was discussed is not known, but based on what happened next it's probable Ruja wanted to discuss a new investor called 'Star Merchants', which she would use to send more money. The next morning, Mark returned to the airport and flew 20 hours back to Florida. Before he took off, he texted his wife: 'Earned another $175K today . . . And hanging [out] with Ruja may be about 25 [million] in next 18 months.'

One week later, Mark messaged Apex to say he'd found another big investor for Fenero: a Hong Kong company called 'Star Merchants' run by a businessman called 'Zhoulong Cai'.[10]

Paul Spendiff didn't like it. He was increasingly unhappy with the information he had on B&N, Irina Dilkinska, and

IMS. And now there was Zhoulong Cai too. He emailed Mark asking for further paperwork. 'Need to talk,' Mark emailed Irina. 'Due to high amounts administrator wants more information. We can handle but need to coordinate.' Even Ruja was nervous, unusually emailing Mark from a long-haul flight demanding updates.

Paul had worked in fund administration long enough to know when something didn't feel right. Over the weekend of 30 June – 1 July, he sat at home examining all Mark's letters, incorporation documents, mission statements and bank accounts, trying to work out the relationship between all the different parties. Anti-money laundering laws require that fund administrators like Paul are confident that a client's wealth has been acquired legally. As he was scanning back through the Fenero files, Paul spotted that Mark had emailed him with a few more documents about this mysterious new investor, Mr Cai.

But Mark had made a big mistake. He had accidently forwarded an email to Paul without first checking the thread that came below it. Fund managers are notoriously busy, and forwarding sensitive emails is a common error. Fund administrators are trained to 'check the thread' because it can be a useful source of information about a client and sometimes even reveals who's really in charge.

Paul scrolled down the thread and spotted an email address he'd not seen before. It was Irina@onecoin.eu.

He started Googling and found a *Daily Mirror* article from a few weeks earlier: 'Who wants to be a OneCoin millionaire?' ran the headline. 'YOU don't – here's why hyped-up web currency is virtually worthless'. The founder, Paul learned, was a Bulgarian woman called Dr Ruja Ignatova. It was a name he hadn't heard before.[11] A few clicks later, he was on the website BehindMLM.

*

By now, BehindMLM had turned into a one-stop-shop for anything to do with OneCoin. Its armchair sleuths – people with usernames like 'Passerby', 'MelaniefromGermany' and 'WhistleblowerFin' – had collectively posted tens of thousands of times about the company, accumulating a publicly accessible goldmine of information about Ruja and her cryptocurrency. They dug up old company records in Gibraltar, scoured YouTube videos looking for familiar names, spent hours researching top promoters. Everything they found they posted on BehindMLM. The site had become such a nuisance to Ruja that she banned everyone who worked for OneCoin from visiting it, a rule they mostly ignored. One particular talent of these citizen journalists was finding and identifying the senior staff who worked at OneCoin's head office. As he scrolled down Oz's slightly old-fashioned looking website, Paul Spendiff learned that Irina Dilkinska wasn't simply a 'wealthy European investor' looking to put her vast wealth into a fund. She was head of legal and compliance at OneCoin's HQ in Sofia.

Why hadn't Mark ever mentioned OneCoin before? And how come an ordinary member of staff had so much money?

When Paul arrived at the Apex London office on Monday morning, he immediately called an emergency meeting with his risk and compliance teams. Now that he suspected foul play, there were procedures to follow. He sent a 'suspicious activity report' to the UK's Financial Intelligence Unit, which is a legal obligation if a firm like Apex believes criminal activity might be taking place. Although Apex could continue to ask Mark questions, they couldn't alert him about their suspicions in case that constituted tipping off. The compliance team agreed that Paul should play dumb, refuse to move any more of Mark's money and secretly record any subsequent calls.

'I am very, very dissatisfied with what's going on here,'

Mark told Paul in a phone call on 9 August, with the second payment to Dr Hui for the Madagascar oil field now overdue. He was clearly panicked. 'We've really pushed to a level of due diligence here that we do not experience in our other funds . . . And we're getting to a point where we have investors who are leaving.'

'We never seem to have a complete picture in terms of the involved entities,' replied Paul calmly. He knew, of course, that the call was being recorded. Everything had to be done exactly by the book. In order to process the second payment, he needed proof of how Irina made her money, and, now, how OneCoin fitted into all this.

'What do you mean *complete* picture . . . ?' asked Mark.

'It's become very difficult to get . . . the due diligence we require to provide us with the comfort in source of funds,' said Paul.

Mark was irate. He threatened to sue. He protested. He complained. He wanted the money out. 'Every little piece of paper was sent to Apex,' Mark shouted. 'You are screwing up our business!'

It's normal for fund managers like Mark to lean on their fund administrators, to pressure them into making payments. But Paul wasn't going to budge. 'No money is going out today,' said Paul. 'And not tomorrow, or until we can clear this up one way or the other.'

The next day Mark cleared it up the only way he could: he fired Apex.

Five days later, Mark was back in the Cayman Islands, where he re-registered the Fenero Funds with a new administrator. (Strict privacy rules in the Caymans make it impossible to know whether the second payment was ever processed. However, according to Dr Hui's spokesperson, Ruja never made the second payment even though the share transfer took place, and he is currently working with the Madagascar government to revoke the deal.)[12]

With the funds re-registered, the money started flowing again too. IMS Singapore sent another €60 million into the Fenero Funds. Within a few weeks, IMS Singapore sent another €34.5 million. Star Merchant, run by Zhoulong Cai, sent €95 million. Now things were back on track, Mark started spending some of his earnings.[13] In October 2016, he paid off the remaining $1 million balance on his house in Coral Gables, Florida. A few days later, he purchased a $2.8 million house in Cape Cod outright. Before the year was out, he'd treated himself to a 2011 Ferrari 599 GTB, a $121,000 emerald engagement ring for his girlfriend and half a million dollars' worth of watches and luxury handbags. In the end, Mark earned around $40 million for his work.[14] But not before the truth would finally emerge about OneCoin's blockchain. News which would transform Mark's cleverly designed Fenero Funds into something else entirely.

Part 4

ANATOMY OF A SCAM

CHAPTER 16

BLOCKCHAIN AND BJØRN

When he was a child growing up in Norway, Bjørn Bjercke used to have a recurring nightmare that his television wouldn't turn off. He'd push the button, pull the plug and even dismantle the box, but nothing could stop it. He sometimes wondered if those dreams were the reason he ended up studying computer science and became an IT security specialist: some mysterious deep-rooted need to regain control over machines. Computers suited his personality too. He liked the precision of code, its exactitude and certainty. In his twenties, when his friends were out partying, he would happily spend hours digging around the latest bit of software, scrolling through the impenetrable languages C++ and Python.

By 2013, around the same time Ruja and Sebastian first met in Singapore, Bjørn's circle of fellow IT guys and hackers in Norway were also talking about Bitcoin. But they were less interested in the price and more interested in the fact it had been running for three years without breaking. 'Bullshit,' thought Bjørn, when he was first told about this apparently un-hackable new technology. '*Everything* can be hacked.' For the next year or so, Bjørn spent his evenings and weekends trying to stop Bitcoin running. For a decade he'd been fixing IT problems at some of the world's top companies, and so knew every hacking technique, every angle of attack. But Bitcoin was so beautifully designed that Bjørn got nowhere. He couldn't break it; in fact, he couldn't even improve one single line of code. It was his nightmare again – a system that couldn't be stopped. But the childish fear was replaced by fascination. Once you're fluent, computer code is much like the written word: it can be jumbled and clumsy, or poetic and elegant. The Bitcoin code was the most perfect Bjørn had ever seen.

As far as Bjørn saw it, the real breakthrough was the strange database that powered it all, the blockchain.[1] It transcended technology; it was about trust and truth. 'When you enter something onto a blockchain,' Bjørn would tell people enthusiastically, 'it's like carving it into stone.' If they struggled with the technicalities, Bjørn sometimes pulled out his other favourite pastime – a Rubik's cube. He would jumble it all up into a multi-coloured mess before solving it again in under three minutes. 'You don't understand how I'm doing this,' he'd say, as his fingers rapidly shuffled the colours back into their rightful positions, 'but you can verify it's correct because all the colours match. Blockchain is the same.' To someone like Bjørn, Bitcoin was a once-in-a-generation idea, the sort of 'upstream' technology that transforms whole societies. The printing press, the telephone, the internet, and now money controlled by the unbending rules of code rather than unpredictable bankers and politicians. 'Why should banks, [who have] not updated their systems and business model for 60 to 80 years, get paid for you to do all the work with your money?' he posted on LinkedIn around this time. 'It is time banks stopped taking advantage of us.'

Although he was in his mid-thirties, Bjørn switched careers and became a full-time Bitcoin consultant, and, by 2015, was helping companies create and use their own cryptocurrencies or blockchains. His particular specialism was to take a company's old SQL or Excel database (often containing customer records or supply chain data) and transfer the entries onto a new blockchain. He was good at it too, and soon became one of Norway's top specialists. So it wasn't unusual when, on 29 September 2016, Bjørn found a private message in his LinkedIn account from a recruitment agent called Nigel Chinnock. Nigel had a client who needed Bjørn's skills – someone who knew how to transfer standard database records onto a blockchain.

'It's a billion-dollar financial firm specialising in crypto-currency,' Nigel said, when they spoke on the phone a couple of days later.[2] 'The salary is around €250 thousand a year plus a new apartment in London and one in Sofia.'

'What's the company called?' Bjørn asked. It sounded intriguing. Especially the salary.

'OneCoin,' replied Nigel, a little coy. Bjørn had the impression Nigel didn't really want to tell him.

Bjørn only vaguely recognised the name, which was strange because he knew every major cryptocurrency, especially those worth over a billion dollars.

'So what will I have to do?' Bjørn asked.

'It's a cryptocurrency company that has a coin, but they don't have a blockchain. They need you to build them a blockchain,' Nigel said.

'*What*?!'

Bjørn was in disbelief. It made no sense. Cryptocurrencies are built on blockchains. A cryptocurrency without a blockchain is like a car without an engine. 'I don't really understand it myself,' said Nigel. 'I'm not technical.' All he knew was they had a 'normal database'. Nigel suggested Bjørn talk to the CEO, a brilliant woman called Dr Ruja Ignatova. She'd explain it.

Bjørn asked Nigel for a few days to think it over. When he went online to research OneCoin, he was even more confused. There were rumours on sites like BehindMLM that it was a scam, a gigantic Ponzi. But then again Ruja's credentials were impeccable, and hundreds of thousands of people had already invested. But Bjørn couldn't escape the killer fact: a billion-dollar cryptocurrency without a blockchain is impossible. Something was very wrong, but he didn't know what.

Bangkok, 1 October 2016

At the very moment Bjørn was mulling over the strange job offer, 10,000 excited OneCoin investors were descending on Asia's second largest exhibition centre, the Muang Thong Thani Impact Arena in Bangkok. (The rock band Queen had played there the night before.) They were there to witness history: the launch of the new 120 billion-coin blockchain that Ruja had promised in London – bigger, faster and smoother than anything the crypto world had ever seen, processing transactions ten times faster than Bitcoin and propelling OneCoin toward global currency status. The same blockchain that Bjørn had just been asked to build.

'Bitcoin cannot go aggressively into payment systems because they cannot do the transactions that they need to do,' Ruja said just before the event. 'Bitcoin is not for the masses.' It was also the moment everyone's coin holding would be instantly doubled, making hundreds of thousands of people rich overnight. Posters around the venue read: *New Blockchain. Double Your Coins.* Whole downlines had travelled together from China, Brazil, Uganda and beyond to be there. 'Watch me double my coin with OneCoin and become rich in two years,' wrote one investor in a Reddit thread about the event. 'I will be laughing at your sorry asses!'

Every week in 2016 was a selling frenzy, but the three months between London and Bangkok were frenetic. Ruja spent most of it on the road, speaking at a succession of huge events all over the world to capitalise on the buzz: Kuala Lumpur in late June, then Tokyo in July, where thousands of Japanese investors turned up, followed by another big event in Sofia in August. It was non-stop. Every promoter went into overdrive pushing the double-your-coins special offer. Kari spent practically every waking hour between flights and events, visiting dozens of countries. Saleh Ahmed in London pressured his downline, telling Layla Begum that she had to put more money in quick in order to benefit from the doubling opportunity, which she did. Ruja even rushed out a brand-new package – a €118,000 'Ultimate Trader' package, which promised returns of €14 million once the new blockchain was launched.

The doors didn't open until 11am but by 9am a queue was already forming. The early arrivals could see Frank Ricketts and Aron Steinkeller, the guy who'd first persuaded Igor to fly to Dubai, doing a last-minute soundcheck. When the venue doors swung open, hundreds of excited OneCoiners flooded in, grabbed their lanyards and buzzed around the foyer chatting to fellow coiners, making the OneCoin hand gesture and loitering by the sleek black Ferrari, which was a prize for that month's top promoter. One team of sellers had made special t-shirts with Ruja's face printed on, which caused a minor commotion. As the motivational talks began, anyone ranked Diamond or above sat down at VIP tables just in front of the stage: Igor and Andreea (wearing matching gold Dolce & Gabbana), Kari Wahlroos and Juha Parhiala took their seats at the front. Further back, the Rubies and Sapphires clustered in their teams. There were a few lucky souls in the crowd who'd bought their €5,000 Tycoon Trader packages in November 2014 when Ruja and Sebastian took their first promotional tour of the region. After today's coin doubling, that €5,000 investment would be worth almost €700,000, a return of over 10,000 per cent in two years. Almost as good as that Norwegian guy who invested $27 in Bitcoin in 2009 and . . . everyone knew the rest.

After the various warm-up acts (including Frank Ricketts announcing that his and Sebastian's old company OPN/SiteTalk would be 'joining the One Family'), Ruja finally walked on stage at just after 4pm local time, wearing a flowing purple gown. There were so many people in the hall that anyone past row 50 could only see her on the hanging 20-metre screen.

'One Family!' Ruja said as she walked out, waving. 'Today is really a very very special day . . . Today we will be switching on the new blockchain!' A cheer went up.

A few eagle-eyed watchers in the crowd noticed that Ruja's appearance was starting to change. It looked like cosmetic surgery, perhaps? Was it her lips, her cheekbones?

'We will become officially the number one cryptocurrency *globally*,' she went on. With the doubling of coins, she explained, the market capitalisation would also double, catapulting OneCoin above Bitcoin into the biggest cryptocurrency in the world. (Market capitalisation is a crude method used in the crypto industry, where total coin circulation is multiplied by coin price to create an approximate total company value.)

At 4.28pm local time, Ruja switched on a live feed of OneCoin's usually top secret blockchain. Nothing was happening. But then a flashing red light on the screen starting blinking.

'I think we are mining about two billion coins now,' she said nervously, glancing at the large screen. In other words, the coins on the 'old blockchain' were – at that exact instant – apparently being transferred to the 'new blockchain'. Just as they had two years earlier, when the original blockchain was turned on, people in the crowd tried to imagine what that actually meant: numbers whizzing through cables and wires from one machine to another? Columns of ones and zeros stacking at the speed of light? A billion coins cut and pasted by a supercomputer? It frazzled the mind just thinking about it.

'Go Go Go – mine!' shouted Ruja. The crowd held its breath.

Suddenly a new message popped up on the screen: 'Genesis Block Is Mined'.

Back in the Sofia HQ, where it was still morning, there was a collective sigh of relief. Everyone's coins had moved from the old blockchain to the new one.

'Yes! We did it!' Ruja shouted, clutching her microphone and staring at the monster screen behind her. 'All of you now should have *double* coins – congratulations!'

People in the crowd excitedly logged into their accounts and within an hour or two there were, as Ruja had promised, twice as many coins as 24 hours earlier. And the price hadn't changed either: each coin was still worth €6.95. As the promoters and investors filed triumphantly out of the Impact Arena that evening, they were twice as rich as when they'd walked in. And OneCoin had a new top-of-the-range blockchain ready to take on the world.

After a weekend of reflection and a couple of chats with close friends, Bjørn emailed Nigel to let him know he wasn't interested in the position. He didn't know anything about the big event in Bangkok where a blockchain he'd been asked to build was being launched. But something didn't smell right about OneCoin. Nigel didn't reply and Bjørn forgot all about it. A few months later he spotted a OneCoin promoter criticising Bitcoin online. Bjørn was surprised the company was still around. A few clicks later he learned that not only was

OneCoin alive and well, Ruja had launched, in front of 10,000 people, the very thing that Nigel had asked him to build. Without giving it much thought, Bjørn dashed off a reply, saying he was confident OneCoin didn't have a 'new blockchain' and that without one the whole thing was a lie.

Within hours, Bjørn was contacted by a Finnish man called Ari Widell who sometimes contributed to BehindMLM. Ari wanted to speak to him urgently. 'This could be *huge*,' he said.

CHAPTER 17

WHAT HAPPENED TO ONECOIN'S BLOCKCHAIN?

Most investors believed a OneCoin blockchain existed, even if they didn't fully understand the technology itself. So did the majority of the Sofia staff and Ruja's small army of advisers. Why wouldn't they? OneCoin was a multi-billion-Euro firm that had sold coins to a million people. On the surface it had everything a cryptocurrency firm needed: audit reports, legal letters, an exchange site, magazine covers and enough money to pay for any technology they wanted. So how was it possible that Ruja was launching a blockchain that hadn't even been built?

Maybe only Ruja herself will ever know the full story. But attempting to answer that question might also unlock the secret to Ruja's motives. The available evidence suggests she was trapped by a blend of success, hubris and irony.

When OneCoin was first launched back in 2014, lots of cryptocurrencies were being created and marketed, often accompanied by unrealistic promises of guaranteed returns. They mostly got away with it too because the law hadn't caught up with this nascent industry. In many ways, One-Coin was just one of a hundred other get-rich-quick crypto schemes. But events turned it into something quite different.

Bitcoin creator Satoshi Nakamoto was obsessed with the idea of 'decentralisation'. He thought many of the world's problems were caused by too much power accumulating to a tiny number of people in government and big banks. Bitcoin's fixed number of coins – the 21 million released (or 'mined') at a pre-programmed rate that even Satoshi couldn't change – was designed to disrupt it. Ruja wanted OneCoin to be part of the same family. Based on the available evidence, OneCoin had commissioned a blockchain when it was first launched in January 2015 – most likely a replica of the Bitcoin technology, except far bigger and faster: 2.1 billion coins being generated at 10,000 per ten minutes. The problem was that selling crypto via MLM turned out to be *too* successful. Her persuasive MLM promoters, the inspired compensation plan, and investor FOMO, combined to create a momentum that exceeded even Ruja's expectations. One possibility is that by early 2015, her blockchain couldn't keep up. Pretty soon Ruja was selling far more than 10,000 new coins every ten minutes. And during the summer of 2015 OneCoin mania, every morning Ruja woke up to find hundreds more Tycoon Trader packages had been sold, containing millions of coins that hadn't actually been created yet. 'This is the implication from the big sales 4 weeks ago', Ruja wrote to Sebastian on 6 August 2015. '1.3 [billion] fake coins. We are fucked, this came unexpected and now needs serious, serious thinking.'[1]

The email to Sebastian implies there might have been a blockchain of sorts in there somewhere, at least at the beginning. But nine months after the January 2015 launch event, Ruja had sold over one billion coins that were not recorded on her blockchain. Numbers appeared in investor wallets just like the 'real' coins, but they weren't backed up by the tech. On the available evidence it seems probable that Ruja scrambled a team to store these 'fake' coins on an 'SQL' database – basically a glorified Excel spreadsheet. Because no one other than Ruja and the IT team were allowed to see the blockchain, it was impossible for investors to know the difference. She might have had a 'real' blockchain: but for months she was selling coins that didn't exist.

Having sold over a billion non-existent coins, Ruja could have stopped activity and waited for her blockchain to catch up. But at the rate of 10,000 coins every ten minutes, it would have taken roughly a year for her blockchain to create the one billion coins that investors had already bought and believed were safely in their wallets. That would have killed the momentum that sellers like Juha and Pehr Karlsson had worked so hard to create, which in turn would have destroyed the company.

In truth, OneCoin was never going to succeed. The mining was fake, and so was the price. But what Ruja did when she realised the full extent of her 'fake coin' problem was a critical turning point. Shortly after the 'we're fucked' email to Sebastian in 2015, investors were briefly prevented from withdrawing their money on the exchange. Maybe this was the moment Ruja surveyed her options: should she come clean? Pause selling and wait for her blockchain to catch up? Pull the plug on the whole thing? But she did none of these things – and from that moment on her fate was sealed. Within days, and without any fanfare, she decided to keep selling and pretend nothing was wrong. The exchange went back online and started periodically paying out again, while promoters continued to sell as fast as before. Just five days after Ruja emailed Sebastian, Christine Grablis from Tennessee bought €15,000 worth of OneCoin packages. It was all thin air.

When Ruja and Sebastian first discussed OneCoin in 2014, she told him her expertise lay in the 'grey zones': those areas where the rules are fuzzy and technology has outpaced the law. Every day she sold coins she didn't have, Ruja moved further out of the grey zone. The most likely scenario is that, in 2014, Ruja and Sebastian spotted an opportunity. Both cryptocurrency and MLM were infused with 'fake it till you make it' culture, where hyped up promises of future profits were normal and failure largely went unpunished. The original plan may have been to pull in lots of initial investment on the basis of future Bitcoin-style price rises, then list the coin on a crypto-exchange with a fake starting price and allow the open market to drive the price down to zero, thereby wiping out any liabilities they owed. This would have been a swift and relatively moderate wheeze, and one which investors and the authorities might have struggled to do much about. By the time of the OneCoin corporate event in Macau in September 2015, she knew full well she'd sold a billion fake coins. And yet she stood in front of 5,000 people wearing a $1 million necklace and proclaimed, again, that OneCoin was the 'future of money'.

Why didn't she simply walk away in late 2015? She might have admitted to over-promising, even creating a fake price: but who didn't hype things up in this industry? No one will ever know for sure, but Ruja had become accustomed to her new life of money and influence. She loved the luxury homes, cars and million-dollar shopping sprees. Suddenly a lot of people depended on her too: she had staff all over the world, some of whom were old friends, and thousands of promoters. Having worked so hard to finally realise her potential, maybe she just didn't want to give it all up. Extreme hubris likely played a part, too. Ruja was supremely self-confident, a character flaw made worse by the constant adoration. 'She always thought she could fix everything with money,' one close adviser said later. It's likely that she believed she could somehow patch over this 'fake coin' problem. Indeed, through much of winter 2015, Ruja searched for a way to reconcile her 'real' blockchain coins and her 'fake' coins. And by the end of 2015, she thought she'd found the answer: the 'new blockchain' plan, which she announced at the June 2016 London event.

But Ruja hadn't reckoned with the imperatives of this new technology. Each new block of OneCoin transactions started, just like Bitcoin's, with a mathematically crunched version of the block before it, which linked them all together into a single unbroken chain. Old entries couldn't be changed or retrospectively added. The fixed supply and immutable ledger of records that underpinned Ruja's promise of a financial revolution were also what prevented her from reconciling her real and fake coins. Ruja needed a first-rate technical specialist to help her solve this riddle. OneCoin's COO Momchil Nikov was a decent IT guy. She had other developers too, like Ivan Slavkov who ran a local IT firm. But perhaps they didn't possess the blockchain expertise needed for such a tricky job and so, in the end, she was forced to contact Bjørn Bjercke. She hoped that he could take her 'fake' SQL database entries and retrofit them onto her new blockchain. If this was done cleverly, maybe no one would be any the wiser.

Unfortunately for Ruja, she'd chosen someone who was a true believer in blockchain technology, and he now wanted to know what exactly Ruja had 'launched' in Bangkok. If it wasn't a new blockchain, then what the hell was it?

CHAPTER 18

THE TEST

OneCoin's new blockchain made no sense to the regulars at BehindMLM either. The contributors to Oz's site were hardly the most conventional armchair detectives. Some were cryptocurrency specialists who felt that OneCoin was damaging the industry, others were reformed believers who'd lost money to other MLM companies. But most had no obvious connection to the case other than curiosity. 'We were all mostly just a bunch of nobodies tied together with a common interest,' Oz would say later. 'Fellow travellers.' What united them all was a desire – although it was more like a hobby or even, over time, an addiction – to find out as much as they possibly could about OneCoin using publicly available information and share it with the world. Each had his or her own unique skills to bring to the table. Tim Tayshun, a Bitcoin specialist from California who attended a OneCoin seminar in 2015 and concluded the whole thing was a scam, would rail against the technical weaknesses of the OneCoin blockchain. 'Semjon' excelled at finding obscure company, web-domain and personnel connections. Inspired by the big-hitting investigations by the open-source journalists at Bellingcat, he'd sometimes spend all night watching YouTube videos of OneCoin events, analysing IP registries or reading through corporate filings, and carefully saved and documented everything he found in a virtual war chest. In another life, he might have been a top-notch private investigator – but like the rest of the BehindMLM contributors, it was a hobby rather than a profession.

Like most of the BehindMLM sleuths, Ari Widell's lack of expertise was compensated by a stubborn fascination with the whole affair. Some days, Ari – a film fanatic in his late thirties – would get home from his day job in advertising, put the children to bed, then stay up until 3am in the morning investigating OneCoin. 'I would just follow the rabbit hole,' he said later. 'And then force myself to bed because I had to get up at 7am to go to work.' He often spent hours contacting banks who'd opened accounts for OneCoin and send them all the evidence he could muster that OneCoin was a Ponzi scheme. But the company always just seemed to brush it off.

As he sat reading Bjørn's LinkedIn post, Ari realised 'instantly' this was the proof everyone at BehindMLM had been waiting for. 'You need to go public with what you know,' Ari told Bjørn when they spoke later that day. 'This might be *big*.' Bjørn agreed to let Ari interview him about what had happened with Nigel Chinnock and Ruja's missing blockchain. The next day, Ari posted the interview on his own blog site. It spread like wildfire and, within hours, Oz had posted it on BehindMLM too.[1] As Bjørn read through the responses, he realised that his part in the OneCoin story wasn't finished. He knew OneCoin didn't have a real blockchain. But now he needed to prove it.

There is a famous saying in science: 'absence of evidence is not evidence of absence'. In other words, proving that something *doesn't* exist is more difficult than proving that it does. That was the task facing Bjørn, who decided he needed to show the world that OneCoin's blockchain was a fraud. It was made harder by OneCoin's secretive design. Bitcoin had a public and open blockchain, which listed every transaction all the way back to the genesis block and anyone could check it. Ruja, by contrast, kept OneCoin's blockchain private and guarded it like the Coca-Cola recipe. But she did concede one tiny morsel of transparency. Although no one was ever allowed to see the complete blockchain, the OneCoin website had something called a 'blockchain display', which showed live transactions between OneCoin wallets as they happened. That small window of openness gave Bjørn an idea. Investors could see their OneCoin balance by logging into their personal account, and those balances were supposed to mirror what was recorded on the blockchain. That meant that if Bjørn could transfer coins between OneCoin wallets, he could check if the same transactions appeared on the blockchain display.

Over the next few days, Bjørn acquired dozens of OneCoin wallets and passwords from disgruntled former investors and online critics, including several from Ari and other BehindMLM sleuths. One evening, he sat down at his desk and nervously opened three browser windows. Outside it was already pitch dark – one of those Norwegian winter nights that last forever. As usual he poured himself hot chai tea with honey and milk in a tall glass.

In the first two windows, he fired up the OneCoin website, and logged into two OneCoin accounts he'd been given.

In the third he opened the blockchain display.

Bjørn then sent three OneCoin between his two accounts. Within seconds a message appeared on his screen: 'Your request was successfully processed'. The coins had left one account and appeared in the other without any problem – just as he expected. If Ruja was telling the truth, if OneCoin really did have a functioning blockchain, that identical transaction should simultaneously appear on the blockchain display too, tucked in among all the other coins that were being sent and received across the network. But if Ruja was lying . . .

Bjørn sat and stared at the blockchain display, watching and noting every transaction that appeared: 0.580 coins moved. 1.121 coins moved. 1.681 coins moved. But no transaction appeared showing his three coins. So Bjørn did it again, this time with a different amount. And then again. And again. Wherever possible he used unusual number combinations that he would easily spot on the blockchain display. He moved 1.234 OneCoin. He moved 11.2233 OneCoin. Sometimes he waited a few hours between his tests, just in case someone from Sofia HQ was watching him. Other times he used his Rubik's cube as a randomiser: in-between transactions he would solve and scramble one, three or seven times so Sofia wouldn't spot his timing patterns. Over the course of several weeks, Bjørn made around 200 transactions on the 'front end' account and watched the 'back end' blockchain display, waiting for a match. But it was always the same result. Money moved between the accounts but never on the blockchain. Not even once.

There was only one, awful, conclusion. OneCoin's blockchain display *looked* like the real thing but it was some kind of pre-programmed 'script', an off-the-shelf piece of kit that was running phoney and meaningless transactions between imaginary wallets. Maybe it was built using 'real' blockchain technology, but what mattered was this: the entries bore no relation to the balance investors held in their wallets.*

---

* Bjørn also noticed that OneCoin's blockchain display contained a serious timing error too. Blockchains contain a chronologically perfect record of every transaction, sometimes down to the nano-second. But a handful of users logged into their OneCoin accounts at 00.01 BST on 1 October 2016 and found that their coins had already been doubled even though Ruja only 'switched on' the new blockchain in Bangkok approximately 16 hours later.

The display was just a clever ruse to fool investors into thinking their coins were held on a brand-new mathematically secure state-of-the-art blockchain. But all they owned were meaningless entries on a database. A million people had bought Ponzi tokens. Monopoly money that was controlled not by computer code, but by Ruja.

Suddenly everything else made sense.

No wonder Ruja could double everyone's coins in Bangkok. She could conjure up as many coins as she wanted, simply by manually changing entries on her database. The absence of a genuine, decentralised blockchain also meant the 'price' of OneCoin (which had gone from €0.5 in January 2015 to €6.95 by the time of the Bangkok event) wasn't based on anything. It wasn't driven by supply and demand, like Ruja had said in the beginning, because she didn't have a real coin to sell. Nor was it based on the 'mining difficulty', like she sometimes claimed, since there was no real mining taking place. The price of OneCoin was just a number invented by Ruja – a number she would periodically increase to keep investors happy.

Her new blockchain was a giant simulation that used the ideas, language and success of Bitcoin to blind people to the truth.

The exchange site xcoinx, which Igor and others had used to exchange OneCoin into Euros, wasn't a 'boutique independent exchange'. It was secretly controlled and run from the Sofia HQ to process periodic Ponzi payouts so people believed in the coin. When Igor sold his coins, it wasn't excited traders on the other side of the deal. It was Ruja's finance team paying him with money from newer investors.

The 'education' packages that people had been snapping up to acquire the tokens to mine the coins were another simulation, like the blockchain. They were pseudo-compliance, designed to confuse regulators into thinking the company was selling education rather than unregulated security investments. Huge chunks of the packages were directly plagiarised: for example, pages 1–18 of education level 3 was lifted word-for-word from the book *Technical Analysis for Dummies*.[2] (That plagiarised 'education' came with the 'Pro Trader' package, which cost investors €1,100.)

And those audit reports OneCoin had published each month since June 2015, which claimed the blockchain was legit? The auditor, a Bulgarian man called Deyan Dimitrov, vanished after a couple of months and, ever since, the audits were written by a company called S-Systems, another firm secretly created and controlled by Ruja herself.[3]

Maybe she'd started with a real blockchain of sorts. Maybe her new 120 billion coin blockchain existed on a server somewhere. But the balances people held in their accounts didn't correspond to it. The price was fake, the auditing company was fake, the exchange was fake and the education packages were fake. Everything was a lie.

Slowly the scale of the scam dawned on Bjørn. By the time he ran his tests in early 2017, OneCoin investors had spent approximately €3 billion purchasing as many as nine billion OneCoin, each of which was now priced at €7.95. That meant up to €70 billion worth of coins were owned by investors from Palestine to New York to Hong Kong to Kampala. Close to a million people thought they'd bought the next Bitcoin, but it was just an old-fashioned pyramid scam.

CHAPTER 19

BILLIONAIRES – ON PAPER

'He who tells a lie is not sensible of how great a task he undertakes; for he must be forced to invent twenty more to maintain that one'

—*Alexander Pope*

On 13 January 2017, thousands of OneCoin investors around the world logged on and checked their wallets and today's price. Things had been going pretty smoothly since the new blockchain launch – the price had continued increasing and thousands of new investors were joining. Checking in on their coins was a daily ritual for some of them – just seeing the numbers somehow made them feel rich already. But anyone who switched tabs and logged into xcoinx that day hoping to exchange a few of their coins into Euros was not greeted with the familiar homepage, but a worrying new message:

The Site is Currently Under Maintenance. XCoinX is currently undergoing a system upgrade, which will bring OneCoin to a whole new level, improving every aspect of the trading experience

Even though there had been technical problems and withdrawal limits on xcoinx ever since its launch in 2015, the existence of a quasi-functioning exchange site was always proof of last resort to investors, evidence that OneCoin had a real-world value. And thousands of investors had successfully 'cashed out' at least some of their coins on xcoinx over the previous year. Overnight, and with no prior warning, even that small pipeline was cut. Some had thousands of OneCoin in their xcoinx trading account, queued up ready to exchange.

For some investors, the sudden closure sparked panic. By this point, Christine Grablis from Tennessee owned one million OneCoin with a nominal value of over a million Euros. She, like hundreds of others, texted her upline (who had recruited her), who told her not to worry – it's just a 'glitch', he promised. But, in truth, the senior promoters didn't know what was going on either and watched in horror as their inbox filled with questions and demands from angry downlines. And Sofia HQ wasn't answering calls.

A simple calculation around this time ought to have persuaded any sane investor that the closure of xcoinx was inevitable. When OneCoin's 'price' hit a new high of €7.85 on 25 November 2016, its 'new' blockchain was mining 50,000 coins every minute. (Bitcoin by contrast mined just 12.5 every ten.) In other words, Ruja's secretive cryptocurrency from Bulgaria was creating over €500 million out of thin air every 24 hours. Even in the high-return world of cryptocurrency, this was absurd. Obviously xcoinx could never pay all that out – even paying 1.5 per cent of that was prohibitively costly. And, little known to investors, after the excitement of the Bangkok coin doubling, revenue from new recruits was drying up, falling from €239 million in November 2016 to less than half that the following month.

There were some people for whom xcoinx's unexpected closure finally tipped the balance and persuaded them One-Coin was a lie. A handful of others had watched Bjørn Bjercke's YouTube videos about his tests, or read the

BehindMLM article that documented Bjørn's discovery a few days after xcoinx went offline.[1] For others, it was a gradual realisation that the reality and the promise were drifting apart. Layla Begum, the council worker from London who'd invested her entire life savings equivalent to around €60,000 by this point, grew increasingly wary of her upline's excuses. Although she'd been told originally that she could get her money out any time, whenever she asked Saleh he was vague and evasive. By late November 2016, she became increasingly panicked and texted Saleh: 'I'm extremely distressed pls return my money'. But although her OneCoin account looked healthy, the money was frozen in space, immovable. 'There is a way u can have that back instantly,' replied Saleh. 'You have to lie though. You have to say to your bank you didn't do that transaction [to OneCoin]'. Layla wasn't prepared to lie to the bank.

But despite BehindMLM's articles, Bjørn's tests and xcoinx's closure, still many investors continued to believe as fervently as ever. Why?

Good scams aren't about facts or logic. They are built on the manipulation of common human irrationalities: hope, belief, greed and, above all, by the nagging 'fear of missing out', FOMO. Websites that say 'currently under maintenance' or YouTube videos by technical experts are no match for these impulses. Although OneCoin investors were victims, they weren't entirely without blame. FOMO is driven by a desire to get rich quick, a willingness to replace work or effort with a risky bet. Many of the top promoters, including Igor Alberts, also felt investors were partly at fault. 'I felt responsibility,' Igor said later. 'Not guilt.' Victims, he thinks, should also have looked into it properly themselves. 'This is the risk of life . . . I told people always: where you can win, you can lose.'

Nevertheless, the sophistication and audacity of One-Coin made it hard to resist. OneCoin was technically three different scams rolled into one. It was primarily a Ponzi scheme, since it was based on the Ponzi accounting trick of paying early investors using money from newer ones. But it was also a pyramid scheme because it recruited new investors using the MLM model, without any real product. Ruja's masterstroke was to take these two well-rehearsed scams and lay a fake cryptocurrency on top. That allowed her to cover the lies with exciting promises of a 'financial revolution' and confusing technical language. The combination rendered facts and logic irrelevant.

Ponzi schemes are named after Charles Ponzi, the genius huckster who conned thousands of Americans in 1920 by promising 50 per cent returns within 45 days if they invested in his clever-sounding 'international postal reply coupon' scheme. When hundreds who put their money in received their 50 per cent back, thousands more rushed to join. It was all a sleight of hand – the new money was just paying the preceding round of investors, who in turn would became unwitting recruiting sergeants for the next round.[2] Charles Ponzi's scam was not the first of its kind. But it became so widely known that the name stuck.

Borrowing from Peter to pay Paul can't work forever, which is why in the end all Ponzi schemes collapse. But a well-run Ponzi can run for years, sometimes even decades, as long as fresh money keeps flowing. The trick is to identify the payout sweet spot that exploits human greed without causing bankruptcy. If a scheme pays too little then no new recruits will join the merry-go-round; but if it pays too much the scam will quickly run out of money. For decades, Bernie Madoff, a well-respected fund manager from New York, had found that spot: his company paid investors a market-busting 10 per cent return for 40 years. In public he said it was thanks to 'sophisticated trading techniques' that only he understood, but behind the curtain there were no investments, no trades, nothing: just a lot of fake accounting and schmoozing. But, just like with Charles Ponzi, investors got their money on time every year, which meant there was always a line of excited Peters and Pauls outside his door. A Ponzi scheme exploits FOMO by making sure enough people really are striking gold so the word gets around. It's one of the most powerful of all human irrationalities. A Ponzi scheme in Albania in the early 1990s hoodwinked so many people that it almost resulted in the whole country tumbling into a civil war.

Unlike all Ponzis before it, OneCoin had *two* payouts. First the weekly 4pm 'Happy Monday' sale commissions, based on the volume of sales generated in a promoter's downline that week. Despite the banking problems faced by Ruja, it normally arrived on time. But only 100,000 or so of the roughly one million OneCoin investors actually recruited enough other people to make decent sales commissions. The overwhelming majority simply bought a package and waited for the value of their holding to grow. This is why the second payout was so important. Until its closure, many OneCoin investors were able to, in theory, exchange their OneCoin on xcoinx for Euros at whatever price was listed at the time: €0.5 in January 2015, €4.45 in January 2016, €7.85 in November 2016. Whereas the commission payments were reliable, xcoinx had those daily withdrawal limits of 1.5 per cent and half the time the website didn't work at all. But the company always allowed *just enough* withdrawals – roughly €10 million a week according to internal accounting documents – to produce a steady stream of believers who would then evangelise to the next round of victims, just as Ponzi and Madoff's investors had done. The lucky ones who managed to withdraw experienced something close to a religious conversion and happily deluded themselves that the balance in their One-Coin wallet was just as real as sterling or yen. It was such a powerful feeling that even when xcoinx went offline, most were willing to believe it would only be a short delay before the coin would finally *go public* on an even bigger, even better exchange.

OneCoin's Ponzi payout system sucked people in, but it was the pyramid recruitment that persuaded them to stick around. Friends would tell each other about this incredible new 'opportunity' they'd discovered. Have you heard about Bitcoin? *Well, there's this new one, which* – Layla Begum recruited her mother and brother; Daniel from Uganda convinced his mother to invest. Entire friend and family networks, some stretching continents, got tied into the scam together because they desperately wanted to share their good luck with their loved ones. But this meant that admitting the whole thing was a fraud would also mean admitting they'd inadvertently scammed their own friends and family. The line between perpetrator and victim in pyramid schemes is not obvious. Many were both. That might have stopped some people from complaining about the people above them, in case the people below them did the same. Christine Grablis, the OneCoin investor from Tennessee, would later confess that it was 'embarrassment' that kept her believing.

In other words, people desperately wanted to believe and Ruja encouraged this self-delusion by always making sure any bad or suspicious news was accompanied by a dazzling new announcement. That's why she doubled everyone's coins (good news!) when she unveiled the new blockchain (bad news).

When xcoinx went offline, Ruja had two exciting new projects ready to soften the blow. First, OneCoin was going to become the first cryptocurrency to be listed on a 'major stock exchange', meaning ordinary people could start buying share options in the company. This would be done via an 'Initial Public Offering', commonly known as an IPO. Ruja invited all investors to go online and turn their coins into share options, which would be redeemable for the share price as soon as the company was listed. (Some advisers at the London RavenR Capital office thought an IPO was a bad idea because there was little prospect that a hybrid MLM-cryptocurrency would clear the regulatory hurdles that come with selling shares to the public.) Second, OneCoin launched a new e-commerce platform, called 'Dealshaker', where investors could spend their coins in exchange for real, physical products. An Amazon or Groupon, but where payments were made in OneCoin.

The key to the OneCoin scam was Ruja's genius for the just-good-enough. Everything about OneCoin was fake, but she somehow always made it appear plausible. The blockchain, the audits, the education packages, xcoinx – even the Cryptoqueen herself – were all imitations that outsiders found risible. But they were always just-good-enough for anyone desperate enough or invested enough or greedy enough.

Nothing epitomised the power of just-good-enough like Dealshaker. The site was created and maintained by Duncan Arthur, the South African bank compliance specialist who would later find himself being questioned at Los Angeles airport with Konstantin. Ruja initially recruited Duncan in late 2016 to help with the IPO but he came up with the idea of creating a sales site instead. When Ruja first announced Dealshaker just a few days after xcoinx disappeared, she promised it would be a ground-breaking, million-merchant platform. 'A huge new e-commerce site,' she said in a slick pre-recorded announcement released on 15 January 2017, which would deliver on the promise of 'cryptocurrency for the masses'. What investors actually found when they first logged on to Dealshaker in February 2017 was a glorified online flea market. Anyone willing to accept OneCoin as payment could sign up and start selling, but nearly every merchant was a OneCoin promoter and there were only a few hundred products for sale, mostly from Russia or China. Typical products included beard oil, online education courses, marketing DVDs, duvet covers and amateur art. Luxury items like five-star hotel rooms or cars were listed, but the links to purchase very rarely worked.[3] And in the unlikely event an investor managed to find something they actually wanted, OneCoin charged a commission of up to 25 per cent. Prices (which were typically set 50 per cent in Euros, 50 per cent OneCoin) were so inflated that the Euro price alone was often more than the RRP price on Amazon. (The HyperX Cloud Revolver gaming headset, for example, cost €107 on Amazon; on Dealshaker it was €200 *plus* 31 OneCoin.) To make things worse, the site was also riddled with its own sub-scams.[4] On day two, Duncan, who was jetting around the world training local franchise holders about how to run Dealshaker in their countries, woke up to find someone had sold a counterfeit handbag. A few weeks later, he deleted a merchant from a small village in China that was selling Louis Vuitton handbags for €19,000 plus 2,000 OneCoin. One morning in March 2017, he removed a Pakistani man who was trying to sell his kidney for 100 per cent OneCoin.[5] The worst of all was when a group of Chinese miners clubbed together and paid €200,000 in real money on Dealshaker for some cars, which never arrived. The miners blamed OneCoin and turned up at the office in Hong Kong, threatening to kill themselves if the money wasn't returned. When the Hong Kong boss Fernando Rhys messaged Ruja about this, she said, 'I will not pay for members' stupidity. I am sorry; this will set a precedent that is simply not acceptable.' Her only concession was to give them double the value of their OneCoin back – which, amazingly, they accepted.

All in all, Dealshaker might have been the worst e-commerce site to have ever graced the internet. Ari Widell, the guy who first contacted Bjørn, dubbed it 'Deal-shitter'. But investors didn't see Dealshaker for the unwieldy, ugly, overpriced, scam-ridden site that it was, just as they didn't see the private blockchain as suspicious, or the xcoinx withdrawal limits as deeply worrying. Hundreds of OneCoin investors logged onto Dealshaker each day and started sending One-Coin (and Euros) to merchants in exchange for insect repellent, pan pipe CDs and nail varnish. Within weeks, One-Coin events included a 'Dealshaker Expo', where vendors would set up physical booths advertising the products they were selling on the platform, and top promoters were instructed by Ruja to start recruiting merchants as well as investors. (Recruiting merchants also generated commissions.) Duncan Arthur later claimed he believed OneCoin was a legitimate business at the time, but would also admit that Dealshaker re-energised the network just at the point it was most vulnerable. 'I was responsible for keeping this scam going for longer than it should have,' he said. Investors believed in it for the same reason they believed in OneCoin: because they wanted to.

Dealshaker was more than a life raft for worried investors; it was also a smart way to draw focus away from OneCoin's increasingly exposed Ponzi-pyramid business model. In one email sent to her legal advisers in January 2017, Ruja said she would 'like to position [Dealshaker] as our main area of business, not the classic education packages, with tokens . . . there is no way on this platform to be a pyramid/Ponzi', before adding 'what are your thoughts how we can utilise this for improving online reputation, standing with regulators, investigations etc???' (Their reply is not known.)

But even with the just-good-enough imitations, the sticky pyramid recruitment and twin Ponzi payouts, nobody expected OneCoin to get as big as it did nor last for so long. But it was helped by an unexpected rival. By 2016, the whole world had the crypto bug, and each week serious magazines wrote how this strange new money was about to revolutionise banking, shopping, land registries, money transfers, international trade, and much else. By early 2017, Bitcoin had entered a self-fulfilling hype cycle. Thought leaders, consultancy firms and other tech cheerleaders all said it was 'the future' for fear of looking Luddite. And it became the future because everyone started buying it on the basis it was.

When xcoinx was taken offline and Bjørn Bjercke started publishing his findings about the OneCoin blockchain on YouTube and BehindMLM, OneCoin should have collapsed for good. But then Bitcoin went on a record-breaking bull run. Its price broke $1,000 in March 2017, then broke $2,000 in May, $3,000 on 12 June, $4,000 on 12 August and $5,000 on 1 September. Suddenly cryptocurrency seemed like it was the future, after all – and the promise that OneCoin would match, and even surpass, Bitcoin's price rally was so tantalising that investors were happy to ignore any lingering doubts. It was nicer to dream than to think.

CHAPTER 20

WELL-SPOKEN PROFESSIONALS

Scammers do not operate in a vacuum. They analyse social trends and spot opportunities to look credible. Since 2010, the world's information output has grown exponentially, and everyone is now bombarded with endless data, graphs, claims and counterclaims. Some of it is from established experts but much of it is not. Working out who to trust is tiring and confusing, especially in novel industries like cryptocurrency where there are no established authorities or agreed-upon qualifications. Ruja took advantage of the uncertainty.[1]

In the summer of 2015, around the time OneCoin released its €12,500 Premium Trader package, and the company topped €1 billion in revenue, Ruja – dressed all in black and wearing red lipstick – appeared on the cover of *Forbes* magazine under the headline 'A Cryptocurrency with Bulgarian Origin'. Over a two-page spread, Ruja talked about the future of finance and the coming crypto revolution. *Forbes* is one of the world's most famous business magazines and for decades aspiring entrepreneurs have dreamt of seeing their face gazing out from its cover in news stands in New York, London and Tokyo. Warren Buffett, Bill Gates, Elon Musk have all made it. When the July 2015 edition was published, OneCoin's social media accounts lit up: 'In her interview for the prestigious magazine Forbes', read one post 'our founder Dr Ruja introduces OneCoin'.

The impact was immediate. Promoters were sent copies to distribute at events. Rubies and Sapphires shared the article with uncertain relatives. In Uganda, wannabe investors were shown photos of the famous cover in seminars and workshops. For anyone confused by the tech (which was nearly everyone) it was a convenient substitute for careful analysis: who needed to understand the intricacies of the blockchain or the mining process when the boss was a *Forbes* cover star?

But Ruja wasn't the *Forbes* cover star at all. Via *Forbes*'s specialised PR firm 'Brand Voice', she'd purchased three pages inside the Bulgarian edition of the magazine and designed an advert that looked indistinguishable from the journalistic content, including a mock-up cover page. (The real cover that month was in fact pop icon Katy Perry, under the strapline 'Pop's Top Export'.) Far from being a *Forbes* front cover star to rival Zuckerberg or Elon, Ruja had paid a few thousand Euros for a simulation. The only way to figure this out at all was to be fluent in Bulgarian and spot the small words 'Brand Voice from OneCoin' next to Ruja's power pose, which indicated it was sponsored content. The vast majority of OneCoin investors could not place Bulgaria on a map, much less speak the language. Sofia HQ purchased hundreds of copies, ripped off the real front cover, and started sending the phoney *Forbes* around the world.

Ruja repeated the clever trick a few months later with an even more esteemed business publication, *The Economist*. In November 2015, she was the keynote speaker at a large conference hosted by the magazine in central Sofia, which was attended by local bigwigs, including the Bulgarian president Rosen Plevneliev. *The Economist* in London had subcontracted its conferences in the region to a local events company called Hazlis & Rivas who sometimes allowed sponsors to speak at conferences. As the delegates filed into the luxurious Hotel Balkans to spend two days discussing economic co-operation and development in south-east Europe, they were greeted with a large poster displaying the sponsors: Dell, CNN, Visa. Top of list and the only 'Platinum' sponsor was OneCoin. The amount she paid has never been disclosed, but she was given a 15-minute speaker slot, during which she wowed the 100 or so participants with her vision of the future of money. 'Our company . . . reached market capitalisation of one billion euros,' she told the audience. 'We take a very active approach of shaping the future of money.'[2] 'I was speechless,' recalled Igor Alberts, who was in the audience. 'She knocked all the other people off.' Ruja ignored Hazlis & Rivas's stipulation that she not use any logos or footage from the event: within days, the OneCoin PR team had edited and released a promotional video of the entire speech. 'Would *The Economist* invite a Ponzi scammer to speak at one of their events!?' promoters would ask. Just as with *Forbes* three months earlier, no one mentioned that Ruja had paid for her turn. (Hazlis and Rivas has since stopped allowing sponsors to speak at events.)

It's impossible to know how many people were persuaded by this technique – but judging by the degree to which promoters pushed it onto investors, it was highly effective. Jen McAdam, a Scottish investor who later spent her father's inheritance of around €12,000 on OneCoin, said that it was *The Economist* speech that persuaded her that Ruja could be trusted.

But the people who most helped Ruja make OneCoin appear credible came from a more trusted profession than journalism. From the outset, Ruja understood the value of having lawyers on tap, and even before the first OneCoin package was sold in summer 2014, she appointed her German lawyer Martin Breidenbach as owner of OneCoin Ltd in Dubai. Toward the end of 2014, Martin's firm Breidenbach Rechtsanwälte published a legal opinion about OneCoin, stating it was 'a legitimate product limited to 2.1 billion coins'.[3] Lawyers are assumed to be trustworthy – which is why their letters and opinions are so valuable. Martin's stamp of approval was circulated widely, appearing in promotional PowerPoints and online seminars.[4] (Martin Breidenbach was approached for comment about his involvement in OneCoin, but had not replied by time of publication.)

Ruja loved lawyers (she was married to one, after all), and by 2017 had a network of at least six law firms working across five countries. Her go-to law firm in the UK was Locke Lord, who she started using in early 2016. Mark Scott's work was done without the firm's knowledge (though he too denies any wrongdoing, and claims that he was misled by Ruja), but Locke Lord's payments specialist Robert Court-neidge, one of the world's leading experts, advised Ruja for three days on how OneCoin should expand, seemingly unaware it was a giant Ponzi. ('At the time I was reviewing [OneCoin], there were many new cryptocurrencies coming into the market,' Robert said later. 'I was told the intention was to create a real competitor to Bitcoin.') A Locke Lord partner, James Channo, administered the purchase of her multi-million-pound London penthouse.

One reason they didn't twig that OneCoin was a Ponzi scheme was the way Ruja used different law firms to advise on different elements of her business. When she wanted advice about whether OneCoin's MLM activities might breach the UK's anti-pyramid trading laws, she didn't ask Locke Lord. Instead she instructed Hogan Lovells, another respected firm based in London, who spent months 'on-boarding' (a legal term for various due diligence checks) the company and then several more months examining the business model in detail. Their team even visited the Sofia HQ, on a 'fact-finding' trip. According to RavenR Capital boss Gary Gilford, Irina Dilkin-ska usually avoided or ignored difficult questions and made herself unavailable whenever possible, which made it difficult for anyone to know exactly what was happening in Bulgaria. (He used to call Sofia HQ's unwillingness to answer questions 'the Bulgarian flu'). In late 2016, Hogan Lovells concluded that, on balance, and subject to several changes, including tighter promoter contracts, 'based on the terms of the MLM agreement... [OneLife] will not constitute a pyramid promotional scheme', although they did add that there were elements which were 'questionable and could create the impression [that it was]'.[5] Ruja was determined to squeeze as much credibility from her lawyers as she could: she read through the report carefully and added a small note in the margin: 'Can we here pls also say that it is not a "Ponzi" scheme??'* (Hogan Lovells later told *The Times* that they were unable to comment on their work for OneCoin, but 'if they saw anything in a client's business which creates a requirement to report to the appropriate authorities then it goes without saying that we would do that'.)

Ruja saw lawyers more like PR than as a source of genuine legal advice. Negative legal advice was usually ignored, while anything that showed the company in a good light was used in marketing materials, or to persuade other organisations to work with her. And it was two of her well-spoken professionals that landed the company's biggest PR coup of all.

As OneCoin grew into a billion-dollar company, Ruja realised her media and comms team in Sofia were not up to the job. They regularly published press releases full of spelling mistakes and unprofessional language about 'haters'. By mid-2016, Ruja decided to get serious about PR. She hired the libel specialists Carter-Ruck, who were known for aggressively

---

* In March 2017, Hogan Lovells sent Ruja, Irina and Gary Gilford a follow-up report entitled 'Good State Report', which contained dozens of sensible suggestions about how to improve its procedures to stay on the right side of the law, including registering with the Direct Selling Association, the UK's industry body for MLM. But most of these were subsequently ignored.

(and successfully) defending the reputations of famous clients, including Russian oligarchs and the Church of Scientology. Via her security adviser Frank Schneider's firm Sandstone, Ruja also hired a London-based 'crisis comms' firm called Chelgate run by Terence Fane-Saunders, a charming and eccentric PR veteran. Chelgate was asked to help improve her image, and work alongside Carter-Ruck whenever needed.

Over the course of late 2016 and mid-2017, Chelgate, Carter-Ruck, Frank Schneider and OneCoin representatives met periodically to consider various PR, legal and media challenges. They often talked about critics, who they described as Bitcoin fans worried by OneCoin's success. They discussed creating an international advisory group comprised of House of Lords luminaries and complained that the City of London Police was unfairly targeting the firm. On one occasion, a briefing note was prepared about the prolific BehindMLM contributor Tim 'Tayshun' Curry. They sometimes emailed whenever bad news popped up. In January 2017, Max von Arnim, an external part-time consultant to RavenR Capital in London, spotted that BehindMLM had connected RavenR Capital with OneCoin. He asked Gary Gilford if 'there is a way to diminish the visual link of RavenR and O[ne]C[oin]?' Carter-Ruck replied there was little they could do legally, while Terence explained that it was 'tricky' to push negative stories down the Google search list, since 'pushing it down really requires burying it under plenty of other stories, each of which need search engine optimisation to push them up'. In a similar vein, one of Carter-Ruck's first jobs, in July 2016, was to send a letter to the editors of the crypto news site Coin Telegraph, which had called OneCoin a Ponzi scheme. 'This allegation is false and seriously defamatory. OneCoin is neither a Ponzi Scheme nor a Pyramid Scheme', wrote the law firm. 'OneCoin sells legitimate products of genuine value such as the OneCoin cryptocurrency . . . Our Client Dr Ruja Ignatova has also been caused serious embarrassment and distress.' They asked that Coin Telegraph remove the article, or legal action would follow. Shortly afterwards, Carter-Ruck did the same thing to former investor Jen McAdam who had also been criticising the firm online. (Neither Coin Telegraph nor Jen removed the criticism.)

Item six on the agenda at the group's meeting in November 2016 was Ruja's latest headache: the UK's financial regulator, the Financial Conduct Authority, had recently issued an investor warning about OneCoin on its website. 'We believe consumers should be wary of dealing with OneCoin,' it read. 'We are concerned about the potential risk this poses to UK consumers.'

Ruja was furious when she heard about the warning, shouting at Irina that she was being 'unfairly' treated. She was right to be worried. Overseeing Europe's biggest financial hub had made the FCA a *primus inter pares* among financial regulators and several other countries issued similar warnings shortly after the FCA's, including Latvia, Nigeria, Uganda, Croatia, Thailand and Spain. Within days of the warning being published, BehindMLM critics started sending it to potential investors, advising them to avoid the company. Ruja wanted the notice removed and, in May 2017, a Chelgate staffer spotted a potential solution. When the FCA was created to regulate London's financial and banking sector after the 2009 crash, cryptocurrencies barely existed and so were not placed under its jurisdiction. As a result, even as late as 2016, no one was responsible for keeping tabs on this fast-growing sector, including the FCA. 'It is not a matter of them acting in breach of their obligations, rather beyond them', read an internal memo from Chelgate. What's more, this strange notice seemed to be more like a press release than an official warning, for which there was no precedent. At some point in summer 2017, Carter-Ruck sent a letter to the regulator stating that the notice should be removed because it was, quite literally, none of their business.

With the scam in full swing and being aggressively marketed in the UK, the FCA removed their warning. The exact reasons are unclear because the FCA refuses to release any correspondence between them and organisations working for OneCoin. Perhaps the understaffed regulator thought Carter-Ruck had a point, and they didn't fancy a scrap with its fearsome lawyers. Whatever the reason, on 2 August 2017, the webpage warning consumers about the biggest Ponzi scheme in the world suddenly vanished.[6]

Ruja was thrilled when she heard the news. Within hours, OneCoin promoters announced that the FCA no longer considered OneCoin a fraudulent company (which wasn't true). From Brazil to Uganda to the United States, promoters incorporated the removal story into their marketing materials. Canada's top OneCoin pimp, Ken Labine, triumphantly told his followers: 'If [the FCA] still thought we were a fraudulent company . . . then, guess what, that warning's not removed. Game over!' Even the BehindMLM crew found it hard to argue.

Some of the sharpest legal minds around – clever enough to spot the technical flaws in an FCA warning, to advise on the minutiae of crypto law, and to structure complex house purchases via offshore companies – were simultaneously unable to see the biggest Ponzi scheme in 20 years staring them right in the face. Money has a funny way of fencing off difficult questions and incentivising strategic and defensible ignorance. It is not corruption *per se*, at least not in the classic sense. But it shows how those with money can, through pressure, legal weight and sponsorship, subtly shape the environment to their advantage.

Unfortunately for Ruja, she soon had far bigger problems to worry about. And this time not even her well-spoken professionals could help her.

Part 5

DISAPPEARANCE

CHAPTER 21

THE LAST HURRAH

Having a baby changed Ruja. Although usually cold and ruthless, she was always capable of being generous and warm. Around the office she would often ask after interns, and, on one occasion, even paid for a colleague to undergo IVF treatment. But colleagues noticed that motherhood had significantly softened her up. After her daughter was born in early winter 2016, the famously meticulous boss started turning up to meetings unprepared and uninterested, showing photos and discussing nurseries rather than sales techniques. And although she rarely spoke about her personal life in public, she made an exception in a short online video published around this time: 'I would like to share very very personal and exciting news,' she announced. 'Last week, my little daughter was born.' Work generally started to take a back seat. When she stayed at her sparkling new Kensington penthouse on a two-week trip to London in December 2016, she spent most days shopping – returning home each evening flanked by two exhausted-looking bodyguards carrying bags of designer dresses and jewellery.[1] She started delegating important decisions to Irina Dilkinska and hired a respectable cut-out Luxembourg banker in his late forties called Pitt Arens as new CEO of OneCoin. Although denied when put to Pitt, it is thought he was paid €750,000 a year to oversee the IPO and Dealshaker projects and was promised a 1 per cent bonus from any IPO sale. (He said later that he had been in charge of product management not sales, and did not control money flows of any kind.) But he was only in post for a matter of months before resigning, citing a 'lack of leeway'.[2]

OneCoin had raised over €2 billion in income over the course of 2016, recruited hundreds of thousands of investors and held events in almost every country on earth. But success brought pressure, and not just from BehindMLM or Bjørn Bjercke. Every week, there was a new problem. Banks periodically closed down accounts because of suspicious activity.[3] Ruja herself had received threats of violence, which prompted her to take on a security detail. She even confided in Gilbert that someone had broken into one of her Bulgarian properties and tried to burn it down. The German police were investigating IMS (Frank Ricketts's infrastructure of companies and accounts that Ruja was using as a feeder fund for Fenero) and there were rumours other police forces were preparing charges too. She still didn't have a Chinese network licence. In late 2016, the Bank of Africa froze one of her bank accounts and detained a handful of OneCoin recruiters and, a couple of months later, Indian police arrested another 18 promoters in Mumbai. In both cases, the police charged the suspects with running a Ponzi scheme. And although Ruja assured worried investors that these unruly promoters had made unapproved promises, a growing sense of unease was spreading in the network, all the way up to Ruja herself.

A year earlier, Ruja might have relished taking on her rivals and enemies, but by early 2017 – and now with a child to think about – she no longer enjoyed the drama. Colleagues found her increasingly nervous and unusually agitated. Her mobile phones proliferated and she started to become paranoid about being kidnapped by angry investors who had grown tired of endless delays to go public. One close friend recalls that she was even afraid for her life. She took her mother's name off some of her companies, increased her bodyguard detail and bought a bulletproof Lexus. One afternoon, she phoned Gary at the RavenR office in London and told him everyone was 'trying to rip her off', demanding that someone be sacked, only to change her mind the next day. Gary sometimes felt sorry for his boss. 'She often seemed quite lonely,' he recalls. Ruja even started to wonder whether Dr Hui had conned her too and sent Gary all the way to Madagascar to check if there really was an oil field. (There was.)[4]

She was also tiring of the network and found her MLM promoters increasingly disobedient and grasping. Although they had built the company for her, she had come to hate Kari's onstage routines and Igor's clownish suits. And although she tightened up promoters' T&Cs following legal advice from Hogan Lovells, it was impossible to control tens of thousands of active sellers all over world, who routinely said anything to drive sales. That was her fault too, because it was Ruja herself who'd said all along that OneCoin would make people rich.

Even her relationship with Sebastian became strained. As co-founder, he was under much the same pressure as Ruja herself, and he secretly resented Ruja for firing his girlfriend after the London birthday party. According to later court testimony, in late 2016, Sebastian snuck into a secret OneCoin flat in South Korea, which stored money, and walked out with millions of dollars in a suitcase. When Ruja found out and threatened to expose him to the network, Sebastian returned the money, but their relationship never fully recovered.

The regulators, the hostile press, the banks, the money, BehindMLM, the closure of xcoinx, the greedy promoters, Bjørn Bjercke, the blockchain, Sebastian, and now a child to worry about – it was all getting too much. And it was about to get worse.

CHAPTER 22

OPERATION SATELLITE

In March 2017, nineteen officials took their seats at Europol HQ in the Hague. The FBI, the Department of Justice and the US District Attorney's office had all made the trip over from America – along with police officers from the UK, Germany, the Netherlands, Dubai and Bulgaria. It was the second meeting in four months for the recently formed 'Operation Satellite'.

Far from being ignorant about OneCoin, law enforcement around the world knew almost exactly what was happening.

Operation Satellite probably all started because of a mistake by Ruja's lover, Gilbert. Back in 2015, when OneCoin money first started flowing into his various bank accounts, Gilbert's job was to move it from his accounts in Dubai or Singapore to his JSC Bank in Tbilisi, from where he processed the weekly commission payments for promoters. But he invested some of it too. One of the companies he invested in was a UK firm called Viola, run by a British businessman called Christopher Hamilton, which specialised in online payments. In November 2015, Gilbert invested $19 million into Viola. 'He was a likeable chap,' Hamilton recalls, although he claims he never mentioned OneCoin or Ruja. As far as he was concerned, Gilbert was an investment manager, and this was simply an investment.

According to Hamilton, a few months later Gilbert sent Viola's Luxembourg investment fund another large chunk of money to invest in renewable energy firms. But some of it came from a company account that Hamilton didn't recognise. He called Armenta and demanded further information about where this money had come from – but within 24 hours Viola's bank HSBC froze his account. Presumably HSBC filed a 'suspicious activity report' to the UK authorities, and pretty soon the City of London Police launched an investigation into Christopher Hamilton and contacted their counterparts in America responsible for white collar crime. From that point on – around February 2016 – the Manhattan District Attorney's Office had Gilbert on their radar.[1]

On 21 April 2016, Hamilton was sitting at his home in south Wales and heard a knock on the door. A postman delivered $30 million in banker's drafts from HSBC – the money that had been frozen. Moments later a dozen officers from the City of London Police turned up, seized the drafts, searched the house, arrested Hamilton and took him in for questioning. According to Hamilton he was quizzed for several hours – including about Dr Ruja Ignatova and OneCoin. 'It was the first time I ever heard of OneCoin,' Hamilton said later. It was the largest ever money seizure by the UK police, although OneCoin was omitted from the police press release – it referred instead to 'overseas crime, including Ponzi schemes'.[2] Shortly afterwards, however, a judge at Hammersmith court ordered the money be returned to Hamilton. (It's not entirely clear why – magistrates' courts do not keep written records; Hamilton only recalls the judge had ruled the seizure as 'unlawful'. Perhaps it was a technicality, or maybe the judge simply decided there was insufficient evidence of any wrongdoing on Hamilton's part. Hamilton was not charged with any crime, and the police subsequently discontinued their investigation.) Either way, the police press release was removed from the City of London's website.

But that wasn't the end of the story as far as the US

authorities were concerned. The Manhattan District Attorney's Office started investigating Gilbert Armenta. By sheer coincidence, a few months later a compliance officer at the Bank of New York Mellon identified several large and concerning transactions that involved multiple Fenero Fund entities and a company called 'International Marketing Services Pte Ltd', or IMS, that were transferring funds via some of its correspondent banks. Another Bank of New York Mellon employee from the 'suspicious activity response team' researched the company and found several articles, including on BehindMLM, that tied IMS to OneCoin.[3] In December 2016, and then again in February 2017, the Bank of New York Mellon reported these 'concerning' wire transfers – including the $30 million involving the Madagascar oil field deal – to the Financial Crimes Enforcement Network at the US Treasury Department.[4] Although the inner workings of law enforcement are mysterious, it seems likely that this is what prompted a second investigation into OneCoin and Fenero, this one led by the US Attorney's Office.

At some point, the US Attorney's Office and the Manhattan District Attorney's Office realised they were working on the same case and decided to pool their resources and make it a federal investigation. The IMS transfers, the Madagascar oil field, the suspicious millions sent to Christopher Hamilton – it was all connected to the same woman: Ruja Ignatova.[5]

This was clearly bigger than Gilbert and dodgy bank transfers – and before long Europol agreed to co-ordinate the efforts of multiple police forces that had also been tracking OneCoin. The codename reflected the global nature of the scam: Operation Satellite.

As the meeting got under way, each team shared the state of their investigations into Dr Ruja and her cryptocurrency. The US team discussed a 'high-placed confidential informant' inside OneCoin and presented several OneCoin bank accounts receiving investor funds. The British police meanwhile had identified around 100 promoters selling in the UK, and had even tried to interview Ruja herself via her UK solicitors – but she ignored their request. The Germans were frustrated that several witnesses didn't want to make official statements about OneCoin because they still believed in it.

Between them, a picture of OneCoin had emerged: a pyramid sales system pushing a cryptocurrency with no real blockchain and a made-up price. Thousands of investors around the world, most of whom still believed in the product. And a sophisticated system of corporate obfuscation and money laundering. But they lacked someone close to Ruja who could provide them with the cast iron evidence they'd need to start arresting people.

A few days after that meeting, Dr Ruja was handed a memory stick. How exactly she got it – and how much she must have paid for it – remains a mystery. Whatever she paid, it was worth it. It contained all the minutes of that meeting, right down to each PowerPoint slide deck presented that day. Ruja had a mole.

CHAPTER 23

CONNECTIONS

Her most pressing issue was money. She'd already moved tens of millions without Mark Scott's Fenero Funds, including buying a penthouse in Dubai, a multi-million-dollar jewellery collection, a fleet of luxury cars, a Sofia townhouse and restaurant. But there were still millions sitting in the Fenero Funds, controlled by Mark Scott. Was this now all at risk? Were the authorities about to seize everything she'd worked for? Ruja asked her advisers and contacts to urgently identify investment opportunities so she could turn the Fenero cash into assets she controlled. What followed was a remarkable six-month spending binge.

On the advice of her Bulgarian contacts, €51 million was invested in a Bulgarian tobacco company called Openmark, which needed money to open a new factory in Thessaloniki, Greece. That was run by Hristo Lachev, the former boss of Bulgartabac.*

Someone at HQ – it's not clear who – identified a horse-racing fund based in Dubai called 'Phoenix Thoroughbred' that was hawking around for investors. Phoenix was a two-year-old fund created by a Bahraini horse fanatic called Amer Abdulaziz to (among other things) buy, breed and race pedigree horses. In

* Hristo Lachev was approached for comment but no response was received at the time of publication.

spring 2017, 11 wire transfers totalling €185 million were sent from the Fenero accounts to the Phoenix Funds Dubai accounts, via the Bank of Ireland.[1] (Phoenix Fund Investments, the parent company of Phoenix Thoroughbred, denies any allegation of wrongdoing.)*

Taken separately these money transfers don't necessarily mean much. Bulgaria's political and business elite is relatively small, and it's inevitable that investments of the size Ruja was making would involve influential people. But taken together, they suggest that, by early 2017, Ruja knew some of the most important people in the country. She was connected – both at home and in Dubai, where many of her companies were based. And there was one deal in particular that likely interested the authorities. Back in 2015, Ruja was involved in a complex property deal, which entailed selling dramatically cut-price land to a pair of Bulgarian supermodel twins called Boryana and Anna Shehtova, via one of her Dubai companies. Boryana was the long-term girlfriend of a notorious Bulgarian drug trafficker based in Dubai called Hristoforos 'Taki' Amanatidis, aka 'The Cocaine King'. Taki was rumoured to have well-placed sources inside Bulgarian law enforcement. Sources that could give him information about ongoing police activities. According to the FBI's analysis of bank statements, which was revealed in a 2019 court case, around the time Operation Satellite kicked into gear a further €6 million went to yet another company owned by Taki's partner. Was Taki the person who alerted Ruja to Operation Satellite?

---

* There were other transactions around this time which suggest Ruja moved large volumes of money quicker than she'd originally planned to. (Only a couple of months earlier, Mark had told his wife Lidia that he thought he could make $25 million with Ruja over the next 18 months.) A Bitcoin wallet Ruja set up in April 2016 to receive payments for OneCoin packages in Bitcoin rather than cash was also emptied of around €2 million in March and May 2017.

By late spring 2017, the Fenero Funds were almost completely empty. It was a remarkable logistical achievement. In little over 12 months, thousands of small OneCoin investments – mostly €5,000 Tycoon Trader and €12,500 Premium Trader packages – had been disguised as large subscriptions from rich Europeans into a regulated fund and transformed into an eclectic mix of shares, properties and businesses. The woman who'd grown up in a small flat above a butcher's in sleepy Schramberg was now a property magnate, a jewellery collector, and a business investor worth close to half a billion Euros.

His job done, Mark started formally closing down the various Fenero entities.[2] He'd worked like a dog, flying to either the Cayman or British Virgin Islands no fewer than 10 times and spending hours each week on paperwork.[3] To celebrate, Mark went on another spending spree: a $1.3 million Sunseeker yacht, two more Porsches, and a $2 million house in the exclusive Hyannis Port neighbourhood in Cape Cod. He immediately commissioned $1.8 million worth of renovation work, much to the anger of his neighbours, who were fed up with gawdy out-of-towners upsetting the feel of the historic town. Determined to fit in, Mark paid for a flattering profile about himself in the local real estate magazine.

As she sorted her assets, Ruja also started to wonder if she could get out of this mess. The easy route would be to sneak off to some exotic island or corrupt kleptocracy where the authorities would never reach her. At this point, it seems likely that Ruja didn't want to actually disappear – she wanted instead to walk away from OneCoin but carry on living the life it had given her. Even as her troubles piled up in early 2017, Ruja spoke excitedly to colleagues about her plans for 2018: to move into the Kensington penthouse and work full-time at the RavenR Capital office in Knightsbridge. She even started researching private schools for her daughter. Maybe it was delusional, but even once it became clear her blockchain problem was insoluble and the authorities were watching her, Ruja still hoped to extricate herself from One-Coin without being directly implicated in it.

In a well-executed con trick, the victim doesn't realise they've been duped until long afterwards. In a perfect one, they never even know at all. It certainly seemed possible back in 2017. That year alone hundreds of new cryptocurrencies and 'blockchain-based' companies were launched, raised millions of dollars from early investors, and then collapsed having delivered little or nothing. Some of them were well-intentioned failures, but others were just smart scams capitalising on Bitcoin's growing popularity. Most fell into the grey area somewhere between the two and in many cases the people in charge walked away with no ramifications.

She had ideas about how to convince the world it was all an honest failure, although all of them were fraught with risk. Her promise to IPO OneCoin on a 'major stock exchange' and get users to trade their coins for share options was one possible way out. From January 2017 on, Ruja told investors that the IPO was the new route for the coin to *go public*. 'If you have coins, you are entitled to become part of the biggest success story, we hope, since Facebook,' Ruja announced to investors around this time. Rather than cashing out on a currency exchange site as she'd always promised, coin holders were now advised by Ruja to 'change as many coins as you can' into share options, which they would be able to sell on for profit to the public once the company was listed.[4] (Confusingly the coin would *also* be listed on an exchange once the company was listed on a stock market.) Within a few weeks, almost half of all coin holders had done as she'd asked and exchanged their OneCoin for share options. It's possible that Ruja really did think the IPO was possible – RavenR Capital consultant Max von Arnim flew to Hong Kong in March 2017 and met with listing advisers there. But according to others involved in planning the IPO, Ruja's hidden motive was to reduce her liabilities. A draft internal document explaining the plan, entitled 'The IPO story', said, 'if users give their coins back to the company, they unite together as shareholders', to which Ruja hastily added a disclaimer: 'No guarantee, risk, blablabla'. The moment OneCoin was listed, the share price would likely crash to near zero, because no members of the public would invest in a company like OneCoin. She would then be able to walk away and blame 'the market'.

Around the same time, Ruja also toyed with simply selling the entire MLM network to a private investor and quietly winding the coin down, leaving her formidable sales force to push more traditional MLM products like health or beauty items.[5] She had staff work round the clock to prepare a 40-slide PowerPoint sales pitch, which portrayed the OneLife network as the sales machine of the century: 'With over 2.2 million paid members and exceptional loyalty to its culture', it read, 'it is unlikely anyone can duplicate Q[ne] L[ife] N[etwork]'s success'. The pitch projected sales of €30 billion 'in the near future' and detailed accounting data claimed that OneCoin's EBITDA (earnings before interest, taxes, depreciation, and amortisation, divided by total revenue) was at least double that of Herbalife's or Avon's. 'The most important thing on her mind at this time was the sale of OneLife,' Gary Gilford said later. 'Nothing else seemed to matter.'

Hopeful that she might have found a clever way out with her IPO or fire sale, Ruja decided it was time to relax.[6]

Sozopol, July 2017

Like many wealthy Bulgarians, Ruja owned a large property in the picturesque seaside resort of Sozopol, a popular holiday spot 20 miles due south of the more touristic Nesebar and Sunny Beach. The grand mansion – which cost Ruja €7.5 million once the refurb was done – boasted a private beach, 20-metre swimming pool and a children's play area. Ruja had large roses painted on the pool floor and custom-made imported furniture flown in from Germany and London. She fitted a gym in the basement and, like many extremely rich people keen on privacy, also bought the neighbouring property. Over the weekend of 7–9 July 2017, a hundred or so of Ruja's friends and colleagues descended on Sozopol to celebrate the christening of her daughter. To mark the occasion, Ruja unveiled her new €6.9 million superyacht (complete with six rooms, an underwater observation lounge, bar and massage room). It was docked at Sozopol's tiny port on the west side of the peninsula, a short walk from the historic old town and its cluttered bars and cafes. The 44-metre boat looked absurd alongside the rusty fishing trailers.

A small gathering on Friday night was followed by an all-day party on Saturday, attended by most of her closest friends and family: Konstantin, her parents Veska and Plamen, her husband Björn – who Ruja was struggling to fit into her increasingly busy life – Asdis Ran, Sebastian, the Dealshaker boss Duncan Arthur, her consigliere Irina Dilkinska, Gary Gilford from RavenR. Gilbert Armenta, her money man and lover, flew over from Florida. Gilbert was usually very convivial, but he seemed out of sorts and spent much of the weekend in the gym chatting to Konstantin about their shared love of sports, dogs and women. Unusually he mentioned his business affairs with Ruja, telling Konstantin that 'the work with your sister is following me around like a big black shadow'.

The party started mid-afternoon with drinks and a conveyer belt of appetisers and snacks. People gathered around the large swimming pool, took small sorties to the private beach and drank champagne. The constant hum of increasingly drunken voices competed with the loud music and echoed off the Black Sea. As the night wore on, Ruja's parents left and the mood loosened. Even Ruja, who very rarely was drunk in public, swapped her customary Diet Coke for champagne. The climax of the night was – just as it had been a year earlier for Ruja's 36th birthday party at London's Victoria and Albert Museum – a famous pop star. For the super-rich, renting celebrities for the night is its own industry, and, the wealthier Ruja became, the more famous her private performers. In 2015, it was a well-known Bulgarian pop star. In 2016, she upgraded to Tom Jones. This time she flew over her favourite artist, the American mega-star Bebe Rexha. Everyone piled down to the purpose-built open stage and danced to Rexha, as she performed her hits as if playing to a sell-out stadium. As a treat, Rexha pulled Ruja on stage to sing her favourite song together, 'Me, Myself and I'. Ruja was embarrassed; 'they're paid to cheer,' she said, smiling at the large audience. 'That's something we have in common,' replied Rexha. One of Ruja's make-up artists was caught cavorting on the beach with someone from the London office and was fired the next day. The Bulgarians broke into folk song and traditional dancing, and, on Ruja's instructions, Gary and Duncan were both thrown into the pool. The whole of the summer continued in a similar vein. Ruja spent most of it in Sozopol, alternating between mansion and yacht, looking after her daughter and welcoming guests. Locals started to recognise the strange crypto woman who threw private parties, and restaurants hoped her high-tipping entourage might roll in. She also made time while in Sozopol to order bespoke Mottahedeh

Tobacco Leaf kitchenware for her London penthouse from Harlequin in west London.[7]

Although Ruja enjoyed the relaxing beach life and break from the pressure of running a billion-dollar company, nothing could fix her problems. In mid-July, she dashed back to the Sofia HQ for a couple of days to host an online webinar with Pitt Arens (the short-lived CEO) and Sebastian, to deal with the continued questions about the blockchain. Nervous investors also wanted to know when the xcoinx.com site was going to reopen – it had been down for six months and counting – so they could cash out whatever coins hadn't been turned into share options. Ruja reminded investors that One-Coin had a unique and powerful 'closed source' blockchain, which was better than Bitcoin, and she complained about 'haters' doing the company down. Sebastian blamed 'fake news' for the negative rumours while Pitt said he was working on getting xcoinx.com reopened. 'Stay with us, be loyal to the company,' Ruja said, 'and you guys will see we will make history.'

The irony of OneCoin was that the very technological revolution Ruja spent three years selling to the world – a fixed money supply controlled by computer code – turned out to be the reason she couldn't escape. Its revolutionary system of unchangeable chronological record-keeping had gone from a tool of liberation to a ball and chain. There was simply no way around the problem. The very technology she'd spent three years promoting kept her trapped. By autumn 2017, her plans to IPO or sell the network had gone nowhere and a final collapse was inevitable. It was just a matter of time. But it wasn't greed or tech that finally pulled the house down, it was her love life.

CHAPTER 24

THINGS FALL APART

Ruja was confident to the point of arrogance in business, but in her personal life she was clueless and wild. 'It's because I'm a Gemini,' she would tell friends when they suggested she be more careful. She should have listened to them.

Ruja had been married to Björn Strehl ever since university. Björn was one of those fortunate people who grow more handsome with age. He had always been tall and striking, but his youthful gaunt had filled out into an attractive feline appearance. His prospects were also improving, and by 2017, he'd carved out a career as a respected real estate lawyer in Frankfurt. Although not a lover of the limelight like his wife, and careful to stay out of OneCoin, Björn enjoyed Ruja's new-found success and attended the carousel of parties, awards and events if work allowed. When Ruja addressed an audience or conducted an interview, Björn would sometimes be found sitting quietly in a corner, looking on admiringly. 'She always has ideas,' he gushed to a Bulgarian lifestyle magazine in a rare interview in 2015. 'And she always makes the ideas happen . . . It's really great sharing life with her.'

Ruja didn't talk publicly about her personal affairs, a habit which probably fanned the many rumours about her love life. But it seems likely that the demands of running an international, multi-billion-dollar company was putting a strain on her relationship with Björn. Then, in the summer of

2017 things would have deteriorated further when Ruja made the mistake of falling in love with the flash Floridian financier Gilbert Armenta. What started as a casual romance in 2015 when Ruja first employed Gilbert to help her process payments via his Georgian bank gradually became something more serious. After spending most of July and August together at Ruja's Sozopol mansion, the pair started talking seriously about leaving their spouses and moving to London.[1]

'She was completely obsessed with Gilbert,' a friend said later. But before she flipped her life upside down, Ruja wanted to know that Gilbert was as committed to the relationship as she was. There was something about him that made her uncharacteristically nervous. It wasn't the first time he was tied up in a risky investment. Years earlier a Caribbean telecoms company called Curanet in which he was the main stakeholder was run into bankruptcy.[2] Even as they relaxed in Sozopol, he was trying to lean on Christopher Hamilton – who was still sitting on the millions Gilbert had sent him in early 2016. Ruja sometimes wondered whether Gilbert was only with her for the money. Although Mark Scott was now handling most of her finances, there was still a vast amount of Ruja's money flowing through Gilbert's web of companies.

In late August 2017, Ruja turned to the one person she employed who could help her figure this out: former spook Frank Schneider. Frank had been managing Ruja's reputation and security since mid-2015 and she'd come to trust him. She valued his calm professionalism and measured assessments. According to Konstantin's later testimomy in court it was Frank who'd suggested she travel to Bishkek to buy a Kyrgyz diplomatic passport. (Bishkek passports were famous in the private intelligence industry. For only a few thousand dollars, anyone could get a diplomatic Kyrgyz passport and use it to travel to certain places without fear of arrest – especially in and out of Russia. She acquired one that summer, shortly after the christening party.) Who better to look into Gilbert than a former spy? His 30-year career was built on finding out other people's secrets. Ruja asked Frank to find out whether Gilbert really was going to leave his wife. (In a later response to the BBC's *The Missing Cryptoqueen* podcast series, Frank Schneider denied any of the following happened).*

Despite the technological advances of the last 50 years, the fundamentals of surveillance work haven't really changed. The best way to spy on someone is the same as it was when Frank joined the Luxembourg intelligence agency SREL in the 1980s: sneak into their home and hide a listening device in the wall or light fitting. Even today, MI5 or the FBI still rely on 'close contact surveillance' when they can't access a suspect's phone or emails. But it's not only state spooks who are listening in any more; private companies and wealthy individuals spend billions each year on private intelligence firms who apply similar techniques to gather information on business rivals, critics, journalists and ex-partners. Most cities have at least one 'spy shop', where anyone can buy recording instruments disguised as calculators, mains sockets or light bulbs. A decent listening device that can penetrate 12-inch-thick walls only costs around £200. For a former head of ops for SREL, covertly listening to a married couple would be child's play.

According to later court testimony, on Ruja's instructions one of Frank's American contacts rented the apartment below Gilbert's in Fort Lauderdale, Florida. He drilled a hole through the ceiling and installed a listening device strong enough to pick up Gilbert and his wife Basia's conversations.

*

* Details about Frank's role in spying on Gilbert are based on Konstantin Ignatov's later testimony under oath in a US criminal case.

Personal life aside, when Ruja returned to Sofia from Sozopol in late August 2017, she found a mixed picture. On one hand her Fenero laundromat had cleaned €350 million, she had a dozen top-end professionals working for her in London, Dealshaker was ticking over, and she had a new respectable CEO in Pitt Arens.

But she still had no blockchain and senior promoters were getting anxious messages every day from their down-lines who wanted her to publish the whole thing in its entirety, rather than the tiny 'display' that Bjørn Bjercke had shown was a fake.

MLM companies possess a shark-like quality. They only survive by moving forwards. Even a moderately profitable year can be disastrous, because the whole industry is built on promises of 'record years' and 'exponential growth'. But smoke and mirrors can't last forever, and, for the first time since mid-2015, OneCoin started to lose its momentum. There wasn't a single moment of collapse, like when SEC agents burst into Bernie Madoff's New York apartment with handcuffs, and OneCoin revenue was still tens of millions a month. But the gradual accumulation of broken promises, delays and blockchain rumours was beginning to bite. The online buzz was quieter and local recruitment events were a shade less energetic. Critics and regulators were becoming more outspoken. Online seminars – which had been running fully booked for months – were now only 75 per cent full. MLM promoters have an acute sense for when a company is on the turn, and some of the top promoters, including Aron Steinkeller, Pehr Karlsson and the New Zealander Ed Ludbrook, started drifting off to newer, fresher projects. In early summer, Juha 'Papa OneCoin' Parhiala himself, co-founder in all but name, also quietly departed. Officially it was due to poor health but there were rumours that he'd been spooked by the spate of OneCoin arrests in India. But no one knew for sure because he practically vanished over-night and wouldn't leave Thailand.

Worse news followed when Ruja quietly dropped her IPO idea. OneCoin wouldn't be selling shares to the public after all. In keeping with her philosophy of smothering bad news, Ruja promised the network it was because she had a better plan: OneCoin would have an Initial *Coin* Offering instead. (An ICO is a lot like an IPO, except it's specifically designed for cash-strapped new cryptocurrency start-ups and has far fewer rules.) Unfortunately it would take a whole extra year.[3]

Just like with the xcoinx closure months earlier, investors panicked when they heard the news. WhatsApp groups were full of worried coin holders trying to figure out what it all meant. Even Kari Wahlroos – the resplendent hype-guy – seemed unsure. 'We as leaders have done everything to provide the correct info', he wrote on his Facebook page. 'Now there is going to be some adjustments . . . I am deeply sorry'. All anyone ever wanted was to buy coins at one price and sell them again at a profit. But OneCoin, supposedly the 'Bitcoin killer' for the masses, had turned into a giant Rube Goldberg machine.

In the pyramid business, products flow down but the money and the questions flow up. With Juha gone, Igor Alberts found himself at the pinnacle – a Black Diamond with a downline of thousands of investors generating over €8 million in sales a month. The chorus of questions was getting louder: When will xcoinx go back online? What's this new ICO all about? And when can we see the blockchain? The Sapphires would ask the Rubies above them, who would ask the Diamonds above them . . . until it reached Igor, and the only people above him were Sebastian and Ruja.

When Igor and Ruja met at the Sofia HQ in September 2017, he told her that investors had a lot of questions. She had to tell the network exactly what was going on, especially about the blockchain. And, if possible, get her legal team to deal with Oz and BehindMLM. People were nervous, he said, including him.

'Please,' Igor said. 'Show the world that we really have what we promised the people.'

'Yes, Igor, we are going to do it,' Ruja replied. As usual, she seemed confident and in control.

'When?' asked Igor. He was the one who had teams of promoters beneath him asking him constantly for updates.

'Sooner than you think. Everything will be clear at the Lisbon event.'

Lisbon was the next big OneCoin event, two weeks away. All the top leaders would be there, including Ruja herself.

Shortly after Igor left Sofia, Ruja received the recordings of Gilbert and his wife Basia's private conversations. Just a few weeks earlier, Gilbert had been in Sozopol with Ruja, lounging by the pool and talking about their future together. But, from the recordings it was clear that Gilbert had little intention of leaving his wife. Ruja was crushed by the betrayal. She imagined Gilbert and Basia laughing at her, using *her* money to fund his private jet. On 24 September 2017 she phoned him.

'I love that footage where you say you aren't going to leave your wife . . .' she said. 'Gilbert, what the fuck is wrong with you, really? I never thought you were like a spineless asshole, are you?'

'Well, the big issue right now is—' Gilbert started.

'No need, *no need*!' Ruja cut back in, regaining her steel. 'I know people can be weak . . . but I don't deserve this and [Basia] doesn't deserve this either . . . there is such a thing as personal integrity. Google it.'

But the recordings revealed something else Ruja hadn't expected: Gilbert was in trouble with the law. Operation Satellite was bad enough. But it sounded like the FBI had Gilbert on a seemingly unrelated charge of extortion.[4] If the FBI was on to Gilbert, how long before they were on to her too? Ruja feared the worst. The FBI would get to work on Gilbert. They'd grill him, shake down his house, clone his laptop, confiscate his phone – they'd turn him inside out. But, still, it was Gilbert. Surely the man she loved wouldn't betray her.

Since 2014, there had been dozens of investigations into OneCoin, and Ruja never seemed fazed. According to one close associate, 'nothing seemed to scare her'. When the UK's FCA put up its warning notice, she called in Chelgate and Carter-Ruck and faced it down. When the German BaFin froze her money in 2016, her lawyers successfully unfroze it. She laughed off the Indian prosecutor's indictment. But the FBI were different. Even her Bulgarian connections couldn't protect her from them.

For the first time since she founded OneCoin, Ruja started to panic. A couple of days after their first phone call on 28 September, Gilbert phoned her on a non-encrypted line. This time she wasn't upset – she was furious. She'd told him several times to only communicate face-to-face. 'Gilbert, you have to be *fucking* careful!' she shouted. 'I can get everything I want within twenty-four hours and if I can they can too. I'm really worried – you have to be really careful with communications.'

But Gilbert was in far more trouble that Ruja realised. When Christopher Hamilton was dramatically arrested in April 2016, Gilbert's money was seized with him. Gilbert got back in touch with Hamilton asking for his money back. When Hamilton delayed, Gilbert believed he was planning to keep it for himself. (According to Hamilton, there was a disagreement over which bank accounts the money should be returned to). The standoff went on for several weeks. To move things along, in around August 2017, Gilbert hired a former army marine to follow Christopher around and send intimidating messages about the debt – including photos of his grandchildren leaving school.[5] In the end, Hamilton sent the money back to one of Gilbert's American bank accounts. But by then it was too late. The FBI had got wind of this behaviour, and started preparing charges against him.

On 12 September 2017, a New York grand jury indicted Gilbert on three counts of extorting Christopher Hamilton.[6] Just a couple of days later, Gilbert was arrested as he disembarked a flight in Connecticut, and immediately agreed to co-operate. The first person he told them about was Ruja Ignatova. And for the next 14 straight days Gilbert sat in a hotel room with FBI agents and told them everything he knew about the woman he loved.

As Ruja lectured Gilbert about the importance of good security in their phone call on 28 September, Special Agent Ron Shimko of the FBI was sitting right next to him, recording every word.

CHAPTER 25

PONZI ACCOUNTING

There is no single correct way to work out the size of a scam because it depends how you define the word 'loss'. The obvious method is to calculate how much money was invested. This is called 'real-world' loss. (Although this isn't straightforward in Ponzi and pyramid schemes because early investors often make money.) There is a second way too, which is how much money investors *thought* they were owed. Although this is sometimes called 'fictitious' loss, it can be just as keenly felt by victims.

Bernie Madoff's Investment Securities is widely regarded as the biggest Ponzi of all time. His fund attracted 30,000 mostly high-net worth individuals or fund managers, who invested approximately $36 billion (€34 billion) in Madoff Securities. About half was paid back out as returns, leaving a total 'real-world' loss of around $18 billion (€16 billion). When the Department of Justice finally made sense of the Madoff paperwork, they found that the money investors thought they were owed – the 'fictitious' loss – was significantly higher. Possibly as much as $60 billion.

OneCoin's precise real-world losses might never be known because much of it was never recorded. Based on internal accounting documents and the testimony of those involved, it's possible to estimate that somewhere around €4–15 billion worth of packages were sold between late 2014 and late 2017. Roughly one third of that was paid back out in returns (either as sales commissions or via xcoinx.com), which places real-world losses at between €2.6 and €10 billion. That's at least five times the size of Elizabeth Holmes's notorious Theranos scam. Nick Leeson's Barings Bank job . . . the infamous *Bitconnect* con . . . even Charles Ponzi's postal coupon swindle – they all paled in comparison to what Ruja had pulled off. Only Bernie Madoff could match it.

Because of its pyramidal structure, however, Ruja scammed far more people than Madoff and they were less able to bear the loss. OneCoin really was shaped like a pyramid, with each layer from Crown Diamond down to Sapphire being deeper and wider than the one above. Only 50,000 or so ranked sellers actually profited from the scheme, and even that was skewed to those at the top: the roughly €1.4 billion that was paid out in commission and withdrawals went to just 5 per cent of the investors, and the majority went to the 0.5 per cent that were Diamond or above. Most of Ruja's victims were not sellers. The pyramid's true base was the roughly one million investors from 175 countries who bought packages but barely recruited anyone else at all – people like Christine Grablis or Layla Begum. Any commission they made was tiny, all they had was coins in their accounts whose returns would arrive when OneCoin finally went public. They were ordinary people from across the spectrum of life – Ugandan farmers, Scottish single mums, Japanese businessmen, Muslim scholars, American car dealers. It was mostly ordinary people who collectively lost almost €3 billion to a scam.

The fictitious losses for OneCoin investors can also be calculated, albeit very roughly. By the time Ruja was shouting down the phone at Gilbert in September 2017, OneCoin had created 21 billion coins on the new blockchain (plus the initial 2.1 billon from the first blockchain), each now worth €15.95 according to the OneCoin website. Although a certain amount had been turned back into cash via xcoinx, and a decent chunk may have been unallocated, there could have been as many as 20 billion OneCoin sitting in people's accounts. *Billions* of coins, each worth €15.95 in the minds of investors. Each one as real to them as the money in their pockets.

It's no wonder Ruja was nervous about the FBI. Bernie Madoff's fictitious losses were around $60 billion (€57 billion). Ruja Ignatova probably owed investors over €100 billion. And it was growing every day.

CHAPTER 26

FLIGHT

Paris, 26 September–3 October 2017

Anyone lucky or rich enough to be staying at the Four Seasons Hotel on Avenue George V during Paris Fashion Week might have spotted the well-dressed businesswoman deep in thought in La Galerie, the hotel's see-and-be-seen dining room. How much trouble was Gilbert in? What might he tell the FBI? Did they already know about Fenero, the fake blockchain, the phoney price? All her other worries – Igor Albert's questions, one million investors, the ICO – seemed insignificant.

Ruja had booked this trip months earlier when things were calmer. Her interest in fashion hadn't waned since school: seeing Dior, Louis Vuitton or Chanel model their latest was one of the few ways Ruja relaxed. One time in Hong Kong, her office manager Fernando Rhys turned up at the Ritz-Carlton and handed her a backpack with one million Hong Kong dollars cash – and she beelined to the nearest luxury mall and blew it on jewellery. To get in the mood for Paris, she'd been on one of her infamous sprees, spending thousands of dollars on a gold crocodile Hermès Birkin bag and a Carolina Herrera Mikimoto emerald-diamond-pearl necklace.[1] Sometimes she wished she'd just opened that cosmetics company 'RujaNoir', like she'd planned back in 2011. Instead she was tangled up in this crypto MLM mess, trying to figure out what to do about Gilbert.

Ever since that angry phone call on 24 September, Gilbert and Ruja continued to speak almost every day. Given he was now working for the FBI as an informant, it's probable that the authorities insisted Gilbert call regularly and tease her with morsels of information to keep her curious. But Ruja wanted to talk face-to-face – like she always said: phone lines weren't secure. Gilbert agreed to travel to Paris to meet Ruja and talk it over, adding that his teenage son would also join. (Konstantin agreed to come to Paris and entertain him so Ruja and Gilbert could be alone. While there Konstantin managed to get a selfie with Cindy Crawford, which he posted on Instagram.)

No matter how impossible the situation, Ruja always thought things could be fixed with enough time and money. Maybe she hoped to sweet-talk Gilbert, maybe to confront him. As a bare minimum she needed to know whether this extortion case involved her, and make sure he didn't do anything stupid. But just before he was due to arrive, Gilbert told Ruja he wouldn't be coming to Paris after all. He didn't mention the reason: the Southern District of New York court had granted him a $5 million bail subject to a curfew, regular urine tests and GPS monitoring. The Department of Justice confiscated his passports and forced him to move from Florida to Manhattan (where he stayed, ironically, at the Four Seasons). He wasn't allowed to leave the borough of Manhattan, let alone fly to France. However, his teenage son did still travel to Paris, and maybe that was what gave it away. Perhaps he let it slip that his dad now lived in Manhattan and was banned from travelling. Maybe one of Ruja's people contacted Gilbert's lawyers and learned about the bail hearing. (The government didn't object to his bail, which is often a sign that a defendant is co-operating.) However it happened, when she should have been enjoying the catwalk, Ruja realised Gilbert was in deeper trouble than she thought. He might already be working for the FBI.

Ruja always tried to keep Konstantin out of her trouble. She cared a lot about her little brother and he was just the PA. Although he travelled everywhere with her, often doubling up as an extra bodyguard, she sometimes ushered him out of the room if anything sensitive was being discussed.

'Something bad has happened,' she told him, uncharacteristically worried. 'Travel back to Sofia without me.'

'What is it?' Konstantin asked.

'I can't tell you,' she replied, trying not to worry her brother. 'I will see you back in Sofia.'

Ruja needed to start planning.

Lisbon, 7 October 2017

Igor Alberts was pacing up and down in his hotel near to Lisbon's popular events venue, the Congress Centre. She wasn't answering her phone, which wasn't like her. He phoned Konstantin, Irina, anyone he could think of from Sofia HQ. No one knew anything. No one had seen her.

'Where is she?' Igor kept asking himself. 'Where is Dr Ruja?'

Two hundred and fifty OneCoin investors and promoters, including some of the biggest names in the network – Kari the hype guy, Latin America's only Black Diamond José Gordo, even co-founder Sebastian himself – had come to Lisbon for the weekend corporate event. Everyone had the same questions that had been festering away for weeks: when are we going public? Will you show us the blockchain? What's happening with the ICO? Igor had told his downline what Ruja had promised him, that she would answer everything in Lisbon.

'How can she not be here?' Igor fretted to Andreea. She'd never been late.

It was true – Ruja did not tolerate tardiness. One time, two promoters had travelled halfway across the world to meet Ruja for a routine meeting. They arrived four minutes late and she sent them all the way back home again. But minutes passed, and then hours, and there was no sign or sound from Ruja – nothing. Emails, WhatsApp messages and phone calls all went unanswered. For the first time ever, Ruja just didn't turn up.

Could it be that those OneCoin critics on BehindMLM were right all along, that this was all just a massive . . . ? No, that was impossible. It would be the biggest scam since Bernie Ma— well, it didn't bear thinking about.

It was too late to cancel so apologies were made and excuses were given. Pitt Arens also failed to show up, and resigned shortly after. The event continued as if nothing was wrong. Saturday was all-day sales training where promoters wore lanyards that read 'live the life of your dreams' and learned the latest pitching techniques. Sunday was motivationals and recognitions. Kari did his usual turn: OneCoin was the 'opportunity of a lifetime' and Dealshaker will be 'bigger than eBay'. But without Ruja the event had lost its oxygen. Kari didn't charge on stage like a steam train saying 'the future's so bright I wear sunglasses' like before. Igor noticed that Sebastian – who for three years had been Mr Positive, Mr We-can-do-it – seemed distant and distracted. His speech at the gala dinner the evening before was rambling and vague. More importantly, there was no new information about going public, no proof of the blockchain, no answers about this strange new ICO plan.

Offstage all sorts of theories were bouncing around the senior promoters. Ruja had been kidnapped. Killed. Igor had told her before that she needed more bodyguards. 'Oh, those fuckers from the traditional banks,' he said to Andreea, between frantic calls. 'This is the trick they do!'

Sofia, 8 October 2017

Ruja sat in her Sofia mansion and watched the missed calls come in from Lisbon.

Ten, twenty, fifty.

It was too risky to go to Lisbon now she knew about Gilbert – and by now she was convinced he'd snitched. With all her connections, she felt relatively safe in Sofia, but if she left Bulgaria, there was a chance an officer with an Interpol red notice would snap her up at the airport. Once she figured out Gilbert was in trouble with the FBI, Ruja started secretly recording her side of their phone conversations too. 'What is it?' she asked in one of their many calls. 'What are you not telling me?' She said she missed him, but then suggested they cool the relationship off. Gilbert played dumb. He said he'd be coming to Sofia to visit her soon.

Konstantin didn't know the details but he knew his sister was extremely worried. Ruja flew off the handle at Konstantin practically every day over minor infractions – the stationery was the wrong colour, her Diet Coke wasn't sufficiently chilled – but she'd always apologise soon after. This was different. She was depressed and lacking energy. To cheer her up, Konstantin turned up at her mansion unannounced with some food, but she'd lost her appetite and looked like she hadn't slept properly in days. Ever since they were kids she was the smart one who always fixed everything. Through all the problems of the last three years she'd never cracked. For the first time, he was genuinely worried about her.

'Ruja, tell me what's wrong,' he said. He'd accepted her vagueness in Paris. But judging from her appearance, whatever it was, it was serious. He wanted answers.

'Gilbert had some problems with the FBI,' she finally replied. 'He wants to make some kind of deal with them. He's planning on giving me to the FBI in exchange.'

Konstantin glanced over at the table and saw a printout. It was a transcript of Gilbert talking about working with the police.[2]

'What's going to happen?' he asked. What the hell were the FBI involved for?

'Don't worry,' Ruja replied, noticing Konstantin's worried expression. 'Everything will be OK. Gilbert's plan isn't going to work.'

Bernie Madoff's biographer Diana Henriques wrote that he had a 'well-defended mind'. He believed he would get away with it, even while simultaneously knowing that was impossible. Madoff sometimes thought that some awful calamity, maybe an earthquake or power outage, might befall New York and his crimes would be forgotten. Ruja also had a well-defended mind. She thought she would get away with it too. But this wasn't New York. It was Bulgaria; the most corrupt country in Europe.

Sofia, 11–24 October 2017

For the next two weeks, little happened. There wasn't much more news from Gilbert. Her Fenero money man Mark Scott was still walking around freely in Florida – if the FBI really knew everything, surely they would have got Mark too?

Sebastian also got back safely to his Ko Samui home in Thailand from the Lisbon event. Maybe Gilbert had kept his mouth shut after all. Ruja started to relax a little and even got back to business, working on the ICO with Irina, talking to Gary Gilford about a partnership with the Ugandan government, and looking for a replacement for Pitt Arens, her recently resigned CEO. She ordered earrings and ceramic flowers and asked Konstantin to pick them up for her. In the background, Ruja also started pulling a few strings. Irina Dilkinska wired €200,000 into one of her Maltese casino bank accounts, called Infinityplay, from the B&N company that had been used to move money into the Fenero Funds.[3]

But there was a lot going on; Ruja just didn't know about any of it. Less than a week after the Lisbon event, a grand jury in New York secretly indicted Ruja on charges of wire fraud and money laundering. In other words, the US legal system had concluded that, with the fresh evidence from Gilbert, she should face charges in America. The indictment was under seal, meaning no one should have seen it. But the net was closing in. It seems likely that at this point – around the middle of October 2017 – the US Department of Justice issued a request for assistance, known as a Mutual Legal Assistance Request, to the Bulgarian justice department. (The other possibility was to issue an Interpol arrest warrant, which would be triggered if she tried to travel on her passport, but given the authorities knew where she was at the time, and Interpol's bad reputation among law enforcement professionals, it seems probable that the MLA route was the preferred one.)

It wasn't only the Americans that had decided to act: German prosecutors were also part of Operation Satellite – Ruja was a German national after all. The North Rhine-Westphalia police had first been notified by a local bank in late 2015 about a large number of suspicious payments connected to one of Frank Ricketts's IMS accounts – and although that specific investigation was ultimately dropped, in September 2016 the investigation was expanded to cover OneCoin and Ruja herself. In the summer of 2017, they formally requested mutual assistance from the Sofia prosecutor's office to raid the OneCoin head office based on the suspicion of unregulated selling of financial and payment services, false advertising and money laundering. In September 2017, the offices of her long-time German lawyer, Martin Breidenbach, were raided. The following month – around the same time as the US Mutual Legal Assistance Request – the German request was also handed up the chain to the more senior Special Prosecutor's Office.[4]

Perhaps unaware that two of the most important police forces in the world had her in their crosshairs, on 21 October, Ruja scheduled a meeting with RavenR boss Gary Gilford for 31 October in Sofia to discuss who should fill the vacant One-Coin CEO role. 'She wanted me over there urgently,' Gary recalls. 'It was really *really* important to her.' But that meeting would never happen.

By late 2017, Ruja had been a member of the Sofia business set for almost a decade, during which time she'd become one of the most well-connected people in the city. She already had a mole sharing details of the Operation Satellite meetings with her. And – according to more than one source – on or around 22 October, Ruja was informed, possibly by a junior police officer, that the police were finally about to move. She faced a choice: either get arrested or get out of the country.

The thought of it! The two-time Bulgarian businesswoman of the year, the Oxford graduate, the Cryptoqueen herself, flown in handcuffs to New York or Münster and dragged through the courts. The whole world watching her humiliated on the stand by lawyers raking over her old emails, her love life, everything. And followed by what? Eighty years behind bars in prison scrubs?

Five years earlier that might have been a simple decision. But Ruja was now a mother. Getting out of the country at short notice would mean being separated from her daughter, which, according to close friends, would have been unbearable. 'Ruja absolutely loved that daughter,' recalls Gary Gilford. 'She would have been heartbroken.'

But she had finally run out of options.

Ruja immediately called an emergency meeting of her top people from the Sofia office. None of the MLM network like Igor or Kari were invited and Sebastian was in Thailand. The London RavenR Capital office didn't know either – she liked Gary but didn't want too many people knowing what was happening. Konstantin sat in her kitchen (which had the best Wi-Fi signal) and let each of her most trusted colleagues in one at a time: Irina Dilkinska; Momchil Nikov, the long-standing IT guy; Veselina Valkova, her head of compliance (Valkova claims she has 'never heard' of these meetings, but was invited to Ruja's house before she disappeared and asked to work on a 'casino project unrelated to cryptocurrency'). For three years, Ruja had more or less run OneCoin from her head, and now she needed to download so things could tick over in her absence. There was so much to discuss: the ICO was still going ahead, the banking issues, the coin price, the Fenero Funds. She promised them she would be back before Christmas. She just needed things to settle down and let this trouble pass.

As soon as the meetings were concluded, Ruja told Konstantin to book her a flight to Vienna in two days' time, 25 October.

'What are you doing there?' he asked. Recently all Konstantin seemed to do was ask his sister questions she only half-answered.

'Don't worry,' she told him. 'I'll be back soon.'

The very next day, Ruja changed her mind. She phoned Konstantin and told him to book another flight for the 25th. This one to Athens.

'Shall I cancel the flight to Vienna?' he asked. He was still technically her assistant, after all.

'No!!' Ruja screamed, flying into a rage. 'I need them both!'

Konstantin quickly logged on and found there were two flights to Athens that day: a Ryanair flight departing at the ungodly hour of 6.50am; and a slightly later, slightly more upmarket Aegean Airlines flight, which took off at 10.45am. With the later one, she might even get a bit of much-needed sleep. But Ruja wanted the earlier flight.

She always knew this day might come. Even before the first coin was mined or the first package sold, Ruja had emailed Sebastian about what would happen if OneCoin didn't work out in the way they hoped. 'Exit strategy,' she'd written. 'Disappear and let someone else take the blame.' She'd never really thought about who that 'someone else' might be. The first president Nigel Allan? Pyramid boss Juha Parhiala? RavenR Director Gary Gilford?

It was never meant to come to *this*, fleeing her own country, her company, her family at a moment's notice. But the hype of Bitcoin, combined with a million people's fear of missing out, had turned OneCoin into a €5 billion monster that was too big to disappear under the radar. It was the scam of the century by mistake.

Sofia International Airport, 25 October 2017

When Ruja woke at around 4am, it was still dark. Outside, a cold drizzle blanketed the city as she waited for one of her

Bulgarian security guys to pick her up. Carrying nothing except a purse and at least two passports, the pair headed to Sofia Airport. At this time of morning, the usually gridlocked roads were empty and the drive took just 15 minutes, barely enough time for her to reflect on the crazy events of the last few weeks.

When she arrived at the airport, there was no one waiting for her: no Interpol red list, no arrest warrant, no agents in suits. At just before 7am, Ruja and her head of security boarded Ryanair flight FR6300 to Athens. Ruja hadn't always been rich – she used to take budget flights all the time as a student. Even in the early months of OneCoin, money was tight. But nowadays she was used to business class and charter. It must have been strange for the Cryptoqueen to sit in a box seat for the package holiday people, but she didn't have much choice.

When she landed at Athens just over an hour later, there were no FBI agents waiting for her there either. Her head of security came back that same evening, alone.

'What happened to Ruja?' Konstantin asked him. He'd booked the flights to Athens. Normally he was in charge of sorting taxies and hotels too – but not this time.

'At Athens airport she was met by some Russian-speaking men,' he replied. 'Then she carried on travelling with them.'

She'd made it out.

Part 6

AFTERMATH

CHAPTER 27

THE DAY AFTER

OneCoin HQ, Sofia, 26 October 2017

There was a strange sense of calm in the Sofia head office on Thursday 26 October. The vast majority of the 50 or so staffers knew nothing about what had happened the day before. Most had never met Gilbert, Mark Scott or Frank Schneider and they didn't pay much attention to the MLM side of the business either. As far as they knew, they worked for a tech start-up with a mercurial founder. If anything, the staff were relieved, since it was always calmer when Ruja was away. Most were too busy to notice. Phase I of the 'ICO' had just started, which was managed by Irina. She'd written an investor document, known in the industry as a 'white paper', which explained how the ICO worked: a three-month sale of tokens after which OneCoin would *go public* and finally – *finally* – get listed on a large crypto-exchange site where it could be bought and sold for real money. It was so full of mistakes that Gary emailed Irina on 2 November 2017 demanding the whole thing be taken down 'with immediate effect'. He also emailed Ruja, saying that Irina was 'destroying the company', but of course received nothing back. Konstantin certainly didn't let on that anything was wrong. On the day Ruja disappeared, he posted a picture of himself on Instagram with his dogs: 'Come and Meet the wretched #goodmorning #dog #instadog'.

Over in London, Gary Gilford didn't know about Ruja's early morning Ryanair flight so assumed he was still meeting her in Sofia in five days' time to talk about who should replace Pitt Arens as CEO. (Gary thought Robert Courtneidge, the payments lawyer from Locke Lord, might be interested.) After hearing nothing from Ruja for a couple of days, he grew anxious and messaged Konstantin to confirm the meeting was still going ahead.

'She's not here, Gary,' Konstantin told him.

'Where is she?' Gary asked, annoyed that Ruja hadn't bothered to let him know. 'Why hasn't she been in touch? I'm trying to help her fix the business!'

'She's had to go somewhere,' he replied, but wouldn't say where. 'She'll be away for a few weeks.'

A few days later, Gary messaged Ruja again, hoping to find out where she'd gone. 'Hi R – are you OK?' But he didn't get a reply. When Gary next spoke to Konstantin a couple of weeks later on a routine catch-up call, he demanded to know what was going on. He was the director of a family office and the head of the family had gone AWOL.[1] For months, Ruja had promised RavenR would receive huge amounts of money to start making large investments on her behalf – all the activity to date had been through Ruja's Fenero Funds – but it never seemed to materialise. And, as RavenR boss, he had rent and salaries to pay.

'She's been gone for weeks. Where is she?!' Gary said, getting angry.

'She'll be back before Christmas, Gary,' Konstantin replied, calmly. He was adamant about it.

'Are you actually *speaking* to Ruja or just emailing her?' Gary asked.

'I'm speaking with her,' Konstantin said.

It was all very strange. But Konstantin didn't seem fazed that his sister had disappeared. Neither did her mother Veska, who was also still working at the Sofia office. 'Actually I went to see her,' Konstantin continued. 'Because if anything happened, we had this plan that she would go to . . .'

But Konstantin stopped himself finishing the sentence, and wouldn't say another word about it. Athens? Or somewhere else, somewhere safer?

Over the following weeks, a slow panic rolled across the network. Top leaders like Igor phoned and messaged Ruja but never heard anything back. If anyone asked Konstantin, he told them Ruja was taking 'late maternity leave', and, if they continued asking, he said it was 'disloyal' to probe. Frank Schneider had more information, but it was scant. He'd claimed that after Ruja had landed in Athens she'd boarded a domestic flight to Thessaloniki in northern Greece, where she'd got into a black Porsche Cayenne with several men – likely Russians or Albanians. But at that point even the spook's sources went cold. Terence Fane-Saunders, the CEO of PR firm Chelgate, was equally baffled, and pretty soon cut the contract with OneCoin. (Fane-Saunders has not responded to my request for comment but in a previous response to the BBC Terence said that 'OneCoin and Ms Ignatova had their own PR/media relation facilities and we were not carrying out any kind of media relations programme. We were among a group of professional advisers providing counsel on a complex and evolving situation.' Fane-Saunders also said he had no evidence of criminal activity by any party.) None of it made sense to Gary. People don't just disappear – not with all the cameras, devices, tracking systems and citizen journalists. But Ruja had left no trace at all.

*

Ruja still hadn't turned up by the next OneCoin corporate event in Bangkok in early December 2017 and rumours were picking up velocity. BehindMLM speculated that she had executed a long-planned and entirely predictable exit, while a Bulgarian website reported she'd been arrested in Germany. One magazine claimed her yacht had been spotted docking somewhere on the Black Sea. The rumours all turned out to be false but investors were getting increasingly jumpy. Cryptocurrency was an unconventional industry with unpredictable bosses, but they don't vanish for weeks on end.

To maintain some degree of continuity, Frank Ricketts, the MLM Rembrandt and boss of the IMS companies that Ruja had used to move money, agreed to step in.[2] (Ricketts later claimed that he was asked just before the Thailand event to put 'motivational and personal development programs together on a global scale as an independent trainer'.) To quell the rumours about Ruja's vanishing act, someone also asked Konstantin if he would address the crowd. In addition to being well-known within the company as Ruja's PA and brother, he had the cushion-cover spiritualism that was popular with the MLM crowd, posting online often about self-improvement, abstinence, self-belief, intuition and meditation. But he was not a prodigy like his sister. He was a gym guy, an Instagram poser who knew nothing about cryptocurrency, finance or even how OneCoin's own technology worked. He asked the IT team several times to describe the blockchain technology and it never made sense to him. Nevertheless, Konstantin liked the idea of being a front man, and, just as in June 2016 when Ruja needed a new PA, he was ready to help the family business. Konstantin had some business cards made and headed to Bangkok.

The OneCoin event at the Crystal Design Centre in downtown Bangkok on 2 December was superficially like previous corporate events in London, Macau or Dubai – there was glitter, professional dancers, motivationals and recognitions. But all the 3,000 attendees wanted to talk about was Ruja's whereabouts. She hadn't been seen for six weeks. They secretly hoped she'd dramatically walk on stage in one of her long ball gowns and explain how the ICO would work or declare that xcoinx was back online. But there were no last-minute surprises. The only Ignatov present was Konstantin, who told the disappointed audience the same thing he told everyone else: Ruja was on maternity leave and sent her 'warmest regards'. Sebastian spoke in cryptic phrases, which undid some of Konstantin's well-delivered reassurances: 'We go through changes . . . without change, you become stale,' he said, slurring his words slightly. 'You don't move forward. So change is good . . .' Igor, who'd agreed to present recognition awards for the Diamonds and Emeralds, thought Sebastian was drunk. The event wasn't the same without the Cryptoqueen. Not even Frank Ricketts (who, as the final speaker, 'sailed' on to the stage on a huge mechanical boat) could lift the mood. Frank's opening words sounded like a legal disclaimer: 'I am not joining the company and am not part of the administration of the company.'

It was obvious to any experienced promoter that the game was finally up. Momentum had been waning for most of 2017 and without Ruja it now slowed to a standstill. Kari Wahlroos left soon after Ruja's Lisbon no show, along with several other Diamonds. But Igor, who'd taken so long to join, also took longer to leave. He'd made so much money from OneCoin, and believed every word of his own MLM-gospel, which classed all criticism as negative energy. But gradually even Igor realised something was seriously wrong and soon after the Lisbon event he told promoters to freeze all promotions until things were clarified. He later claimed watching the movie *The Wizard of Lies* about Bernie Madoff convinced him that it was possible to fool millions of people for years, although it seems unlikely that one of the world's biggest MLM sellers first learned about Bernie Madoff in late 2017. Whatever the trigger, in the weeks after Ruja's disappearance, Igor contacted former colleagues, blockchain specialists and legal experts to ask for their advice. They told him that he needed to find out if OneCoin really had a proper blockchain. If it didn't exist, he'd been selling the world a duff.

Soon after the Bangkok event, Igor travelled to Sofia for one last go at finding out the truth. He half hoped to see Ruja herself, but instead Veselina Valkova and Konstantin greeted him at the Crypto Centre and took him up to one of the meeting rooms on the fourth floor. With Ruja gone, Veselina, Konstantin and Irina (who wasn't around that day) were the most senior people left. That alone was a red flag. Veselina, a relatively recent recruit who specialised in online casinos, had quickly become a high-ranking member of Ruja's inner circle, but Igor knew Konstantin as the bodyguard and PA – and now he seemed to be in charge of the whole company. As he walked through the office, Igor took a look around. Sofia HQ had always been full of energy and buzz. But now everyone seemed worried and uncertain. Another red flag.

Igor had spent the previous weeks preparing the questions he wanted to ask: about the ICO, the IPO, going public. For him, there was one question above all that needed answering.

'Veselina,' Igor said, 'do we have a blockchain or not?'

'Yes, we do,' Veselina replied. That wasn't enough. Everyone at Sofia HQ always said 'yes' but never actually offered any proof.

'Look me in the eyes,' Igor went on. 'Don't lie to me. Tell me honestly. Have you seen it?'

'No. I have never seen it,' Veselina replied.

According to Igor, Veselina's answer was the final straw.

'How is this even possible? How can it be with all the money there is no blockchain?!'

'We don't have any money left,' Veselina replied. 'The money is all with Ruja.'

'This is worse than Bernie Madoff! Investors will come to the office and find you!' Igor said, getting angry. His whole career – 30 years in the industry – was on the line. (According to Veselina, she told Igor that she was 'the wrong person' to ask about the blockchain, and that Ruja's disappearance 'makes no difference', since the company was still going.)

Igor resigned on the spot (OneCoin HQ later told investors he had been fired). In truth, money wasn't the problem. Even with all the gold in Fort Knox, it was impossible to retrospectively build a blockchain. Igor got in touch with the top promoters in his downline, just as he had 18 months earlier, and told them: it's over.

CHAPTER 28

THE RAID

OneCoin HQ, Sofia, 18 January 2018

Given the events of the last few weeks, if OneCoin were to continue it needed a reboot for the new year. In early January, Frank Ricketts convened a large meeting in Frankfurt of the remaining top promoters. There were lots of problems, but OneCoin still had a huge network of enthusiastic and talented sellers, which was priceless in the MLM world. It was agreed that OneCoin needed a rebrand. No more clowns like Kari or Igor. No more sunglasses on stage and Lamborghinis parked out front. Better training materials. And, finally, Konstantin should take on more of a leadership role. It was called the 'New Generation' and a small cabal of top promoters formed a 'Global Leadership Group' to drive the new direction. For now, at least, OneCoin would continue selling. Almost immediately, disaster struck.

The Bielefeld public prosecutor's request to raid the OneCoin office, which was originally filed in the summer of 2017 just before Ruja disappeared, had been delayed several times. Finally, on the morning of 18 January 2018, a joint Bulgarian–German police team entered the side door of 6A Petko R. Slaveykov Square armed with a search warrant. They found around 20 confused members of staff working at their desks. One of the German officers noticed an oversized picture of Ruja hanging on the wall. She was still there in spirit, although not in person.

Over the next several hours they confiscated laptops, servers and thousands of documents – anything that might serve as evidence for the German prosecutor's allegations of money laundering, false advertising and illegal selling of financial products – including the computers that contained the elusive blockchain. It was after midnight before the operation was over. The next morning, German and Bulgarian police interviewed several employees, including Veska, Irina Dilkinska and Veselina Valkova. Veska told them she didn't know where her daughter was, and, although she'd been managing director, only received 'a very small' salary. No arrests were made, and Ruja never turned up (nor did Konstantin).

Two days later, Sofia HQ rushed out a press release claiming the whole affair was yet more unfair treatment, more fake news:

> '. . . [I]t is a demonstration against One Network Service Ltd., the virtual currency OneCoin and its creator Dr. Ruja Ignatova. We see a purposeful media campaign to discredit the reputation of the above-mentioned and deliberate concealment of important features from the company's business, which presents us in a totally negative light.'

But the routine was starting to wear thin, even for the staff. At least three decided enough was enough and simply didn't turn up for work the next day.[1] Momchil Nikov, the IT guy since 2014, was also spooked. Shortly after the raid, Konstantin went to see him to discuss how serious this police investigation was.

'Is there something we should be worried about?' Konstantin asked. He'd never really paid all that much attention to the technology side of the business until now. He'd left that all to Ruja.

'The blockchain is . . .' Momchil replied, cryptically, '. . . not exactly what it should be.'

'What do you mean?' he asked. 'Can we fix it? Let's try to make it work.'

But Momchil was facing the same problem that had stumped Ruja. And if it was beyond her, it was certainly beyond him. Although Momchil was a decent IT professional, he was no blockchain specialist. According to one former colleague, Momchil was harassed and bullied by Ruja and 'made to do things he wasn't comfortable with'. A few days after his chat with Konstantin, Momchil left the office as usual after work and never came back. According to at least one former employee, he also took whatever limited technology the company still had.

The January raid was also the last straw for Sebastian Greenwood. He stopped promoting OneCoin entirely, cut ties with the head office and ensconced himself in Thailand, safely out of reach of European law enforcement. In March 2018, he purchased a large defunct holiday resort on the island of Vanuatu with a mysterious British businessman from Bangkok called Geoffrey Bond.[2] He starting spending his time racing fast cars – he'd always loved Formula 1 – and relaxing in his large mansion in Ko Samui.

Four years after that first frenetic summer when Juha, Sebastian and Ruja hashed out the comp plan and dreamt of revolutionising money, all three founders were out.

One quiet afternoon in May, some of the staff at the Sofia HQ were starting the weekend early with some drinks. Irina was usually very discreet and considered, but she had one weakness: when she drank, she talked.

'Konstantin,' Irina said, a couple of drinks in. 'I need to tell you something about our blockchain.' Konstantin, who was teetotal, didn't usually get involved in drunken conversations about the business. But this time he listened, because Irina was one of the few people who knew everything. 'We have been distributing more coins than we have been mining.'

'So what have we been selling people?!' Konstantin asked. His blood ran cold. The 'new blockchain' had now been running for 18 months. Although sales were slower since Ruja left, millions of coins had continued to be sold to investors.

'We have been selling people thin air,' said Irina.

This was probably the last moment Konstantin could have walked away from OneCoin. He might have pleaded ignorance like Igor Alberts would eventually do, or even disappeared to the Far East like Sebastian and Juha. Although he was starting to take on more responsibility, on paper he was still just a junior staffer who'd only joined the company in the summer of 2016. But OneCoin was the Ignatov family business. His mother Veska still worked there as the office manager, and Konstantin was loyal to his family. Back in 2011, when Ruja and her father ran the Waltenhofen Gusswerks into the ground, Plamen fell ill. Even though he had nothing to do with the affair, it was Konstantin who left university and moved back home to look after him. Not Ruja – she headed back to Sofia to carry on with her career. The whole family owed everything to this company and he refused to believe that his sister had left him in charge of a tech company with no real technology and hundreds of billions of dollars of theoretical investor liabilities. He felt duty-bound to carry on.

One evening around this time, Konstantin left the office

late after another long day of work. It wasn't unusual for him to work into the night and it was dark and cold. As Konstantin made his way to the back road where his car was parked, he felt a cold metallic object being pushed into the back of his head. A voice told him to carry on walking. He knew immediately it was a gun.

CHAPTER 29

MONKEYS

Konstantin's problem was money. Investors all over the world now wanted their coins turned into real money and cashed out. Some could be fobbed off with the usual excuses, but not all. The people who'd put a gun to the back of his head took him to a minivan, broke one of his fingers and told him that, if Ruja had disappeared with their money, 'we will come back and kill you'. Going to the police wasn't an option either – they threatened to 'cut a body part out' if he did. A few weeks later, Konstantin found himself in a hotel room in Zurich with members of the Hells Angels gang who'd also invested. This time a gun was put into his mouth. 'You have to make sure every promise is fulfilled,' they told him. 'The money we've invested in [OneCoin] is worth far more than your life.'

Konstantin texted Gary Gilford around this time. 'It's really, really bad over here,' he told him. Things were getting serious.

The issue wasn't money *per se*: it was getting hold of it. Ruja knew every loophole, every shady jurisdiction and corporate trick used by the rich and infamous to keep their assets hidden, and it turned out she'd used all of them. Shortly after Ruja's disappearance, Konstantin found himself looking at one of the most complicated corporate structures ever created. The multi-million pound properties, the €6.9 million yacht, the company shares, the bank accounts – it was all mostly intact. Konstantin just couldn't get it. Ruja's assets were all hidden inside a labyrinth of phoney directors, offshore firms, and strangely named holding companies.

Although she had companies all over the world, where OneCoin was concerned, the most important were based in Dubai. She had a favourite 'formation agent' there called 'Europe Emirates Group', run by a man called Adrian Oton. Its offices were in the Jumeirah Lake Towers, an 80-skyscraper mega-construction that circled one of the city's artificial lakes. Europe Emirates Group specialised in setting up companies for those who wished to operate in the Emirate, where the law states overseas businesses need a local corporate structure. The company signed contracts on Ruja's behalf, and set up several of her companies there, including RISG, OneCoin Limited and Meteora Holdings.

A typical set-up went something like this: when Ruja purchased the elegant nineteenth-century townhouse on Sofia's famous Narodno Sabranie Square in 2015, she registered ownership to a Bulgarian company called One Property. That in turn was owned by her Dubai company RISG Limited. But that was just the half of it. On 27 September 2015, Ruja handed all 1,000 shares in RISG Limited, and the famous townhouse it owned, to Elva Marga Bolivar de Rodriguez and Eduardo Enrique Harris Robinson, two quiet churchgoers from the small town of Tocumen just west of Panama City.[1] But before receiving their shares, Eduardo and Elva will have almost certainly signed an undated 'blank stock transfer document', in which they resigned with immediate effect and agreed to return all shares back to Ruja Ignatova.[2] Ruja probably held a physical copy of this document in her safe in Sofia. If anything bad happened, her assets would be unconnected to her, safely out of the authorities' reach. But whenever she wanted to take back control, all Ruja had to do was retrospectively date their resignation letters.

She called these people her 'monkeys'. And she used monkeys with RavenR Dubai and RavenR Capital London too. Both were technically owned by two ordinary Cypriots. Thomas Christodoulou was a former cook in his thirties whose previous work experience included being a cook at Cyprus Airways and the manager of a branch of Pizza Hut. Andri Andreou was a woman in her mid-twenties with practically nothing whatsoever to her name.[3] (At some point, Gary had realised that Ruja's name wasn't on the official company documentation. 'Don't worry,' Ruja had told him. She had explained that there were a few technical issues that needed ironing out because everything had grown so quickly – and it was easier to just keep her name off the paperwork for now.[4] Later, Gary would regret accepting that answer. 'I wish I'd delved into it more,' he says.)

These corporate games were designed to protect Ruja and confuse outsiders. But the consequence of Ruja's prolonged and unplanned disappearance – combined with OneCoin's declining revenue – was that Konstantin was also baffled. He was struggling to access the assets that might have been useful to pay off debtors, keep the company going and avoid getting 'a body part cut off'.

What he really needed was a power of attorney – a legal letter signed by Ruja in the presence of a lawyer that could confer him access to her assets. Even that might not be enough, because some countries and banks have very strict rules about their use, but it would certainly be a start. According to the FBI, Konstantin had a power of attorney from his sister signed by her on 8 February 2018. Konstantin would later claim it was a forgery knocked up by Irina Dilkinska. But Gary Gilford recalled Konstantin spending weeks desperately trying to get hold of the power of attorney in early 2018. If it was real, then Konstantin knew exactly where his sister was – and might even have gone to see her too. But where?

CHAPTER 30

ARRESTS

Barnstable, Massachusetts, 5 September 2018

At 5.30am, FBI Special Agent James Eckel and IRS Agent Kristine Fata met with local police officers at a pre-operational briefing meeting at Barnstable Police Department, a small municipal building on Phinney's Lane, which housed the 100 or so police staff for the county. Brian Guiney, a heavy-set Barnstable detective with a thick Bostonian accent, was the local lead on the case. It was a warm late summer morning, and Cape Cod was still just about in season, with enough wealthy holidaymakers to keep the shops and cafes open. The local cops were more used to dealing with tourists asking directions to the local restaurants or President Kennedy's old haunts than financial fraud and money laundering.

From there, a small unit – the two federal agents plus local officers – took Phinney's Lane northbound toward the coast. It took five minutes to reach Sunset Lane, one of the town's most desirable streets. Number 133, 'Villa Meeres-blick', was a stately coastal property with a large backyard that looked out over the inlet of Cape Cod Bay, close to where British pilgrims on the *Mayflower* first made landfall in 1620. As they drew close, Agent Eckel received word over the police wire that the suspect was driving nearby in his new BMW. They hit the sirens and rushed to intercept him.

When they pulled the car over, the driver politely told officers that there was a .40-calibre semi-automatic handgun loaded with 13 rounds of ammunition in the glove compartment.[1] Detective Guiney identified himself and told the driver they were revoking his gun licence. 'Mark Scott, you are under arrest You have the right to remain silent and refuse to answer questions. Anything you say may be . . .'

Mark Scott was too tired to argue. He probably hadn't slept for days. Over the last few weeks, he seemed to have grown increasingly paranoid and edgy. 'No Trespass' signs adorned his backyard, much to the frustration of local residents, who were usually relaxed about walkers wandering through gardens to enjoy the long tidal flats.

As Mark was driven back to Barnstable police station for booking, Detective Guiney and the two federal agents continued to Mark's home on Sunset Lane. His wife Lidia answered the door and FBI Agent Eckel flashed the search warrant. On entering the building, Detective Guiney spotted a loaded, unsecured semi-automatic handgun on the living room table and a small child playing nearby. Lidia was arrested too on charges of wanton or reckless behaviour, and the child swiftly placed in the custody of the authorities. Detective Guiney soon found several more guns dotted all over the house: a revolver with six rounds in a desk drawer; a handgun; a shotgun; and 150 rounds of ammunition. In a town that was a virtual crime-free zone, it looked like Mark was preparing for a siege. Detective Guiney had been a police officer in this state for 30 years; this was not a routine case.

It wasn't even 7.30am by the time Mark Scott was sitting across from Agents Eckel and Fata in an interview room at Barnstable police station. It all happened so quickly that Mark didn't have time to get his lawyers to join – if they had, they would probably have told him to keep schtum. The two agents had 40 years of experience between them. They knew how to play this.

'I wanna say, off the top, that I'm, like, absolutely surprised at what's going on,' Mark said, staying cool.

'Who are the investors in Fenero?' asked Agent Fata, not skipping a beat.

'Well, there are a bunch of, uhh, companies,' replied Mark.

'What about B&N Consult?' That was Irina's company. Alongside IMS, Star and Fates, it was one of the four companies that had sent almost €400 million into Mark's fake fund. (And €200,000 into the online casino company.)

'B&N Consult is one of the investors,' said Mark.

'Who is that?'

'Ummm, Irina,' said Mark.

'What's the last name?' replied Agent Fata.

'I can't remember it right now,' Mark replied, stumbling his words. 'I don't, I mean, I'm sure she's a, she's a, from Bulgaria, but I can't tell you the last name off the top of my head. Dil, dil, dil . . . something ka. Ahh, I just don't know how to spell it right now.'

Mark Scott had worked with Irina Dilkinska constantly for two years. They were even co-directors on two of the Irish companies.

'Tell us a little bit more about Irina,' Agent Eckel said.

'Umm, she was introduced to me by . . . another person that Gilbert [Armenta] brought to me, which is, umm, she is very famous because she does all this crypto stuff now. Umm, uhh, Ruja, and . . . she—'

'That's her first name?' Eckel interrupted. It was impossible not to notice Mark was umming and ahhing a lot.

'Ruja is her first name,' said Mark, who was rambling. 'And, umm, she was involved in some cryptocurrency. She had one of those Bitcoin, or has one of those Bitcoin type of deals . . .'

'So where is Ruja?' asked Agent Fata.

'I have no idea . . . don't speak to her any more.'

'So, Fenero was not involved with OneCoin at all?' asked Agent Eckel. They knew of course that it was. They had recordings of Mark's calls to Apex, hundreds of subpoenaed documents and bank records, and Gilbert Armenta's testimony. They knew everything. This interview was mainly to see what Mark Scott would tell them about it. Would he lie? Did he have something to confess?

'No.'

'Not at all?'

'I mean, no contracts or anything as far as I know, no.'

'OK, *funded* by OneCoin?'

'Not that I know of . . . We had a, we had one company that got close where we knew they had a, they had a relationship in terms of processing. They were doing accounting for, for OneCoin.'

Bingo! Mark Scott was lying to the FBI and IRS. It was time to change tack.

'We're going to be honest with you here,' said Agent Eckel. 'You have a very small window of opportunity to help yourself, OK? . . . We know that OneCoin was involved in Fenero, OK? We have that information . . . And we can't help you if you're not going to be forthcoming with us. Do you understand?'

'Yeah,' said Mark.

'Is there anything else you want to tell us about any of this?' asked Agent Eckel.

'Well, no. I'm, I'm, I'm really . . .' Mark stuttered. 'I appreciate that and, and, and, but I'm telling you when we started . . . I would not view [OneCoin] as involved as you might . . . think, and that's what I'm trying to explain . . .'

Mark was being evasive and vague. Agent Eckel had dealt with this before. He'd been at the Bureau for over 30 years – during which time he'd investigated anarchists, organised crime and political blackmail. He could handle Mark Scott.

'I'm going to ask you one more time,' he persisted. 'OneCoin and Ruja were not investors in Fenero?' Agent Fata, pushing on Mark's conscience, added: 'This is your one opportunity. You have a small child at home. You have your wife. I'm sure you have a life that you want to live. This is your one opportunity to help yourself. So just think about that for a moment before you answer.'

'Yeah, I would love to discuss this further. I really would,' replied Mark. 'But I'd like to have a lawyer help me with that.'

Mark wasn't going to say anything more. Had his lawyer been present, he would have told Mark that he'd already said too much.

Later that day, Agents Eckel and Fata returned to 133 Sunset Lane. Mark's 2018 White Porsche 911 GTRS2 was parked in the driveway.[2] The FBI search and seizure team meticulously combed the house for evidence. After a couple of hours, they walked out with piles of bank and financial records, seventeen phones, six laptops, three memory cards, two iPads and five flash drives. In total it was three terabytes of data – equivalent to hundreds of thousands of documents. Another search and seizure team at Mark's home in Coral Gables, Florida, grabbed a further two terabytes and another four guns.[3] They also confiscated any items that might have been purchased using the proceeds of crime: three Porsches plus his Sunseeker Predator 57 yacht from the nearby Hyannis Port.

When news of Mark's arrest reached Sofia a day or two later, Irina Dilkinska almost fainted.

'I'm fucked,' she shouted at Konstantin when she arrived at the office, panicking. 'I'm in all documents with Mark Scott!' she said. 'When they get him, they'll also get me!'

Later that day, Irina went home and started burning documents. Over the past 18 months, she'd acquired dozens of legal documents relating to Ruja's and Mark's affairs, many with her name on: a Venezuelan machinery deal, which mentioned her Florida-based company H&H CA Corp, her joint-directorship of Payments Card Technology with Mark, the paperwork that proved her ownership of B&N Consult. That evening anything that linked her name to Mark and Fenero went up in flames.

Little known to anyone, two months before Mark Scott's arrest, another police operation took place 6,000 miles away. This investigation, however, was far more low key. It had been slowly making its way through the various diplomatic channels. There were no press releases or public indictments. No one even knew this had happened at all until months later. Ruja had got away; but the FBI weren't going to let it happen again. US agents, along with Thailand's notorious Crime Suppression Division, had tracked their target to a villa on the party island of Ko Samui. Inside was Sebastian Greenwood.

CHAPTER 31

GOING PUBLIC

Melbourne, 8 October 2018

As the counter approached T-minus one hour, about 200 OneCoiners were gathered at the Convention and Exhibition Centre in Melbourne, Australia. No one inside knew that Mark Scott had been arrested a month earlier, or that a US grand jury had secretly indicted Ruja Ignatova on fraud and money laundering a whole year before, or that Sebastian was sitting in prison in Thailand. As far as attendees were concerned, it was a day to celebrate. Finally OneCoin was *going public;* it was the day the ICO was formally concluded, which Sofia HQ had promised was the final step to getting OneCoin listed on one of the major exchange sites like Kraken or Poloniex. The dedicated ICO website was projected on a large screen and the song 'The Final Countdown' by the rock band Europe played. A cruise for the top promoters around Melbourne's coastline was planned that evening to celebrate.

'Going public' had taken on an eschatological quality over the previous four years. Although it technically referred to the moment that OneCoin would be listed on a public exchange site where it could be freely traded for real money, it was much more than that: it was vindication. For investors like Christine Grablis in Tennessee, it meant turning her roughly one million OneCoin into €30 million. But it was

also about self-respect. For three years she'd insisted to sceptical friends and family that OneCoin was real, that she was
most certainly not a gullible fool who'd blown everything on
a Ponzi scheme.

'Three . . . two . . . one . . . !'

Although the audience was mostly made up of low-level
promoters and investors from Australia and south-east Asia,
where OneCoin still had a solid network, there was still a
euphoric atmosphere. They cheered and whooped. Some
raised their arms in the air in celebration, muttering under
their breath. Some hugged. Others could hardly believe the
moment had arrived, and immediately phoned their uplines
and downlines: 'It's happened! OneCoin is g*oing public*!'

Despite the celebrations, it was a long way from the hal-
cyon days. Investors had always assumed the 'going public'
event would be bigger than London or Bangkok. But Ruja
wasn't there to witness it, nor was Sebastian, Juha, Nigel
Allan, Kari Wahlroos, Igor Alberts. Everyone had gone. Even
Konstantin didn't make it. He told the audience via a pre-
recorded message that his plane broke down in Doha. The
highest-ranking OneCoiner was now a man called Simon Le,
a quietly spoken Black Diamond from Vietnam who'd been
sucked up the pyramid with each departing leader. He was a
good seller, but not in the same league as people like Igor or
Kari. But so what? There were people in the room who held
thousands, *millions*, of OneCoin – each now worth €26.95.
And they would finally be able to sell those coins for real
money.

The next day, investors excitedly logged in to their One-
Coin accounts, expecting to find instructions on how exactly
to cash out their millions. But nothing had changed. The
only difference was on OneCoin's dedicated ICO site, www.
onecoinico.io. The 'countdown clock' had been replaced
with a new message:

Please be informed that a new email for the Offering has been created, namely: SUPPORT@ONECOIN-ICO.IO. In case you have any inquiries, do not hesitate to contact us. Please be patient, the Offering is about to start really soon!

OneCoin: the really-soon company. It was always the *future* of payments and never the present. A few days later, Sofia HQ quietly announced it wasn't going public just yet after all: in fact, it would take at least another year for all the various admin to be completed.

The ICO, like everything else OneCoin did, was just another jam-tomorrow delay. But, for Sofia HQ, it created one final opportunity to scam a few more people before everything collapsed for good.

CHAPTER 32

BANKING THE UNBANKED

Entebbe International Airport, 17 October 2018

Wearing his 'Twins MMA' t-shirt, a gift from the local mixed martial arts centre where he trained, Konstantin walked out of arrivals at Kampala's Entebbe airport. Even though it had just passed 3am in the morning, there were dozens of people waiting for him, wearing OneCoin t-shirts and waving Dealshaker flags. It was more like the arrival of a rock star than the boss of a tech firm. When Konstantin finally made it past the mêlée, a police motorcade accompanied him to his hotel.

The trip to Uganda was Fred Ntabazi's idea. Fred was a former street preacher in his thirties turned hotshot local promoter. While many OneCoiners talked in loosely spiritual terms, Fred took it literally. In 2016, he founded the 'One-Light Ministry', which combined religious worship with MLM. Fred had risen to Diamond by pushing the coin through his church of around 100 fervent OneCoin believers, who would turn up to the fourth floor of the Padre Pio building in central Kampala every Sunday to listen to his unique blend of crypto prosperity gospel and Pentecostalism. '*Dealshaker*,' Fred would shout. '*Game Changer*!' they would reply. His sermons would sometimes last for hours as he jumped between financial emancipation, the power of prayer, Ruja's vision and lines from the Bible. He occasionally asked

his followers to pray for the coin to *go public*. When parish-
ioners asked him when exactly that day would come, he
would tell them to wait. 'Those who are patient will go to
heaven,' he used to reply. 'God has told me that the coin is
genuine.'

Konstantin had agreed to travel to Uganda because
OneCoin needed money. Having a gun pushed into the
back of his head had shaken him up, and he spent most of
2018 on the road desperately trying to hustle up more sales.
Trying to release funds from Ruja's puzzle of assets was
proving almost impossible. The more mature markets like
Europe, America and China were drying up even before
Ruja left, and, once she vanished, most believers in Glasgow
or New York or Tokyo weren't willing to pour more in. In
2018, Konstantin visited 40 countries (and took 200 flights),
and many of them were places where there was less information about OneCoin: Colombia in March; Malawi and
South Africa in May; Brazil, Trinidad and Argentina in July.
In these newer markets, OneCoin was still growing. In
Uganda alone, there were at least a dozen local OneCoin
offices and over 50,000 investors, who continued to promote the coin using the *Forbes* cover or FCA notice as
'proof'. Although some had heard rumours that Ruja had
left, many didn't speak English and were reliant on their
uplines for information, who told them that everything was
fine. By the time Konstantin arrived, OneCoin was a household name in large parts of the country, possibly even more
famous than Bitcoin itself. As soon as his visit to Kampala
was announced, investors from South Africa, Tanzania,
Congo, Nigeria, booked bus tickets, flights and borrowed
cars, just to get to there. For some of them, it would be a
three- or four-day trip.

For three days, Fred drove Konstantin across the country
in his white Range Rover. He visited schools and met

politicians. He addressed the OneLife East Africa Summit and promised a financial revolution for the millions of people without a bank account. At a large orphanage, he donated 100 OneCoin tablet computers and told the children that, 'Every day you spend in school, you're building your future.'

On day two of his visit, Konstantin and Fred travelled to Mbarara, a fast-growing city in the prosperous farming region in the west of the country. OneCoin had spread to Mbarara almost as soon as it arrived in Uganda, following the path laid out by other MLM companies who'd been targeting wealthy farmers for years. As they crossed the equator on the four-hour drive west, Konstantin noticed the young men loitering on rebuilt motorbikes, who always seemed to be waiting, the roadside livestock searching for clumps of grass, the billboards advertising mobile money, the banana plantations that lined the roads . . . this was how far his sister's vision had travelled. Even in Sofia, Ruja was no more than a minor celebrity, a half-famous businesswoman whose face occasionally graced the trashy papers. But half a world from home, Ruja Ignatova was a household name. She had never actually visited places like Mbarara – her OneCoin universe was five-star hotels in Dubai, Macau, London and Hong Kong – but somewhere out here, Konstantin had found the bottom of his sister's million-person pyramid – down dirt tracks off a road 400 miles from Kampala. It was a long way from Ruja's Sozopol mansion, Igor's Dolce & Gabbana collection, or rooms stacked with cash. But these people had paid for all of that.

In one way, the trip was invigorating. OneCoin was on the ropes everywhere. Regulators were getting more aggressive, BehindMLM continued to target the firm, and whatever investors remained were growing even more restless. But in Uganda, Ruja's disappearance, the German raid, the blockchain revelations – it was as if none of it had ever happened.

But he knew he was ripping these people off, promising a financial revolution while pushing them deeper into poverty. He later admitted that he was racked with guilt when he spoke at the school and orphanage. In Uganda, lives depended on OneCoin. People had staked their entire savings on his sister's promises. Some were running from the bank, others had pulled their kids out of school. He knew that one day all these people would realise that the money was gone.

It had now been almost a year since anyone had seen Ruja. Shortly before Konstantin was in Uganda Gary met up with Ruja's spook Frank Schneider – perhaps he knew something. In fact, in June 2018 James Channo from Locke Lord had written to Ruja explaining that 'further to our discussion with Frank Schneider, we believe it is important to revisit the manner in which you hold your real estate interests in the UK'. (A statement provided by Locke Lord and James Channo said the letter was an offer of legal services 'in a standard form', that 'there was no resulting engagement and no work was carried out' for Ruja, that the letter was disclosed by Locke Lord to US prosecutors, and that there was no suggestion during the trial that the letter demonstrated any wrongdoing.) It seems the reply placed Frank and Konstantin in charge: 'You have given us instructions that we are to correspond and take instructions from Frank Schneider . . . and your brother Konstantin.'

If Frank was acting for Ruja somehow, perhaps he knew something, *anything*, about her whereabouts. But Frank told Gary around this time that he'd called his contacts, applied his techniques and even had people searching through morgues for women Ruja's age. But even the experienced spook had found nothing.

But to Gary, it made no sense. If Ruja was dead, why did

Veska or Konstantin never seem upset? She was the family star and they were carrying on like nothing had happened. And how come Konstantin said he had seen her? Was this Ruja's way of telling everyone: 'I'm not coming back. Don't wait for me'?

CHAPTER 33

ALWAYS PLAY STUPID

Los Angeles International Airport, 6 March 2019

As he dawdled around Los Angeles airport waiting for his now delayed Turkish Airlines flight back to Sofia, Konstantin told Duncan Arthur – the South African Dealshaker boss – that he was planning to slow down. His partner Kristina was pregnant, and Konstantin was tiring of the MLM world, just like his sister had two years earlier. He liked seeing new places, but 2018 had been exhausting. He'd only just recovered from a mammoth trip around Latin America, trying to arrange a deal to sell apartments that had been built for the Olympic Games using 100 per cent OneCoin. He was hoping to do what Ruja had attempted just before she vanished: sell off the MLM side of the business.

Ever since Konstantin had taken over OneCoin in June 2018, he and Duncan had become unlikely friends. Duncan was a heavy-drinking IT guy and Konstantin was a vegan tee-total fitness fanatic but for some reason they got on. The pair stopped off at the duty-free shop, where Konstantin bought a baseball cap. They talked breezily about the game they'd watched a couple of days earlier at the Staples Center: the Los Angeles Lakers lost to their local rivals the Clippers in a tight match. But at least Konstantin had seen the legendary

LeBron James score 27 points. He sent a couple of posts on social about heading home.

Konstantin should have known something was wrong when they landed at San Francisco a few days earlier. Duncan, who always carried both a South African and Irish passport, sailed through passport control on the latter. When he looked around, Konstantin wasn't behind him. Ten minutes later, the younger man emerged, carrying his passport in a ziplock bag, looking worried. He was wanted for some enhanced questioning. Duncan waited around until a tough-looking border patrol officer told him to 'fuck off', unless he 'wanted some of what your friend is getting'.

Duncan flew to Las Vegas, where he got into the silver stretch limo waiting for him and headed directly to the Bellagio hotel, where some top American OneCoin promoters were waiting. Six hours later, Konstantin finally arrived, having talked his way in by saying he was in America to train at a specialised mixed martial arts gym. Homeland Security returned his laptop, but kept his phone and all his clothes. 'How did you get in?' asked Duncan when they reconvened at the Bellagio reception. 'Always play stupid,' Konstantin replied, with a smile.

Little did he know that the FBI had downloaded the entire contents of his mostly unencrypted laptop. Including a power of attorney, signed by Ruja on 8 February 2018. Four whole months after she'd disappeared.

Rather than realising the game was up, Konstantin got straight to work.

Over the next couple of days, in one of the hotel's innumerable meeting rooms, there was the usual business talk about how to grow Dealshaker in the US. Other leaders turned up. When one of them asked Konstantin when One-Coin would finally go public, he exploded. 'If you are here to cash out,' he responded, 'leave this room now, because you don't understand what this project is about.'

Duncan thought the American promoters seemed twitchy. Although Konstantin and Duncan were here to discuss Dealshaker, one of them kept changing the subject to a strange new idea called 'priming the pump', which seemed to involve some kind of complicated price manipulation. Every time Duncan and Konstantin tried to go for lunch or a walk around Las Vegas's famous casino 'strip', the Americans insisted on joining them. The only time Konstantin could escape was when he borrowed Duncan's AC/DC t-shirt and went for a jog. During a coffee break, Duncan took Konstantin to one side and said he thought they were being set up. 'Do not agree to anything,' Duncan told him. 'Especially this priming the pump plan.'

Once the meetings were over, Duncan wanted to get back to London as quickly as possible. But Konstantin insisted the pair spend a couple of days relaxing in Los Angeles first. After flying to LA, Konstantin dragged Duncan to Chinatown, the Walk of Fame to see the film stars' names in the pavement, to the famous Hollywood sign, to the Lakers game. Eventually, they were ready to return home. But now their flight was delayed too.

'Would Konstantin Ignatov and Duncan Arthur please report to the counter?' blasted the airport speaker system.

That was the moment the FBI agents pounced. As three of them whisked Konstantin away, two IRS agents calmly walked Duncan Arthur into a second interrogation room. 'Oh fuck,' thought Duncan, as he felt a heavy hand on his shoulder.

They sat him down at a long steel table. He wasn't being arrested, they said sternly. Just questioned. At least for now.

'Where is Ruja?'

'I have no clue,' Duncan replied in his thick South African accent.

'How does the blockchain work?'

'It's a centralised immutable add-only database, which is mined by super computers, and tokens buy you computing power.' Duncan noticed the agents actually looked slightly embarrassed for him. 'They know more about this company than I do,' he thought to himself.

'How is OneCoin priced?' It was question, question, question. They weren't messing around.

'I have no direct knowledge but I was told that it is a complex algorithm.'

'You're a fucking idiot,' said one of the agents.

After about 40 minutes, the agents took a photo of Duncan's passports, warned him that he might be summoned back to the US soon, and let him go. They accepted that he was only responsible for the Dealshaker platform, not One-Coin itself. He wasn't the person they were looking for.

'Where's Konstantin?' Duncan politely asked one of the agents, as he left.

'Don't worry about him,' he replied, and firmly suggested Duncan stop asking questions and get the hell out of the country.

Duncan boarded the next flight back to London via Istanbul, alone. Sofia HQ rushed out a press release, saying that 'Mr Ignatov has not been formally charged with a crime'. That was another lie, of course. He'd been charged with wire fraud. Duncan never saw Konstantin again.

BehindMLM was, as usual, the first website to break the news. *Konstantin arrested, criminal charges filed against Ruja Ignatova*, ran Oz's article, a couple of days later. 'FINALLY,' wrote WhistleblowerFin, one of the regulars, in the comment thread below.

Every investor had their own breaking point. For some it was the coin doubling in London, for others it was Ruja's disappearance or xcoinx shutting down. Typically, though, there wasn't a single trigger or epiphany. Instead, their psychological defence mechanism, which had shielded them from the consequences of the hard truth, was gradually worn down by the weight of evidence.

Christine Grablis had a nagging feeling ever since xcoinx was shut down, but she preferred the excuses. Her doubts grew when she logged on to the ICO website in October 2018 to find it would be another whole year before going public. But Konstantin's arrest was the final straw. A friend forwarded her the BehindMLM article, and she immediately texted her upline, the person who'd recruited her. 'Why did they arrest him[?] R we still safe with onecoin[?] That article is frightening.'

'The charge is wire fraud,' he replied. 'Everything is business as usual for the rest of the world.'

Christine carried on reading more and more BehindMLM articles – the stuff she'd dismissed as 'fake news' for so long. In the same way she had once searched for and found comforting evidence that OneCoin was real, as soon as the spell was broken, the reverse happened, and she found proof everywhere that OneCoin was a scam.

'Is this true about onecoin? Being exposed as a Ponzi scheme?' she texted.

'Only allegations. OneCoin and OneLife still operating globally . . . as far as I know everything is moving forward.'

'This is the first time I'm nervous. I put in $135k. When can we start taking money out[?] Any news on going public[?] Is this a Ponzi scheme[?]' Deep down, Christine already knew the answer, but she wanted him to tell her himself.

'All I have done is try to help you and others to understand what's going on and why we must all be patient.'

Something snapped. Not only was the money gone, she had to accept she'd been a naïve fool.

'You are one pathetic asshole,' wrote Christine, 'May you rot in hell.'

It suddenly all seemed so *obvious*. 'I just couldn't believe I fell for it,' Christine said later. 'I'm not the sort of person who would fall for a scam.'

Nearly everyone who lost money to OneCoin described the moment of realisation in the same way. It was a physical sensation, an actual *feeling*. All Layla Begum could think was that her upline, her friend Saleh, was 'a bastard'. She felt let down, sick, betrayed and anxious. She cried, and screamed down the phone demanding her money back, to little avail. 'Why didn't I look into this before sending my money?' she asked herself over and over. It wasn't just money that was gone, though. A whole future went up in smoke. 'My world was over.' The immediate physiological experience was often followed by an even worse thought. Pyramid scams incentivise people to recruit those they care about. Most OneCoin investors, whatever their exact moment of realisation, were angry with the people who'd recruited them. But they also faced the dawning realisation that they had recruited people too. How do I explain this to the people I recruited? they wondered. Will they be as angry as I am? 'I felt like I'd let my whole family down,' Layla said later.

CHAPTER 34

CO-OPERATION

The *Los Angeles Times* once called the Metropolitan Correctional Centre in downtown Manhattan 'The Guantanamo of New York'. The 12-storey building, which is home to almost a thousand inmates, is a dirty, claustrophobic, understaffed hellhole. The cells are tiny and usually shared with vermin. For years, activists have tried to get something done about the conditions, but no one cares about prisoners.

The MCC was the new home of inmate number 77737-112, Konstantin Ignatov.

The day after his arrest in Los Angeles, a Californian district court judge ruled Konstantin should be detained and sent to New York, where the original charges had been made. (For historic and political reasons, high-profile white collar crime cases are often led by the Southern District of New York.) Three weeks later, Konstantin was sitting in his cell, wondering what had just happened, and what he was going to do next.

He might not have realised that Sebastian Greenwood was sitting just a few cell blocks away.

Konstantin had already decided he would protest his innocence. One of the first things he did on arrival at the MCC was head to the secure computers on the second floor and email his fiancée and his mother to tell them he'd done

nothing wrong. They hired Konstantin the best defence lawyer that money could buy: Jeffrey Lichtman. Ever since he'd
secured the acquittal of New York mafia boss John Gotti Jr on
racketeering charges in the mid-2000s, Lichtman was known
as the sharpest criminal lawyer in New York. When the drugs
kingpin Joaquín 'El Chapo' Guzmán was arrested in 2018, he
hired Jeffrey Lichtman.

Lichtman's first job was to get Konstantin out of the
MCC. He proposed the most stringent bail conditions
imaginable: full-time, self-funded armed guards, a $20 mil-
lion personal bond, $8.5 million cash, no mobile phone and
24/7 GPS monitoring. He urged friends and family to write
letters of support. (His father Plamen wrote that Konstantin
had looked after him when he was ill. 'Without him I wouldn't
have managed to successfully cope with my sickness . . . even
after the surgery and during the recovery period, Konstantin
continued to support me, his mother, and his family the way
he has always done.')

The prosecution countered that no bail conditions on
earth were strong enough to stop Konstantin vanishing. He
had too much money and too many connections – just like
his sister. The judge agreed, and in June 2019 Konstantin was
refused bail. Even Bernie Madoff had gotten bail.

After reviewing the charges and the evidence against
him, Lichtman told Konstantin that if he wanted to see his
partner he had one option: plead guilty and co-operate. Otherwise he would be prosecuted, and he would lose. For every
defence of his sister he mounted, the FBI could produce an
email, a recorded call, a private text message that took it
apart. The government tightened the racks, adding wire
fraud, conspiracy to commit money laundering and conspiracy to commit bank fraud to the existing conspiracy to commit
wire fraud charge he was arrested for. Combined, that was up
to 90 years behind bars.

The authorities were open to a plea deal. There were bigger fish than Konstantin, and his testimony could help them. Work with us, they told him, and you might see your family again. We might even be able to get you on the witness relocation programme.

Konstantin had looked up to his sister since they were children. He considered Ruja as his best friend, even if she did shout at him all the time.[1] Co-operating with the authorities would mean telling the truth about everything – the blockchain, the pricing, the Fenero Funds, the Uganda trip. But the more evidence he was shown about OneCoin, especially the early emails between Ruja and Sebastian, the more Konstantin must have realised that when Ruja had said she would one day 'disappear and let someone else take the blame', that person had turned out to be him.

Conditions at the MCC can break anyone. In August 2019, four months after Konstantin's arrival, Jeffrey Epstein hanged himself a few cells away. On 4 October 2019, with his lawyer present, Konstantin pleaded guilty to all counts, and signed a co-operation agreement. In exchange for – he hoped – a reduced sentence, Konstantin agreed to turn state witness.

When you sign the plea deal, you sign away everything. The word 'co-operation' is misleading. Total subjection is more accurate. They can call you when they want, and wheel you in and out of court whenever they need. And if they suspect for a moment you're lying, the deal is off. You don't even know if you'll get a reduced sentence either, because a judge decides that after you've done your work. Signing a deal means submitting to the system, including your own safety. 'It is understood that Ignatov's truthful cooperation with this office is likely to reveal activities of individuals who might use violence, force and intimidation against Ignatov, his family, and loved ones', read the agreement.

But what it really meant to Konstantin was that he would have to testify very soon against Mark Scott. And maybe later against Sebastian Greenwood.

And, if she were ever caught, against his sister too.

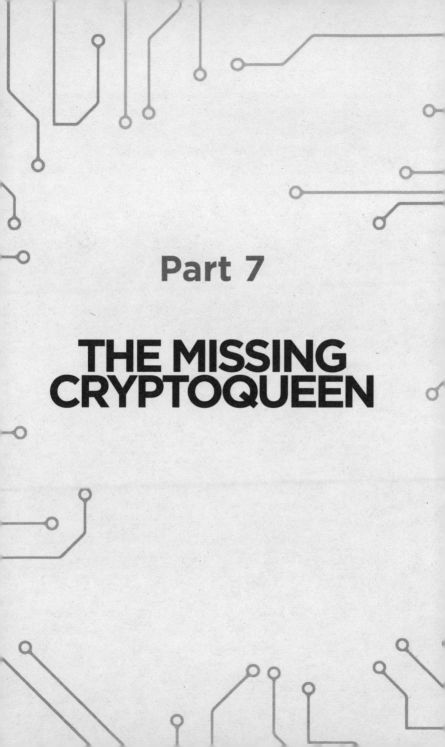

Part 7

THE MISSING CRYPTOQUEEN

CHAPTER 35

THE MISSING CRYPTOQUEEN

In November 2018, just a few months before Konstantin's arrest, I received an email from a BBC audio documentaries producer called Georgia Catt. Earlier that year she and her partner had been out for dinner with some friends and one of them had told them about an 'exciting new cryptocurrency' he'd just bought. He even suggested they consider investing themselves. But they quickly realised there was something off – even in the wild west of cryptocurrency. Money couldn't be withdrawn, it just sat there in investor's accounts. Its promoters drove Lamborghinis but knew little about technology. Events were like religious conventions, and wide-eyed investors seemed more ordinary than the typical crypto-enthusiast. And, above all, the enigmatic visionary behind it hadn't been seen in public for over a year.

For the next six months, Georgia became obsessed with understanding what had happened – why so many had put their faith in a coin they couldn't spend – barely believing the testimonies of those who'd been roped in. She also realised the story could be the perfect way into the niche, hyped world of cryptocurrency. Her editor, Philip Sellars, agreed. Over the next few months, they dug more into the story.

Georgia had read a few articles and books I'd written on Bitcoin and told me about OneCoin and its missing founder

'Dr Ruja', asking if I'd like to team up on the investigation and go in search of the missing cryptoqueen.

When we started working on BBC's *The Missing Cryptoqueen* podcast series in January 2019, neither of us imagined how it would take over our lives. We spent the next three years travelling all over the world, trying to piece together the scam and the whereabouts of its mastermind: to Sofia and the OneCoin HQ, of course; to Sozopol where her €6.9 million yacht was anchored and manned by a handful of unfriendly staff; to Igor Alberts's eight-storey mansion near Amsterdam; to Scotland to interview Jen McAdam, who'd lost her father's inheritance to OneCoin; to Uganda to pin down the dodgy pastor Fred Ntabazi, and meet Daniel in his mother's small village; to the Waltenhofen Gusswerks and its angry union boss Carlos; to an enormous OneCoin event in Bucharest where we somehow managed to talk our way in. We reviewed hundreds of leaked documents and interviewed almost as many people. Lots of them wanted to stay anonymous, like the husky-voiced debt collector who'd spent months tracking down stolen OneCoin money in south Asia and wouldn't tell us his name.

We wanted to understand how so many people could fall for such an audacious scam and how promoters blinded investors with techno-babble and false promises. But, above all, we wanted to know what happened to Ruja after she took Ryanair flight FR6300 from Sofia to Athens on 25 October 2017.

Tracking down someone who doesn't want to be found depends to a surprising extent on attentive members of the public. Every week, especially after our podcast was released and Ruja's face was all over the internet, Georgia and I received sightings and tip-offs. Some were probably OneCoin supporters trying to throw us off track, such as one widely circulated rumour that Ruja had fled to Belize and was now living openly in Brazil. Others were honest mistakes. For weeks we investigated a lead from a builder who was certain he'd seen Ruja at a mansion he was renovating in north London, which happened to neatly align with a very credible sighting at Heathrow Airport. After a lot of digging, it turned out the home belonged to a wealthy Russian with a passing resemblance to Ruja. A former politician from Serbia told us she'd been hiding in Serbia all along, protected by powerful politicians. But he refused to say more unless we told him what we knew in return. According to an old friend of hers, Ruja was even at the OneCoin event we attended in Romania, pulling the strings from behind the scenes and sussing out the two BBC journalists in the corner holding a microphone in the air. It was sometimes nerve-wracking following leads. I had to delete social media accounts and scrub the internet of any clues about my personal life. And although Georgia and I tightened up our online security and only communicated via encrypted messaging apps and secure email systems (like Ruja, ironically), we often felt on edge. It didn't help when someone started banging and screaming on my front door at 3am on the same day the podcast was released. 'They've found me *already*?!' I shouted at my sleeping partner as I frantically dialled 999. But it was someone at the wrong house.

We knew the promoters wouldn't be happy because many of them were still selling OneCoin even while we were investigating it. Predictably enough, they did everything they could to undermine us. Before the first episode aired, OneCoin HQ co-ordinated a mass complaint to the BBC about how unfairly we were treating them. That didn't bother us: it was just more evidence of the cult-like grip OneCoin had over believers. But a more worrying moment occurred as the series starting climbing the global podcast charts. A top promoter called King Jayms filmed himself firing a gun, saying, 'I'm not going to name no names but you know who you are.' A message below said: 'Pretending I see the OneLife haters'.[1] Having told millions of people that OneCoin was a giant Ponzi scam, there was little doubt Georgia and I were now firmly in that camp.

The vast majority of people who got in touch were former investors who'd personally lost money and were grateful we were trying to uncover the truth. But nearly all of them said the same thing: OneCoin is still going. People are still investing. People are still losing everything. It was true. In mid-2020, Ruja's mother Veska headlined a large OneCoin event in Romania, where she promised yet another re-launch of the e-commerce site Dealshaker. Facebook and WhatsApp were still full of people pushing the coin or advertising upcoming seminars. Where was the money going? Was Ruja still somewhere, secretly pulling the strings? No one knew. OneCoin was like a monster from a horror movie that simply refused to die.

Finding Ruja and preventing more victims getting fleeced started to feel like one and the same thing. As long as Ruja was still out there, believers still had hope. They could claim she'd never been convicted of anything and might one day return to fix everything. And, until then, our reports could be dismissed as 'fake news' and 'BBC propaganda'. Even in her absence, Ruja still held sway over so many people that actually finding her seemed the only thing that could kill OneCoin for good. When we started making the series, I never really thought we had any chance of finding Dr Ruja. But it soon felt like we had to.

The first thing journalists usually do when trying to find someone is the old adage: 'follow the money'. But that wasn't much help here. Ruja's web of companies and accounts encompassed practically every dodgy jurisdiction on earth.

Despite frequent government initiatives and high-profile pledges to crack down on corporate secrecy and tax evasion, it's still easy for rich people to squirrel money away. All her Dubai-based companies were dead ends. The best we could usually find was the names of frontmen – nobodies who'd been paid to keep her name off any public paperwork. Both RISG and OneCoin Limited were 'owned' by unknown Panamanians who were untraceable. (In fact, when Ruja did her Bitcoin deal with Sheikh al Qassimi, it was via her 'monkeys', or 'nobodies', Cesar Degracias Santos and Marisela Yasmin Simmons Hay.) The director of RavenR Dubai and RavenR Capital, both firms at the heart of her plan, was the Pizza Hut guy Thomas Christodoulou. Her secret Maltese gambling firms were bulletproof, usually ending up with a Curaçao trust company. Her penthouse in London was owned by an offshore Guernsey company, which had three other Guernsey companies, called Aquitaine Services Limited, Certidor and Treodoric, as directors.

Following the money ended with us chasing Pizza Hut managers, formation agents and shell companies.

It was infuriating. Ruja was everywhere but nowhere. It was always rumours and speculation. No one had proof. There were no photographs, no documents. No one willing to go 'on record'.

The task was made harder by the fact her appearance had almost certainly changed too. Ruja started having plastic surgery from mid-2015 and, by the time she absconded, looked very different to the woman who set up OneCoin with Sebastian and Juha three years earlier. A top London plastic surgeon explained to us how someone like Ruja could easily buy new cheeks, a new jawline, new nose, new lips. Although she would still be recognisable on close inspection (if you knew who you were looking for), he said, at a quick glance she could pass for anyone. One well-placed source told us that, by early 2018, Ruja had also lost several pounds and dyed her hair blonde. Worse: she was probably using an alias and travelling on a high-quality fake passport, possibly the Kyrgyz diplomatic passport she bought on Frank Schneider's advice the summer before she vanished, possibly on a new Bulgarian passport she'd bought from bent border officials.

We also had to consider the possibility Ruja had been murdered and we were chasing an apparition – finding connections and clues that weren't really there. Maybe angry investors got to her before the authorities. There were always rumours about 'people above her': Russian mafia or Bulgarian organised crime syndicates who'd spotted OneCoin's success early and used it to launder money – and wouldn't think twice about getting rid of her if needed. And although there was never any strong evidence pointing this way, given who she was and what she'd done, we couldn't rule it out. After all, it seemed impossible that someone so high profile could simply vanish into thin air.

But the uncomfortable truth is that hundreds of criminals evade justice every year and go on the run just like Ruja. Europol, SOCA and the FBI's Most Wanted lists include hundreds of criminals that are currently at large. Croatian Marko Nikolić is wanted for aiding a murder – and has been on the run since 2001; convicted Austrian killer Tibor Foco has been evading justice since 1995 when he escaped prison. Some vanish to faraway countries, while others take up new identities and fade into obscurity closer to home. Shane O'Brien murdered Josh Hanson in London in 2015, fled the country on a private plane and spent the next three years travelling around Europe with fake ID, new hair and fresh tattoos (he finally handed himself in to Romanian police in 2018). Others rely on the support of powerful backers: former Wirecard COO Jan Marsalek has been missing since June 2020 and is thought to be somewhere in Moscow under the protection of the GRU. Even the most high-profile can stay underground for decades. Until his arrest in Sicily in 2023, Matteo Messina Denaro, the *capo dei capi* of the Italian mafia, had been on the run, seemingly on the island, for 30 years.

According to specialists, the trick is discipline: you must avoid contacting family and friends if possible, stay away from official authorities and never slip out of character. If you have a new identity, plenty of money and iron will, evading capture is not as hard as it seems.

But all it takes is a small lapse of judgement. And, in the end, everyone makes mistakes.

Gradually, Georgia and I were able to piece together a rough outline of her movements after her flight to Athens. There were gaps and unknowns, but after a careful assessment of the various sightings, rumours and tip-offs, by late 2020 we had a working document: a 'best guess'.

When Ruja stepped off her Ryanair flight at Athens International Airport on the morning of 25 October 2017, she drove (or possibly flew) to Thessaloniki in northern Greece, where she part-owned a large tobacco factory.

She stayed in Thessaloniki for a couple of days. Maybe she visited the picturesque old town, or found time for some shopping in the swish Tsimiski Street. Perhaps she even visited her factory and took a look around.

Then she did the last thing anyone would have expected: she turned around and went back into Bulgaria. One plausible scenario is that Hristoforos 'Taki' Amanatidis, aka 'The Cocaine King', helped arrange safe passage by car via one of the well-known smuggling routes between the two countries. (Thessaloniki is on the road route from Athens to Sofia, less than 100 kilometres from the Bulgarian border. The Greek/

Bulgarian crossing is one of Europe's great cigarette smuggling hotspots – and is also known for people smuggling too.)

We don't think she was planning to disappear for good at this point, but simply make people *think* she'd left the country so she could lay low in Bulgaria. She had plenty of influential contacts and several houses there, including the luxurious Sozopol mansion. Places where she could safely plan her next move.*

However, the German police raid on the Sofia HQ in January 2018 persuaded her that Bulgaria wasn't the safe haven she thought it was. The authorities were not going to let this drop – and it wasn't only the Americans who had her in their sights. And now it was only a matter of time before the EU's most powerful country would discover the truth about her phoney blockchain.

Over the next several months, Ruja was spotted multiple times in Dubai – in a luxury shopping mall, at a restaurant, on a private yacht. After London and Sofia, Dubai was the place Ruja felt most at ease. She'd lived there on–off ever since 2014 and even held a residency permit. She owned a 5,000-square-foot luxury penthouse flat in the exclusive Palm Jumeirah area, popular among rich Bulgarian expats. How she travelled from Sofia to Dubai is unclear – possibly via a private jet, since it's only a five-hour flight. Some sources told us she was living in Dubai quite openly at this time, confident that, even if the Germans or Americans did know where she was, the chances of extradition were practically zero. While the US authorities do manage to extradite the occasional

---

* A second possibility is that she took a connecting flight from Athens to Cyprus, where her two 'owners' of RavenR Dubai and RavenR London lived. From there she could have travelled to Northern Cyprus, a well-known refuge for fugitives due to its lack of extradition treaties with the EU and America.

criminal from the new 'Costa del Crime', it is the exception rather than the rule.

Former FBI Special Agent Karen Greenaway spent 20 years investigating transnational organised crime and knows this world inside out. If Ruja was in Dubai, reckons Karen, it's 'entirely possible' the FBI knew. But even they wouldn't have been able to swoop in and arrest her. If Ruja was spending good money in the country and not causing any trouble, it wouldn't have been in Dubai's interests to hand her over. And if she had any connections with powerful people – for example, Sheikh al Qassimi – a formal request for assistance from the FBI would likely have ended up at the bottom of an unanswered pile of papers in an office somewhere. 'It happens all the time,' says Karen. 'The FBI cannot override [any protection Ruja might have]. I can tell you that from experience.'

Ruja living in Dubai in 2018 would certainly tally with the fact that neither Konstantin nor Veska ever seemed remotely worried or upset about her.

But if she was in Dubai, then where exactly?

CHAPTER 36

THE DUBAI MANSION

Georgia and I had heard rumours that Ruja owned a secret mansion somewhere in the city, a luxury pad inside a private compound. In a later court appearance, Konstantin mentioned a 'Dubai mansion' that cost around '20 million dirhams'. He even said he'd visited it once. A Dubai mansion inside a private compound is exactly the sort of place someone like Ruja might like to hide. But no one knew where it was.

On 15 February 2018, just as he was taking over the top job from his sister, Konstantin posted a selfie on his Instagram account. Konstantin often posted selfies on Instagram – with his chiselled jawline and sporting physique, he'd once considered a career in modelling. He was wearing a black t-shirt, cap, and the modern selfie smoulder. 'Just woke up and already have 200+ messages,' he wrote. 'You crazy guys. Birthday mode on!!!' It was tagged Sofia, Bulgaria.

But in the far distance there were skyscrapers visible, including one that looked like a bottle opener, and a mosque minaret. It looked more like the Middle East than the Balkans. Was it possible that Konstantin was in fact at his sister's secretive mansion? It seemed like a long shot. But I noticed the date again: 15 February 2018. When Konstantin was stopped at San Francisco airport in 2019, the FBI found a power of attorney on his laptop apparently signed by Ruja herself. It was dated 8 February 2018. Just one week earlier.*

We drafted in a BBC open-source specialist called Aliaume Leroy to take a look at the photo. Even innocuous social media posts sometimes contain valuable digital bread-crumbs and people like Aliaume specialise in making sense of them.

First, he labelled every distinctive image in the back-ground of Konstantin's selfie: every building, tree, lake and wall. He then meticulously searched through hundreds of photos using Google and Yandex reverse image search, look-ing for a match. It didn't take him long to discover the 'bottle opener' building was not in Sofia. It was the Amesco Tower in the Jumeirah Lake Towers waterfront district, Dubai. His only stumbling block was several confused hours trying to figure out why the skyscrapers around the Amesco Tower didn't line up in the way he expected – until he remembered it was a selfie. Konstantin took the photo with the front facing camera of his phone, which created a mirror image. From there he matched up every other visible building and, using Google Earth Pro's satellite imagery and basic geometry, started to calculate Konstantin's likely 'line of sight'. He went from buildings to lakes to trees to fences, narrowing down the location metre by metre. After days of non-stop sleuth-ing, he emailed me a password-protected document.

'Good news,' he said, in a gross understatement. His document included an exact address in the Springs 1 neigh-bourhood of Dubai. 'Konstantin's photograph was taken in the back garden.'

---

* Konstantin later claimed in court that he thought the power of attorney was probably fake: forged by Irina Dilkinska. However, if Konstantin knew it to be fake, then why would he have kept it on his laptop?

'*What*?!' I said. 'How on earth . . .' I wasn't expecting an exact address.

'People don't realise how much we can find from a photo,' Aliaume explained. 'I knew I'd find the address as soon as I saw it.' I've hardly posted a single photograph online since.

Based on a careful analysis of the various states of construction of the bottle opener building, Aliaume could even pinpoint when Konstantin took the photo: some point between September 2017 and 15 February 2018. In other words, very likely *after* Ruja vanished.

Armed with the address, we found a 2016 estate agent listing for the property – the year it was sold to Ruja. The property is a 6,700-square-foot villa with five bedrooms, an infinity pool, sunken pool bar and five reception rooms. The asking price was 17 million dirhams – very close to the 20 million number Konstantin later mentioned in court. We also found a partial Dubai property register that had been leaked on the dark net, which luckily for us included the same address. The named owner was . . . Sebastian Greenwood. Ruja and Sebastian sometimes used each other's names with their companies, including in Dubai.

Thanks to one careless Instagram post, we had the address of a secret Dubai mansion, which Konstantin visited weeks or months after Ruja vanished, and which on paper belonged to her closest business partner.

It was the strongest lead we'd ever had but it wasn't conclusive. It's possible Konstantin was in Dubai visiting Sebastian or staff at the OneCoin Dubai office, and via intermediaries Ruja had arranged for him to stay at her mansion. But based on the available evidence – the date on the power of attorney, the fact Gary Gilford distinctly recalls Konstantin saying he'd seen Ruja in person, the persistent rumours she was in Dubai around that time – another possibility is that Konstantin travelled to Dubai in early 2018 to visit his missing sister and pick up a power of attorney.

If this was the UK, we'd have staked the property out, monitored comings and goings, and, in the end, simply knocked on the door. But you can't show up in Dubai with a microphone and doorstep people. According to the World Press Freedom Index, the United Arab Emirates ranks 131st in the world for press freedom and criticising the ruling classes; harassing residents, or even working undercover, can land journalists in jail. Trusted colleagues, journalists who knew the region, wisely but firmly told us not to go. If Ruja was in cahoots with the authorities or paying someone off, they said, the police would find a trumped-up charge to arrest us before we cleared customs. And there were certainly signs she was being protected by someone. Following the Dubai bank freezes in late 2015, a public prosecutor issued a warrant for Ruja's arrest in December 2016. But it was never executed. She even spent New Year 2016/17 in Dubai at her penthouse without any trouble.

Part of me wanted to ignore them: I could have pretended to be a foreign tourist and hung about expensive bars and Chanel stores, just in case she turned up on one of her infamous shopping sprees. But much as I wanted to find Ruja, I didn't want it at any cost. It was bad enough worrying about Bulgarian organised criminals, former spooks and angry OneCoin promoters – I didn't need Dubai intelligence agencies added to the list. Besides, a trip would be pointless, since the mansion was tucked inside a private compound protected by a large security detail. We tried via intermediaries to check the property out for us – but all we learned was that the bins were occasionally changed. We contacted neighbours, private investigators, former residents and even local Airbnb hosts: no one would talk. We even managed to get some Krispy Kreme doughnuts sent to the house via a food delivery app. We spoke to the driver over the phone as he banged on the front gate – but no-one answered. (And even to this date, we don't know if the property still belongs to Ruja or Sebastian – it might even have been sold on.)

But protection in Dubai is only ever temporary. According to former FBI Special Agent Karen Greenaway, if Ruja was in Dubai in 2018, Konstantin's arrest by the FBI in March 2019 (plus her own indictment, which was published on the same day) might have changed her calculation. Maybe her relationship with Sheikh al Qassimi was turning sour. Soon after the enterprising Sheikh tried and failed to unfreeze Ruja's bank accounts, he moved the company HQ and made himself sole shareholder.[1] According to Dubai Commercial Court filings, al Qassimi then tried to cash the cheques that Ruja had handed over when she sold him the company in 2015. When Ruja found out, she cancelled his power of attorney, and by 2019 the case started making its way through Dubai's legal system.[2] Entangled in a messy dispute, and now publicly wanted by the Americans, it's possible that Ruja decided, for one final time, she had to get out.

One tantalising possibility is that the Dubai authorities simply threw Ruja in prison the moment they saw the arrest warrant, and she's sitting there right now while the authorities decide if it's in their interests to extradite her. That doesn't rule out the secret Dubai mansion, but it makes it less likely to be the safe haven it might have been in 2018. That left us with one final, incredible, possibility.

CHAPTER 37

FREEDOM?

About 500 years ago, as international trade and mercantilism were starting to expand, there was a serious problem: no one knew who was in charge of the sea. A general agreement held that waters close to a coast – roughly the distance a cannonball could be fired – were under the jurisdiction of the closest country, but, beyond that, there was only force. In 1609, as the Dutch and Spanish quarrelled over access to the lucrative spice and silk markets in the East Indies, the philosopher Hugo Grotius argued that the sea should be subject to no legal jurisdiction at all: 'For even that ocean wherewith God hath compassed the Earth is navigable on every side round about, and the settled or extraordinary blasts of wind, not always blowing from the same quarter, and sometimes from every quarter,' he wrote in *The Free Sea*, 'do they not sufficiently signify that nature hath granted a passage from all nations unto all?' By the mid-nineteenth century, as global commerce accelerated, the 'freedom of the sea' became an accepted principle of international law. In 1958, the United Nations signed the 'Convention on the High Seas' and the informal cannonball rule was extended to 12 nautical miles.

If you stay 12 nautical miles (about 13.8 common miles) from a coastline, you are technically nowhere: no country has jurisdiction over you and no police force has the legal authority to arrest you. And even if you're closer in, police operations at sea are expensive, and collecting intelligence on private yachts and luxury cruisers is almost impossible. While there are a few exemptions – notably for piracy – the majority of planet earth is technically lawless.

In early 2021, as we pondered what to do with the Dubai address, an anonymous source got in touch claiming that someone he knew had spotted Ruja Ignatova at some point in 2019 on a boat in the Med – but couldn't remember when or where exactly.

We might have filed that as just another 'maybe'. Except it tallied with something we'd learned a year earlier when a private investigator called Alan McClean advised us to start looking in the last place Ruja was seen. 'There's a reason she flew to Athens,' he said. 'The Mediterranean.' Two of Alan's former colleagues were working there and he asked them to visit a few top-end restaurants with photos of Ruja. Incredibly, staff in one of the restaurants told them Ruja had been there around six months ago with a large entourage. We emailed the restaurant with a few more picture the following day to confirm. 'Lady in photo is familiar to staff,' replied the manager. 'They all remember this lady with a party of 6–8.' That would have been some point in April or May 2019.

Soon after, another well-placed source told us she'd been spotted more than once in summer 2019 near to Saint-Tropez in France, moored somewhere out at sea in a large yacht, occasionally visiting land by speedboat.

As we collated and analysed these sightings, Georgia Catt and I started to form a working theory about what Ruja had done after stepping off that RyanAir flight in October 2017.

Initially she was living secretly in Bulgaria, having gone

to Greece – before turning back round and sneaking straight back over the border. With Operation Satellite gaining pace – and then Gilbert's betrayal – Bulgaria was the safest place for her.

But things got too hot for her there too – especially once the German authorities raided her office and started interviewing her staff. She moved to Dubai for a while, but Konstantin's arrest in February 2019 changed her calculations again.

Travelling on fake identity documents, Ruja returned to Europe – hopping between land and sea in and around the Mediterranean.

Ruja returning so close to the scene of the crime seems strange in some ways. Wouldn't it be safer to vanish somewhere further afield – a tropical island? Russia? Isn't it more likely she'd been killed, either by angry investors or organised crime groups?

But there is a useful rule of three in journalism: if three separate sources tell you the same thing, it's usually worth pursuing. And three unrelated sources were saying the same thing: Ruja wasn't dead, hiding in Sofia, or living in a Dubai mansion – she was in and around the Mediterranean. Was it really possible she could be living at sea?

In mid-2021, Georgia Catt and I asked an investigative journalist called Rob Byrne to help us investigate the 'Med boat' theory. He contacted different ports and analysed the movement of several superyachts, using specialised marine tracker software. None had been to our key locations around the dates we had. (Annoyingly, it turns out a lot of private yachts simply turn their trackers off, although it's technically forbidden.) He even posted several photos of Ruja in the handful of private Facebook groups that cater to yacht crew, asking if anyone recognised her – adding that she might look a little different these days. Nothing seemed to work until one day he got a reply out of the blue:

'Hi Rob. She is on the yacht I work on right now. Why are you looking for her?'

'Hey,' Rob replied. 'Are you 100% sure?'

'Yes, she's here, right now . . . she talk[s] about crypto all day . . . She use[s] 3 computers in her room but never in saloon.'

'OK, whereabouts are you?'

'We are in Greece right now. Anchored. We call her Jaru.' Ja-Ru.

'If there is any way you can verify she's on the boat it would be really important. Or the boat name or where you are going next?'

'I'm sorry I don't want to get her into trouble.'

And then, like so often, the line went dead: the mysterious boat woman vanished. There were hundreds of boats anchored in Greece, far too many to individually check.

When I first published this 'Med Boat theory' in June 2022, I wasn't sure what the response would be. It was outlandish – and even I was a little sceptical. But it was the best we had. I also wondered if the police – especially the FBI – would turn up at my house asking questions. If I was wrong, I could live with it. But what if I was right? What if the FBI had secretly tracked Ruja to somewhere around the Med – and I'd accidentally tipped her off?

It didn't take long to get an answer. Within a fortnight of this book first being published, the FBI were in touch. But not with me. With the whole world.

CHAPTER 38

THE WORLD'S MOST WANTED WOMAN

Since its creation in 1950, over five hundred wanted criminals have appeared on the FBI's Ten Most Wanted Fugitives list. That includes some of the world's most notorious names: Osama Bin Laden, James 'Whitey' Bulger and El Chapo. On 30 June 2022, a new name was added: Dr Ruja Ignatova. 'Ignatova is being sought for her alleged leadership of a massive fraud scheme that affected millions of investors worldwide' read the notice.

Even though I'd been looking for Dr Ruja since late 2018, I was as surprised as anyone by the new development. I watched the press conference in New York slack-jawed, as FBI Special Agent Michael Driscoll announced a $100,000 reward, and asked that 'anyone with information about her whereabouts . . . call us'. The notice itself a classic mugshot with details of the case – had been translated into Russian, Bulgarian, German, Albanian, Greek and Arabic. All places we'd been interested in too. 'Ignatova is believed to travel with armed guards and/or associates' it read.

The amateur sleuths on BehindMLM were watching too, of course. 'OneCoin scammers on Facebook are desperately trying to delete comments about this' wrote the prominent poster WhistleblowerFin. For this rag-tag gang, who'd done more than anyone, including the police, to bring the scam down, it was vindication. 'We tried to warn you!'

*

As the only female on the list, Dr Ruja had suddenly become the world's most wanted woman, subject of an international global manhunt. I felt slightly silly – as if Georgia Catt and I could really have found someone that had eluded the world's most powerful police force! There was relief too – for almost four years it felt we were the only people actively looking for Dr Ruja, which sometimes made me feel quite exposed. There is safety in numbers.

But fairly soon I had a different realisation. Was there more to this than the FBI wanting to catch a crypto-scammer? Was Ruja involved in something bigger, something darker? And, by extension, was I?

When I interviewed FBI Special Agent Paul Roberts a few weeks later, he told me that the FBI believes Ruja does indeed have affiliations with organised crime groups. And those affiliations 'factored' into their decision to add her to the list.

'What do you mean factored into your decision?' I asked.

'It's not just a financial crime . . . she has these organised crime connections and potentially information about her could lead to information about these organised crime groups.'

'Is it your belief they were involved in her disappearance and maybe still involved in her ongoing disappearance?'

'It's certainly possible.'

I started this investigation in late 2018 because I thought it was an interesting crypto story. A cautionary tale of techno-hype, greed and the strange madness of crypto-investors. I never expected – or wanted – to be digging around organised crime groups. I'd spent a lot of time talking about the naivety of OneCoin investors, not realising that I'd been extremely naïve myself.

In the weeks that followed, there was renewed coverage and interest in the story. Suddenly everyone was looking for Ruja. Investors who'd put their money into OneCoin started to get organised – some created victim groups in the hope they might recoup some of their money. I wrote an article with Rob Byrne for the BBC's website about Ruja's secretive ownership of the large Kensington penthouse and the very next day a court in Guernsey issued a restraint order on the company that owns it. A glimmer of hope.

In some ways the renewed coverage helped us. There were more leads and more sightings to investigate. That also has its downsides. Once someone appears on the FBI's Ten Most Wanted list, suddenly every other person has seen them: in Greece (this time in a swish bar), in Brazil, in Dubai, in London. And, nearly always, they're wrong.

But when Ruja's former security chief Frank Schneider agreed to talk to me in August 2022, it was different. He was one of the only people who might know where she'd gone. I was surprised he'd agreed to talk at all. Ever since he was arrested at gunpoint by French police in 2020, Frank had been fighting an extradition request from the US for his alleged role in the OneCoin scam. When I arrived at his house in France, he showed me his electronic tag – one of the conditions of his house arrest. It beeps if he walks past his front gate. '[Awaiting extradition] is comparable to being told you have a very serious illness' Frank said, in perfect English.

Frank gave me a new account of Ruja's disappearance. She did board that RyanAir flight, he said. But it wasn't her choice – she was forced to leave. When Ruja told him one day in October that she was leaving Bulgaria for a while, he repeatedly asked her why. 'You don't understand' she replied. 'I have to do what certain people tell me what to do.'

When Ruja arrived in Athens, Frank says she was met at the airport by a man who flew with her to Thessaloniki. She was then told to wait. A car would be coming to pick her up soon.

And how does Frank know this? Because, he says, Ruja

phoned him up while she waited. She'd been shopping in Thessaloniki. She was bored.

'I thought you were the boss?' Frank asked.

'So did I,' Ruja joked back.

A couple of hours later Ruja texted Frank, with just two words: 'home safe'. He says that was the last he heard of his old boss.

Who are these 'certain people?' I asked. Was it Taki, the so-called 'Cocaine King'? Was this why Ruja had sent Taki's partner all those millions? For protection of some kind?

Frank said he didn't know. Simply that they were powerful people at 'the very top' of Bulgarian politics: the same people who'd helped Ruja learn about Operation Satellite. Not him.

But why would those people want Ruja out of the country? There was soon a potential answer to that question, too.

In early 2023, I was walking to a meeting in central London when my phone started beeping frantically. That's usually a sign something bad has happened – and it was. A respected Bulgarian media outlet called Bird.Bg had just reported that Dr Ruja wasn't in hiding. She was dead: murdered in November 2018 on the orders of the Cocaine King Taki.

The article also alleged something I'd started to suspect, but couldn't prove: that Ruja was using OneCoin to launder money for Taki's smuggling empire. OneCoin wasn't simply a crypto-currency scam. It had become a convenient cover story for a vast money laundering operation. According to Bird.Bg, Operation Satellite and then Gilbert Armenta flipping had spooked Taki. He started to worry that if Ruja were ever to be caught, she might bring him down with her. He couldn't take the risk.

The details were graphic, grim. One of Taki's guys had killed Ruja onboard a yacht off the Greek coast. He chopped her body into small pieces and dumped it into the Mediterranean. I'd been right with the Med Boat theory – but not in the way I thought or wanted.

Ruja was dead? And all this time we'd been searching for . . . What? Shadows? Figments of our imagination? Was it really possible that all those sightings were mistaken identities? It didn't make sense. Both RavenR boss Gary Gilford and Duncan Arthur recall Konstantin speaking to Ruja on the phone after that date. We'd also received another strong lead in late 2022: according to a top Greek journalist, the police there had conducted a raid on a property following a credible tip-off that she was travelling around the country. And would the FBI have added Ruja to their Ten Most Wanted list if they thought she was dead?

As we dug deeper into the latest rumour, it started to blend into the others, another elusive 'maybe'. The source of the story was an unsigned, untitled piece of paper that was found in the safe of a murdered Bulgarian police officer. The paper claimed one of Taki's guys was overheard drunkenly talking about her death, a year after it happened.

I've now spent five years looking for Ruja. I've spoken to hundreds of people, travelled around the world, reviewed untold tip offs, leads, sightings and rumours. I still don't know for sure what's happened to the Cryptoqueen. It's certainly possible that Ruja is dead. She might be in Russia, holed up in Dubai, or living as a faceless rich woman in the Seychelles. With Ruja, anything is possible. But at the time of writing, the most plausible theory – for me at least – is one of the most unbelievable. As her countless victims – the people who believed her promise of a financial revolution – face ruin and heartbreak, and as those who helped her to get away with it face serious jail time, the Cryptoqueen is floating somewhere on the high seas with a new name and a new face.

Perhaps she spends her time sailing leisurely from place to place, surrounded by opulence and luxury. Maybe she's trapped somehow – in exchange for her safety, she is forced to use her knowledge of finance and cryptocurrency to help the organised crime groups who once helped her: moving money between secret Bitcoin wallets, foreign exchange companies, phoney Maltese casinos and fake frontmen. Passing her day in front of three screens just like she used to at McKinsey.

I lie awake some nights imagining Ruja making land periodically and carefully, meeting with close family and friends for dinner here or there, where she reminisces about her crazy life, and asks after Konstantin. She spends much of her time planning how and when she can next see her daughter safely. It's risky, but so was everything she's ever done. No-one would look twice at the wealthy well-dressed woman as she hops on her speedboat and heads back out to sea: it could be anyone. There's a flicker of recognition, perhaps, but all her papers and documents are present and correct. As untraceable but omnipresent as cryptocurrency itself.

AFTERWORD

Trials

Although OneCoin is ostensibly a Bulgarian company, it is a global story. Ruja herself was both a Bulgarian and German national and grew up in the latter; Sebastian Greenwood was both a British and Swedish citizen. The earliest promoters were Finns and Swedes – most notably Juha Parhiala. While the HQ was technically in Sofia, her London, Hong Kong and Dubai offices were all important too. The top MLM pushers were the most diverse set of people you'll ever meet: Italian brothers, born again American Christians, British Muslims, Ugandan doctors, Australian businessmen. Her companies and assets were dotted in every jurisdiction on earth: Malta, Frankfurt, Dubai, Sozopol, London, the Caymans, Florida. That was all part of the trick. The scam was global, but law enforcement is still limited by borders and jurisdictions. OneCoin slipped through the cracks, and it took years for the law to catch up with it.

But, as this book was going to print, it was finally getting there.

Mark Scott was the first, in November 2019, just one month after Konstantin signed the co-operation agreement. It took place in the famed Courtroom 318, a large ceremonial court with high ceilings and wood-panelled walls, on the third floor of the federal courthouse in Foley Square, Manhattan. Despite the fact this was the biggest Ponzi scheme since Bernie

Madoff, only a couple of bloggers showed up – the press weren't that interested. The mainstream press thought OneCoin was a cryptocurrency story – far too complicated to excite the public. The specialised crypto press, by contrast, thought OneCoin was an old-fashioned Ponzi scheme, and so not really their business either. Even until the very end, OneCoin avoided detection.

Mark pleaded innocent, and while he didn't speak during the trial, his lawyers argued that Ruja had lied to him, just like she'd lied to everyone. Konstantin Ignatov was the star witness for the prosecution and, for three days, he stunned the court as he told the story of OneCoin. The jewellery, the spies, the flats stacked with cash, the properties, the parties. When the court played the recordings of Ruja shouting at Gilbert Armenta over the phone in September 2017, it was too much for Konstantin. He started to cry. And when he explained how Frank Schneider had made secret recordings of Gilbert and his wife, only to learn about the FBI investigations, there was an audible gasp in the room. One of the court employees present said later it was the most remarkable thing she'd heard in 20 years of watching trials.

It only took the jury four hours to find Mark Scott guilty of bank fraud and money laundering. As they read out the verdict, his wife Lidia let out a wail. Mark Scott, portly and tanned, remained sanguine. He leaned over the railings and hugged her before being led out. At the time of writing, Mark Scott still claims he is innocent, and is appealing his conviction. In late 2021 Scott's counsel applied for a re-trial based on the allegation that Konstantin Ignatov perjured himself during Mark Scott's trial. It is not clear when Scott's motion for a new trial will be decided.[1]

In October 2021, Mark Scott's assistant, David Pike,

who worked with him on the Fenero Funds, pleaded guilty to conspiracy to commit bank fraud.

Next was Gilbert Armenta, who'd been arrested in September 2017 and agreed to co-operate. In January 2018 Armenta pleaded guilty to conspiracy to commit wire fraud, three counts of conspiracy to commit money laundering, and conspiracy to commit extortion. In February 2023 Gilbert was sentenced to five years in prison for his role in the One-Coin scam. In their sentencing submission, the Department of Justice mentioned the BBC's Missing Cryptoqueen podcast as evidence of the global impact of the scam.

On 16 December 2022, after having spent four years in custody, Sebastian Greenwood pleaded guilty to wire fraud, conspiracy to commit wire fraud and conspiracy to commit money laundering. As this book was going to print, sentencing had not yet taken place.

In 2022 a UK judge approved a US request to extradite Christopher Hamilton on a money laundering charge related to these transactions. At the time of writing, Hamilton is appealing the request.

On 29 April 2021, Frank Schneider, the former spy who was Ruja's security adviser, was dramatically arrested by French special forces at the request of the FBI. Armed police surrounded his car on the school run and put a gun to his 13-year-old son's head. 'I thought we were about be assassinated on the spot,' Frank said later.[2] On 19 January 2022, a French court ruled Schneider should be extradited to the US. At the time of writing, he is appealing the decision.

On 20 March 2023, Irina Dilkinska was extradited from Bulgaria to the US to face one count of conspiracy to commit wire fraud, and one count of conspiracy to commit money laundering, in connection with OneCoin.

Over in Germany, the Bielefeld prosecutors had their day

in court too. In October 2020, Frank Ricketts was charged with providing unauthorised payment services for OneCoin. The trial started in September 2021. At the time of writing the case is ongoing. The same month the lawyer Martin Breidenbach was charged with money laundering, in connection with the purchase of Ruja Ignatova's London penthouses. The trial started in September 2021. At the time of writing the case is also ongoing.

In October 2019 Konstantin Ignatov pleaded guilty, pursuant to a cooperation agreement with the government, to conspiracy to commit wire fraud, substantive wire fraud, conspiracy to commit money laundering and conspiracy to commit bank fraud. At the time of writing, he is yet to be sentenced. Just like his sister, Konstantin's whereabouts are unknown.

At the time of writing, OneCoin continues to be marketed and sold around the world.

NOTES

Chapter 2: Ruja and Sebastian

1 Himmelheber, Martin, 'Die Cryptoqueen aus Schramberg' (*NRWZ*, May 2020). Much of Ruja and Konstantin's early years in Schramberg have been pieced together in a series of articles by Himmelheber.

2 Post on 'Cryptoqueen' (@Dr.RujaIgnatova) profile page (Facebook, 20 March 2015): https://www.facebook.com/766500173402431/posts/business-woman-of-the-year-2014-dr-ruja-ignatovalet-me-introduce-you-to-a-very-b/905216542864126/

3 Hässler, David, 'Pyramidpengar bakom bröllopskupp' (Realtid.se, June 2010)

4 Ekström, J. and Wisterberg, E., 'Sebastian Greenwood pekas ut som hjarnan bakom OneCoin – riskerar 20 års fängelse: "Var en svärmorsdröm"' (BreakIt, 8 May 2020): https://www.breakit.se/artikel/24885

5 Gjernes, Knut and Skaalmo, Gøran, 'Pyramidepredikanten' (*DagensNaeringsliv*, June 2010)

6 'Sebastian Greenwood, SiteTalk Convention, Slovenia 2011' (YouTube, 28 March 2011): https://www.youtube.com/watch?v=5Q89YJ-C9Pg

7 Engert, Marcus, 'OneCoin konnte Milliarden stehlen, obwohl Banken die Behörden informiert hatten' (Buzzfeed,

September 2020): https://www.buzzfeed.com/de/mar-cusengert/onecoin-banken-fincenfiles

8 'Businesswoman Ruzha Ignatova: I invested in the salon of the transvestite Ursula' (headline translated) (Blitz.bg, 1 November 2011): https://blitz.bg/article/27717

9 Bulgarian company records show that Ruja was director or manager of several companies which were owned by CSIF: Multineshanal Aset Portfolio Salport, Keptial Apartments, Teres Fond, Slavyanska Rial Isyeyt. CSIF was the company owned by Borislavova.

10 'BIOEFFECT EGF Serum - парти 20.07.2011' (YouTube, 22 July 2011): https://www.youtube.com/watch?v=8fk11 CV3p2c/

11 Björn Thomas was Sebastian's partner in both Towah Group Cyprus and Loopium. Towah was a notorious payment pro-cessor for several pyramid schemes in Scandinavia, which shut down some time in 2011. The Cyprus company reg-istration is available here: https://opencorporates.com/companies/cy/HE287205. The exact relationship between Towah and Towah Group Cyprus is unclear.

12 Gibraltar corporate registry: https://www.datocapital.com.gi/companies/Loopium-Ltd.html

Chapter 3: Bitcoin and BigCoin

1 The first email exchanges about Bitcoin are archived by the Satoshi Nakamoto Institute: https://satoshi.nakamotoinsti-tute.org/emails/cryptography/12/#selection-89.0-89.125

2 Zetter, Kim, 'FBI Fears Bitcoin's Popularity with Criminals' (*Wired Magazine*, 9 May 2012): https://www.wired.com/2012/05/fbi-fears-bitcoin/

3 One of the few early mentions of BigCoin is from a Chinese blog site: http://blog.sina.com.cn/s/blog_13785f6da0102 vbfj.html

4 The author has been told by three separate people that Ruja and Sebastian first met at a 'cryptocurrency conference', likely in Singapore in late 2013. This was also described by Tommi Vuorinen in a 2016 talk. There are frustratingly few precise details. 'Tommi Vuorinen OneCoin esitys' (You-Tube, 29 February 2016): https://www.youtube.com/watch?v=Uk1g2KwECJo

5 Ekström, J. and Wisterberg, E., 'Sebastian Greenwood pekas ut som hjarnan bakom OneCoin – riskerar 20 års fängelse: "Var en svärmorsdröm"' (BreakIt, 8 May 2020): https://www.breakit.se/artikel/24885

Chapter 4: MLM Meets the 'Bitch of Wall Street'

1 Loopium legal letter sent February 2014, complaining about funders (author's copy).

2 One of Ruja's first jobs was to register a new company at the same Cyprus address as Loopium, which would become the vehicle for the new project. It was called Zooperium, which was then renamed OneCoin. Gibraltar company details for Loopium are available here: https://www.datocapital.com.gi/companies/Loopium-Ltd.html

3 Ekström, J. and Wisterberg, E., 'Sebastian Greenwood pekas ut som hjarnan bakom OneCoin' (BreakIt, 8 May 2020): https://www.breakit.se/artikel/24885

4 Ekström, J. and Wisterberg, E., 'Sebastian Greenwood pekas ut som hjarnan bakom OneCoin – riskerar 20 års fängelse: "Var en svärmorsdröm"' (BreakIt, 8 May 2020): https://www.breakit.se/artikel/24885

5 *United States Government Sealed Complaint v. Konstantin Ignatov* (6 March 2019)

6 Juha Parhiala was born in Finland in 1958, but the family crossed over the border when Juha was three years old.

7 Different MLM companies use different techniques to measure sales, and Juha proposed OneCoin use a 'binary' model. This meant that each promoter would create two teams, called a 'left leg' and a 'right leg'. The business volume commission each week would be based on the sales generated by the weaker leg, with the remaining difference between the two carried over into the following week. There were small conditions and exemptions. Promoters who purchased larger packages would receive larger percentage payouts down the pyramid. The trio also placed a weekly cap of no more than €35,000 earnings each week, although this varied depending on how high you were in the network. If a seller reached their ceiling, it was called 'maxing out'.

8 'Bangkok OneCoin – Event Guest Speaker Mr. Juha Parhiala' (YouTube, 3 March 2015): https://www.youtube.com/watch?v=WK5VhCRb78Q

9 Ruja set up a new company called Zooperium in Gibraltar, which she then renamed OneCoin Ltd. Ruja also set up a OnePay website, which provided MLM payment solutions – 'a global commission payment solution, enabling direct sales companies to pay millions of distributors worldwide instantly'. This suggests that one early idea for OneCoin was to continue with the Loopium idea of providing a payments service to MLM companies. In May 2014, Ruja renamed one of her old Bulgarian companies as BigPay Ltd – possibly to convince John that this was part of a plan to help BigCoin. But then she sold it to a company owned by her mother, Veska.

10 RISG's address was 1203 Jumeirah Towers, Dubai. OneCoin Limited's address was just down the hall, at 1209 Jumeirah Towers. The Towers serve as a kind of postal address for companies. Martin Breidenbach, a German lawyer that Sebastian had employed while working for Loopium days, agreed to be secretary.

11 'OneCoin Presentation by Nigel Allan' (YouTube, 12 May 2015): https://www.youtube.com/watch?v=fakVq9UhuDw

12 Early version of the OneCoin homepage, from WayBackMachine: https://web.archive.org/web/201408 23011912/http://www.onecoin.eu/

13 The 'Bitcoin fork' theory is supported by later court testimony of an IT forensic specialist from the State Criminal Police Office in Germany who had access to the original blockchain.

Chapter 5: We Sell Education!

1 Nigel Allan's wordpress page: https://nigelsallan.wordpress.com/page/2/

2 Järvinen, Petteri, *OneCoin – Suuri Bittirahahuijaus* (Docendo, 2020)

3 In some accounts of this early meeting, Pehr and Petri were presented with two MLM ideas: one was OneCoin; the other was an iteration of Ruja's original pension plan idea. It is not clear whether Ruja was present at this first meeting.

4 According to the Federal Trade Commission: 'Pyramid schemes now come in so many forms that they may be difficult to recognise immediately. However, they all share one overriding characteristic: they promise consumers or investors large profits based primarily on recruiting others to join their program, not based on profits from any real investment or real sale of goods to the public.' Some critics do not like this distinction and argue that even with a real product a company can still be a pyramid if they make misleading claims about success. In the most well-known case regarding MLM – '*In re Amway Corp*' – the FTC ruled that Amway was not a pyramid because a consultant must sell 70 per cent of their inventory each month to at least ten different customers to get the performance bonus – and there were

opportunities to sell back to Amway. This is known as the 'Amway Safeguard' and, in the US, this became the standard test of whether an MLM is functioning as a pyramid scheme.

5 Technically speaking, the Tycoon Trader package came with 60,000 tokens. However, the Tycoon Trader package tokens also 'split' twice, so any investor who waited a few weeks would have 240,000 tokens. In late 2014, the token-to-coin exchange ('the mining rate') was 5 tokens per coin, which meant 240,000 tokens generated 48,000 coins. However, within a year or two, the mining rate had increased to over 20, and so would generate fewer coins. As such it's not possible to say how many coins each package came with – it depended on when the package was bought and the 'mining rate' at the time.

6 Level 1 Education (these were known as 'OneAcademy'); OneCoin homepage on February 2015, available on Way-BackMachine: https://web.archive.org/web/2015020600 0933/http://www.onecoin.eu/page/details/about One-Coin.eu

7 The Starter Pack came with 1,000 tokens; Trader – 5,000 tokens; Pro Trader – 10,000 tokens; Executive Trader Trader – 30,000 tokens; and Tycoon Trader – 60,000 tokens.

8 Järvinen, Petteri, *OneCoin – Suuri Bittirahahuijaus* (Docendo, 2020)

9 'OneCoin Ruja Ignatova in Malaysia' (YouTube, 25 November 2014): https://www.youtube.com/watch?v=fe76hk4jQ4M

10 Author interview with one of the participants who attended the event itself.

Chapter 6: The Genesis Block

1 Examples from Facebook include: https://www.facebook.com/makeincomedaily/posts/7099352091 22099; https://www.facebook.com/groups/546215405482356/permalink/609648362472393

2 For Sebastian's speech at the launch event, see 'onecoin launch programme in hongkong' (YouTube, 2 February 2015): https://www.youtube.com/watch?v=fpTAKw-f9N6g. He helpfully listed the top ten countries in the network: China, Thailand, Malaysia, Finland ('It's quite small,' said Sebastian, 'but it has dedicated leaders'), Vietnam, Sweden, India, Russia, Indonesia and, surprisingly, the United States.

3 https://www.flashback.org/t2546019#. Author translated from the original. ('*Jag kan inte mer än hålla med, Ja tror verkligen på denna valuta och jag vet folk som verkligen tjänar stora pengar bara på att sprida budskapet. Så ta chansen och bli en del av detta innan det är försent . . .*' Also: '*Vet dock 2 stycken som inte har någon anledning alls att ljuga som berättade att dom har tagit ut pengar redan.*')

Chapter 7: Selling the Dream

1 'Igor Alberts Celebrates 32 years in MLM With $110 Million In Lifetime Earnings' (Business for Home, 19 October 2019): https://www.businessforhome.org/2019/10/igor-alberts-celebrates-32-years-in-mlm-with-110-million-in-lifetime-earnings/

2 Taylor, Jon M., 'The Case (for and) against Multi-level Marketing' (Consumer Awareness Institute, 2011): https://bit.ly/3EeT6Oq

3 Aron was one of three brothers (the other two were Christian and Stephan) from German-speaking Switzerland. Aron had been a level above Igor in Organo Gold. The Steinkellers had started their own MLM company called Coligus when they left Organo Gold in 2014, which they sold to OneCoin in early 2015.

4 Worre, Eric, *Go Pro – 7 Ways to Becoming a Network Marketing Professional* (Network Marketing Pro Inc, 2013), p. 50

5 Järvinen, Petteri, *OneCoin – Suuri Bittirahahuijaus* (Docendo, 2020)

6 This included working with Russian Israeli billionaire Arcadi Gaydamak. The affidavit is available here: http://www.less-entiel.lu/lup/06_2013/sandstone_affidavit.pdf

7 'OneCoin Review: 100-5000 EUR Ponzi point "cryptocur-rency"' (BehindMLM, 23 September 2014): https://behindmlm.com/mlm-reviews/onecoin-review-100-5000-eur-ponzi-point-cryptocurrency/

Chapter 8: Money Troubles

1 Taylor, Jon M., 'The Case (for and) against Multi-level Marketing' (Consumer Awareness Institute, 2011): https://bit.ly/3EeT6Oq

2 Liu, Heidi, 'The Behavioral Economics of Multilevel Mar-keting (*Hastings Business Lay Journal*, 2018): https://repository.uchastings.edu/hastings_business_law_journal/vol14/iss1/3/

3 The following endnote is another one for the reader with a genuine interest in MLM mechanics. OneCoin operated something called a 'matching bonus' system. A promoter would receive a 10 per cent commission from the sales of the people they'd brought in, plus 10 per cent of the recruits *those* people brought in; and then *20 per cent* of the recruits *they* brought in. In other words, the further down the down-line, the higher the commissions. Matching bonuses created an incentive to ensure a promoter helped those below him or her build a team.

4 The US Securities and Exchange Commission decided Bit-coin was a commodity on 18 September 2015, which likely precipitated this change in policy.

5 Igor appears to have misunderstood the phrase. It comes from Shakespeare's play *Hamlet*, and the protagonist's famous

soliloquy in Act III, Scene I: *For in that sleep of death what dreams may come, when we have shuffled off this mortal coil.*

6 Emem, Mark, 'OneCoin Scam Victim Files New York Lawsuit after $760,000 Loss' (CCN, 10 July 2019): https://www.ccn.com/onecoin-scam-victim-files-new-york-lawsuit-after-760000-loss/

7 Somerville, Hannah, 'Ex-council employees among those embroiled in alleged global scam' (*East London Advertiser*, 19 April 2019): https://www.eastlondonadvertiser.co.uk/news/crime/onecoin-promoted-to-east-london-residents-3624864

8 There are conflicting stories about how and when OneCoin entered Uganda. According to Dr Saturday David, it was via David Lombardi, an Italian OneCoin promoter. According to Petteri Järvinen, it was via someone called Jouko Juvonen.

9 'Corruption Perceptions Index 2018' (Transparency International, 2018)

10 In Uganda, it was common for investors to pay in cash in one of the offices, where they had an account set up by their uplines, and were given a code to access it. In Europe or the US, investment was usually done via direct bank transfers.

11 In fact, her foray in Maltese gambling companies started earlier. In May 2015, Ruja created an online gambling site called Coin Vegas, which was marketed as part of the OneCoin family, although very little actually happened with it.

12 The 'Sale Agreement of OneCoin Limited' which sets out this deal, is dated 1 October 2015. Technically the deal was signed between al Qassimi and Cesar Degracias Santos and Marisela Yasmin Simmons Hay, who were the on-paper nominal owners of OneCoin Limited. An undated 'Acknowledgement', signed by Ruja, elaborates on the nature of the deal: 'I, Ruja Ignatova, acknowledge that I have received 4 (four) USB flash memory drives (flash drives) from HE Sheikh Saoud Faisal al Qassimi

containing 230,000.00 Bitcoin, representing the full payment to buy OneCoin Company Limited.' The Acknowledgement also explains that she is handing over three cheques to al Qassimi, totalling 209,868,010 AED dated 7 September 2015, 20 September 2015 and 6 October 2015. (As of 7 October 2015, this amounted to €50.719 million according to xe.com's historic exchange rate data.) There is however some uncertainty over the precise dates. The 'Sale Agreement' refers to bitcoin being transferred to Ruja Ignatova in batches between 2014 and May 2015. It is possible therefore that the deal was agreed some point before October 2015. There are also at least two powers of attorney involving al Qassimi: one was granted from Cesar Degracias Santos and Marisela Yasmin Simmons Hay to al Qassimi, and notarised in the Seychelles on 4 October 2016. A separate power of attorney from Ruja herself to al Qassimi was notorised in Dubai on 27 September 2016.

13 This calculation is based on the bitcoin to dollar and dollar to Euro exchange rates on 1 October 2015. The four memory sticks contained 43,618, 30,850, 60,700 and 94,832 bitcoin respectively. Price calculations are based on the exchange rate and bitcoin price at the time of the deal. According to internal bank documents from Mashreq Bank, Ruja had around $50 million and €15 million in her OneCoin Mashreq accounts. Based on the available evidence, the deal appears to have revolved around the Mashreq accounts. The balance of any other Dubai-based company accounts is not known.

14 Letter from al Qassimi to Essam Issa al Humaidan, Dubai Attorney General, in late 2016. This is addressed from the 'Intergovernmental Collaborative Action Fund for Excellence' (ICAFE) of which al Qassimi was 'Extraordinary Ambassador'. Leaked documents also include a photocopy of Ruja's 'diplomatic identification' for ICAFE, in which she is referred to as 'special adviser'. Ruja's charity, the 'One World Foundation' is cited.

15 Letter from al Qassimi to Essam Issa al Humaidan, Dubai Attorney General, in late 2016. The letter included the notarised power of attorney. Essam Issa al Humaidan's response is not known.

Chapter 9: The Fenero Funds

1 Gilbert's company Zala Group originally arranged the pre-paid cards through a bank in the Caribbean, using a different name (OneNet). When that fell through, he issued cards through his own bank, JSC Capital Bank. OneCoin promoters could register to get a card, pay a few Euros, and then each week their commission was paid directly onto their card – which they could then use like a normal Mastercard.

2 *United States v. Mark S. Scott*, S10 17 Cr. 630 (ER). According to later court testimony given by Rosalind October, a Senior Financial Intelligence Analyst in the Major Economic Crimes Bureau, four transfers totalling $85 million were made in September 2015 from RavenR Dubai Noor bank account to Zala Group's account at Comerica Bank. In October 2015, two transfers totalling $13.9 million were sent from the Comerica Bank to Zala's Regions Bank account.

3 Lehmann, John, 'Boris Makes Racket over $1m deposit' (*New York Post*, 23 January 2003): https://nypost.com/2003/01/23/boris-makes-racket-over-1m-deposit/.

4 While not privy to the call itself, I have assumed this was discussed, since Ruja wrote this in a follow-up summary email she sent to Mark immediately after the phone call.

5 Robert Courtneidge worked a small number of days for Ruja advising on the cryptocurrency side of the business, most notably writing a detailed 'road map' in early 2016 to advise on how OneCoin could 'become the mass market crypto currency' with a 'stable price'. But from late 2016, Ruja no longer required his services.

6 *United States v. Mark S. Scott*, S10 17 Cr. 630 (ER), Document 318

7 They were: Fenero Equity Investments LP (which was formally incorporated on 1 March 2016), Fenero Financial Switzerland, Fenero Equity Investments II and Fenero Equity Investments (Cayman) I.

8 Mark had already contacted a Dublin law firm called Mason Hayes & Curran to act as secretary for the Irish entities. (On 11 March 2016, Mason Hayes & Curran introduced him to Bank of Ireland executives, who then opened several bank accounts for him.)

9 Fenero Equity Investments LP and Fenero Switzerland had accounts with DMS Cayman; Fenero (Cayman) and Fenero Equity Investments II at Deutsche Bank Caymans.

10 Author's private copy of agreements between IMS Singapore (25 March 2016), IMS Germany (21 March 2016) and IMS UK (15 March 2016) and Europe Emirates Group DMCC, represented by a formation agent called Adrian Oton. It describes that IMS will provide 'implementation, logistics and establishment of new corporate structures and banking in different worldwide jurisdictions'.

11 In fact, B&N Consult was a pre-existing company that Irina purchased. She became the limited partner of B&N Consult on 29 February 2016.

Chapter 10: London Calling

1 The London penthouse address was Abbots House, 23 St Mary Abbots Terrace.

Chapter 11: Waltenhofen Gusswerks

1 RilaCap was a consultancy Ruja founded around this time. The website read: 'RilaCap EOOD turns problems into opportunities. We are a company that actively invests in

distressed companies and creates value by operational optimisation i.e. allowing companies to focus on high profitable areas.' See internet achive (2011): https://web.archive.org/web/20111014235641/http://www.rilacap.com/pages/view/22

2 Beck, Sabine, 'Hoffen auf Gerechtigkeit' (*Schwäbische Zeitung*, April 2016): https://bit.ly/3paSWTX

Chapter 12: Happy Birthday, Cryptoqueen

1 According to the US government, Konstantin was earning over €10,000 per month and Ruja bought him a €3 million house in Sofia. Konstantin himself claimed he was paid only €3,000 a month to work for Ruja and that his house was worth only around €150,000.

Chapter 13: Money In

1 Under the BVI Approved Funds Act, regulated private equity funds need to appoint an administrator.

2 The agreement with Apex stipulated that the general partner (Mark Scott) had a legal obligation to notify Apex if he had any concerns or doubts in connection with the investors relating to money laundering, or if there were any changes in the status of the investors.

3 Paul was first introduced to Mark Scott through email in April 2016, via an Apex colleague in the New York office. In fact, Mark had tried to register his funds with another fund administrator first called Appleby, but he failed their due diligence test. Apex also administered a second fund called Fenero Financial Switzerland LP, but there was little or no activity on that fund under Apex's management.

4 As mentioned, Mason Hayes & Curran, a respected law firm in Dublin, acted as the company secretaries for Mark's Irish companies. They got in touch with the Bank of Ireland to set

up his accounts. According to the questionnaire Scott filled in for Bank of Ireland, this Irish company expected turnover in its bank account to be between €10 million and €25 million a year.

5 Apex sent DMS Bank Caymans a comfort letter on 9 May 2016.

6 *United States v. Mark S. Scott*, S10 17 Cr. 630 (ER), 14 November 2019, p. 152

7 *United States v. Mark S. Scott*, S10 17 Cr. 630 (ER), 31 August 2020. Gilbert's Fates Group sent almost $10 million in three wires to Fenero Equity Investments II between June and September 2016, but this appeared to be a distinct fund – this was the only money it received.

Chapter 15: Project X

1 Raonimanalina, N. and Fitzgibbon, W., 'Chinese oligarch could face scrutiny in Madagascar oil land grab' (*The Africa Report*, 8 January 2014): https://www.theafricareport.com/4903/chinese-oligarch-could-face-scrutiny-in-madagascar-oil-land-grab/

2 Yingzhi Yang, 'China prosecutes 98 people, recovers US$268 million in OneCoin cryptocurrency investigation, report says' (*South China Post*, May 2018)

3 Author's personal copy of the term sheet agreement.

4 Author's personal copy of the power of attorney

5 Originally the bank transfer was meant to go from Fenero Equities Investment LP to CryptoReal Investment Trust and then on to Barta Holdings. But Mark asked Apex if it could be wired from Fenero to Barta directly.

6 *United States v. Mark S. Scott*, S10 17 Cr. 630 (ER), 8 November 2019

7 The 'Venezuela deal' is one of the more mysterious aspect of Ruja's spending. In June 2016, Ruja emailed Mark saying,

'Mark, we need a pof [proof of funds] for 100 m. The entity does not matter. Until tomorrow. R.' 'To whom should it be addressed?' asked Mark. 'What's the deal? And please do not use LL email for these matters.' Max von Arnim, part-time external consultant to RavenR, replied, 'It is about the oil deal in VZ. Addressee is PDVAS. Thank you.' This deal may relate to the purchase of 29 pieces of oil extraction machinery in Venezuela. According to a 'reasonable expenses agreement' seen by the author, a Hong Kong company called 'Jacky Tacson' agreed to send a Venezuelan company called 'H&H CA Corp' approximately $500,000 a month for machinery maintenance. H&H CA CORP was also listed in Florida, with Irina Dilkinska as president: https://www.corporationwiki.com/p/2ejz92/hh-ca-corp. It is not known whether these deals ever took place. It has been explained to the author by a source close to Max von Arnim that his intended role was to provide analysis and advice on investment opportunities to RavenR; that his involvement with RavenR was limited as the necessary KYC documentation was never provided to him; and that Max von Arnim did not work for OncCoin and was never involved in receiving or directing any money flow.

8 Engert, Marcus, 'OneCoin konnte Milliarden stehlen, obwohl Banken die Behörden informiert hatten' (Buzzfeed, 26 September 2020): https://www.buzzfeed.com/de/marcusengert/onecoin-banken-fincenfiles

9 In a slightly skittish email on 13 July, Ruja emailed Mark and Gilbert saying: 'As I am having a lot of she-said he-said new issues popping up daily and unfortunately no visible results or clear schedule on what is happening on our project this is why I want to meet you both in person next week'.

10 Mark's email on 29 July 2016 read: 'We are just about to introduce another investor out of Hong Kong, documents coming your way later today, to subscribe for the majority of the remaining financial Fenero Switzerland Fund in tranches.'

11 In fact, Ruja's name had appeared on the contract between Dr Hui and CryptoReal Investment Trust, but Paul assumed that was just an authorised signatory, probably a lawyer.

12 Within a few months, however, Mark started having the same problem with their new administrator, Dave van Duynhoven at JP Fund Administration in the Caymans. In March 2017, David was asking Mark about Irina's source of wealth. 'Hi Irina,' wrote Mark. 'How will you show that you personally own tens of millions of dollars???? And have banks verify that?'

13 On 16 September 2016, Mark returned to Sofia and met Ruja at The Residence, a private members club where she often entertained visitors. No one knows what precisely Mark and Ruja agreed, although it seemed likely they discussed setting up a separate investment fund for Anatoly and Anton who were working at the RavenR office (Ruja called the pair her 'golden Russian boys') and creating a foreign exchange fund for Ivan Ivanov – another RavenR employee. After the meeting he texted his wife Lydia to say he'd just closed a 'huge deal' with Ruja.

14 *United States v. Mark S. Scott*, S10 17 Cr. 630 (ER), 8 November 2019. Preliminary Order of Forfeiture as to Specific Property and Substitute Assets / Money Judgement.

Chapter 16: Blockchain and Bjørn

1 'Bitcoin at its most fundamental level is a breakthrough in computer science,' wrote Silicon Valley's most famous investor, Marc Andreessen, in 2014. And blockchain finally solved the problem of 'how to establish trust between otherwise unrelated parties over an untrusted network like the Internet.' Andreessen, Marc, 'Why Bitcoin Matters' (*New York Times,* 21 January 2014): https://dealbook.nytimes.com/2014/01/21/why-bitcoin-matters/

2 Bjørn was not the only person they contacted regarding the role. On 4 October 2016, Nigel Chinnock found another blockchain specialist called Gijs Wouters, who Nigel's colleague contacted (also through LinkedIn), explaining they had a 'C Level Role with our client, a billion-dollar financial firm specialising in cryptocurrency'. The founder, explained Nigel in a later email, 'is a very sharp lady by the name of Dr Ruja'. Gijs looked into it and said he thought OneCoin was a scam and declined.

Chapter 17: What Happened to OneCoin's Blockchain?

1 *United States Government Sealed Complaint v Konstantin Ignatov* (6 March 2019).

Chapter 18: The Test

1 'OneCoin was trying to recruit a blockchain specialist last year' (Scam Detector, 23 February 2017): http://kusetukset. blogspot.com/2017/02/onecoin-was-trying-to-recruit.html
2 In level 2, for example, at least 1,623 out of 3,812 words were plagiarised, including the following sections: 1.1 'how does the stock exchange work' (copied from Yahoo Answers and disnat.com); 'The NASDAQ' (from *How Can I Get Started Investing in the Stock Market*); section 1.2 'stocks, mutual Funds and IPOs' (copied from *Personal Finance for Canadians for Dummies*).
3 'OneCoin 2015: Interview with Auditor Deyan Dimitrov 2015' (YouTube, 21 August 2015): https://www.youtube. com/watch?v=1pzDoT092q8

Chapter 19: Billionaires – On Paper

1 'Blockchain Dev: OneCoin using SQL database script to generate coins' (BehindMLM, 24 February 2017): https://

behindmlm.com/companies/onecoin/blockchain-dev-onecoin-using-a-sql-database-script-to-generate-coins/

2 In point of fact, it *was* possible to make a small profit from international postal reply coupons, but not at the scale Charles Ponzi was claiming.

3 OneCoin claimed to have 80,000–90,000 vendors on Dealshaker. But manually adding up every single available deal and vendor gave a far lower number. Duncan Arthur later told the BBC that there was never more than 10,000 vendors. These calculations are based on data collected by OneCoin critics, who monitored all listings available on the Dealshaker site. read: On 19 May 2017: 13 sellers together owned over 10 per cent of all the open deals in Dealshaker. According to OneCoin, there were 31,000 registered businesses back then – but there were only 10,800 open deals. Ari Widell ran a blog criticising OneCoin (and Dealshaker in particular). See: kusetukset.blogspot.com

4 'Duncan Arthur, London Dealshaker Training' (YouTube, November 2018): https://www.youtube.com/watch?v=-zD-npB0yfj4. Dealshaker worked on a franchise model. Duncan appointed franchise holders in each country, who were responsible for ensuring the deals were legal, followed the 'know your customer' anti-fraud rules, and were in line with Dealshaker's T&Cs.

5 'Fraud Plagues OneCoin's Dealshaker Platform' (BehindMLM, 28 April 2017): https://behindmlm.com/companies/onecoin/fraud-plagues-onecoins-dealshaker-platform/?sckattempt=1

Chapter 20: Well-spoken Professionals

1 According to internal accounting files, approximately 20 per cent of OneCoin's outgoing was on events and marketing (author's copy).

2 Dr Ruja Ignatova at the 4th EU Southeast European Summit by *The Economist*

3 According to the Solicitors Regulatory Authority, carrying out a form of due diligence on a company in which you have a 'financial interest' can give rise to conflicts of interest.

4 See for example, 'OneCoin Presentation by Nigel Allan' (YouTube, 7 May 2015): https://www.youtube.com/watch?v=fakVq9UhuDw

5 Memorandum: 'Regulatory aspects of multi-level marketing activities conducted by the OneLife Network' (October 2016)

6 Bartlett, Jamie, 'Why did the FCA drop its official warning about the OneCoin scam?' (BBC News, 11 August 2020): https://www.bbc.co.uk/news/technology-53721017. At the time the notice was removed, the FCA told one person who queried the decision that 'it had been on our website for a sufficient amount of time to make investors aware of our concerns'. This was a strange argument given OneCoin was still being actively promoted in the UK, and several alerts have remained live on the FCA's website for years. In a later statement to the BBC, the FCA said it was because it did not require FCA authorisation – and the decision was made in conjunction with the City of London Police. The City of London Police, however, told the BBC it was the FCA's responsibility.

Chapter 21: The Last Hurrah

1 Testimony of the live-in porter at Abbots House when Ruja lived there.

2 Pitt Arens replaced Pablo Munoz, who had taken over as CEO very briefly in late 2016. Munoz was a former Amway top seller in the United States. However, he found the pressure too great, and quickly left. Technically Pitt's contract started on 9 December 2016, but, for reasons that are unclear,

it wasn't announced until weeks later. See 'OneCoin Leaks: Ruja Ignatova's passport + Arens' contract' (BehindMLM, 25 January 2020): https://behindmlm.com/companies/one-coin/onecoin-leaks-ruja-ignatovas-passport-arens-contract/

3 Around late 2016, the national bank of Georgia revoked the banking licence for Gilbert Armenta's JSC Capital Bank for failure to comply with anti-money laundering rules.

4 Gary took a small propeller plane from the capital Antanana-rivo to a makeshift airstrip near the oil field and drove another three hours to Area 3112. Knowing nothing about oil fields, Gary saw a bit of machinery in the middle of some fenced off land, spoke to a couple of Dr Hui's people, and took a video on his phone. (He left satisfied that Ruja did in fact own a real oil field.)

Chapter 22: Operation Satellite

1 *United States v. Mark S. Scott*, S10 17 Cr. 630 (ER). Man-hattan District Attorney's Office senior financial intelligence analyst Rosalind October says that the department received a 'tip' in February 2016 about suspicious activities relating to Viola Accounts. (This was Christopher Hamilton's company.) She adds that some months later the United States Attorney was running a separate investigation. I assume this relates to the 'suspicious activity report' that the Bank of New York Mellon filed on 9 February 2017, which related to $350 million worth of suspicious banking activity. Fairly soon the two offices pooled their resources.

2 The original report of the raid here: Hawken, Abe, 'Police make biggest EVER UK money seizure as they arrest man, 58, with £30MILLION of banker's drafts in south Wales' (*Mail Online*, April 2016): https://www.dailymail.co.uk/news/article-3551654/Police-make-biggest-UK-money-

seizure-arrest-man-58-30MILLION-banker-s-drafts-south-
Wales.html

3 *United States v. Mark S. Scott*, S10 17 Cr. 630 (ER)

4 Details of these suspicious payments were published as part
of the 'fincen files' series: https://projects.icij.org/investi-
gations/fincen-files/confidential-clients/#/en/ruja-
ignatova/

5 According to later court testimony, UK law enforcement notified the Manhattan District Attorney's Office about the
Armenta/Viola Assets payments in February 2016. According
to Rosalind October, the senior financial intelligence analyst at
the Manhattan District Attorney's Office, 'approximately 13
months into our investigation [March 2017] we were working
parallel investigations [with the United States Attorney's Office]
and it was more useful for us to pool our reseources together
and be able to collaborate since we were investigating the same
targets'. It's not clear when the US District Attorney's investigation started, but the dates suggest it was likely sparked by the
Bank of New York Mellon reports, which were filed in December 2016 and February 2017. According to some reports, this
joint operation was known as 'Operation Satellite'.

Chapter 23: Connections

1 According to the Department of Justice, the money went from
Fenero Equity Investments LP's DMS Caymans account to
Fenero Equity Investments Ireland's Bank of Ireland account,
then to Fenero Securities Trading's Bank of Ireland account,
and finally via 11 wire transfers to the Dubai bank of 'Phoenix
Funds'. It wasn't always plain sailing. Mark even emailed Irina
in February 2017 saying 'things are not looking good . . . they
know pretty sure OneCoin/OneLife behind it.'

2 According to the *Cayman Gazette* and British Virgin Islands'
Gazette, Fenero Fintech Europe LP was struck off 28 June

2017 and the liquidation of Fenero Equity Investments started on 23 June 2017. (I have not been able to locate the others.) Mark then dissolved the three key Irish companies (Fenero Securities, Fenero PCT and Fenero Tradenext) in mid to late 2017. Fenero Equity Investments, however, continued to function. As late as January 2018, Mark changed directorship and added his own lawyer, Nicole Huesmann, as director. (This may have been because there was outstanding paperwork that needed completing before he could strike it off.)

3 *United States v. Mark S. Scott*, S10 17 Cr. 630 (ER).

4 'Dr Ruja Ignatova on OneLife STOCK IPO, XCOINX EXCHANGE and New Business Model at Macau – May 7, 2017' (YouTube, 8 May 2017): https://www.youtube.com/watch?v=dMUxAfbAy1M

5 Author's personal copy of the PowerPoint slides, entitled 'Investor Presentation'.

6 There were concerns that neither of these plans would work if she couldn't fix her blockchain. Any potential buyer would probably send round technical experts to analyse OneCoin's tech credentials. Similarly, listing shares on a public stock exchange would require full disclosure of company accounts, not to mention independent audits of the blockchain. At the OneCoin corporate event in Macau in May 2017, Ruja decided to address it head on. Her new CEO Pitt Arens told the 5,000-strong crowd that the company had commissioned a blockchain 'audit' from a Singapore company called DX Markets, which had reported that OneCoin had a functioning blockchain. 'Here is the statement, we have the blockchain,' Kari Wahlroos told the audience, standing beside a large screen, which displayed a sentence from the audit, which read 'The OneCoin private blockchain system ... has been designed to satisfy the company's requirements'. (Pitt claims he was given assurances by the IT

team in Bulgaria that there was a brand new blockchain 'ordered and paid'.) Bjørn Bjercke would later contact the CEO of DX Markets, a young tech specialist called Marcello Casil. Marcello admitted he hadn't been granted access to OneCoin's technology and hadn't seen any blockchain. His 'audit' was in fact simply a paper about *theoretical* technology DX Markets could potentially build for OneCoin in the future. DX Markets was a blockchain company based in Singapore run by Marcello Casil. Casil was an adviser for a company run by Jed Grant. Grant was a co-founder and partner of Frank Schneider's Sandstone. Casil signed an NDA and quickly wrote a report describing what kind of things a future, retroactively fit blockchain might do. The 'OneCoin private blockchain' Kari described didn't actually exist. (Marcello Casil later admitted, 'I don't know what they have or had . . . the work I've done was not based on their existing IT systems'.)

7 In case you're curious, she wrote: 'Pls make it however for 18 and make sure there are 3 bowls / plates each and two soup terrines. We will need one coffee can and two tea-pots . . . also what are these epergines? Maybe you send a catalogue of the non standard pieces?' This is proof (should any be needed) that even criminal masterminds are interested in kitchenware.

Chapter 24: Things Fall Apart

1 Gilbert's private jet, a Gulfstream IV aircraft, flew into Shannon, Ireland, en route to Sofia on 21 Jul 2017 (and then back on 28 July 2017); and returned to Shannon on 13 August 2017, and back again on 8 September 2017.

2 'Ad Ernstig Mismanagement MIO' (*Knipselkrant*, December 2012): https://knipselkrant-curacao.com/ad-ernstig-mismanagement-mio/

3 Pitt Arens announced the news to a group of senior OneCoin

promoters at a special meeting at the Sofia office in early September, telling them that a new company called 'Golden Gate Investment' would formally run OneCoin's ICO, which would start in October with an 'information phase', followed by a brand-new token sale, to last for another year; at this point the coin would finally go public. See 'OneCoin Affiliates Claim IPO Dropped' (BehindMLM, September 2017): https://bit.ly/3miNJHM. Irina Dilkinska was put in charge of running the ICO. She set up a new website (www.onecoinico.io) on 25 September 2017, incorporated a new company in Panama called AHS Latam, and used the same director – Andri Andreou – who was director of both RavenR London and RavenR Dubai. AHS Latam was the holding company that owned the ICO tokens. To make things more confusing, Ruja called the new ICO tokens OFCs, which was the same name they'd used for the IPO shares.

4 *United States v. Armenta Indictment (Sealed)* – Document 4 (Docket Number: 1:17-cr-00556). This was filed 12 September 2017, but was made public in April 2020.

5 In a subsequent court case in Wales, the former marine employed by Gilbert Armenta admitted trying to persuade Christopher Hamilton to return the money but the jury ruled it didn't constitute harassment.

6 *United States v. Armenta Indictment (Sealed)* – Document 4 (Docket Number: 1:17-cr-00556).

Chapter 26: Flight

1 *United States v. Konstantin Ignatov*, S7 17 Cr. 630 (ER), Document 91

2 This is according to the testimony of Konstantin Ignatov given under oath at the trial of Mark Scott. Whether or not this was a transcript of the secret recordings, or a transcript of his court proceedings, is not clear.

3 Around one month before her Ryanair flight to Athens, Ruja emailed Konstantin, asking him to organise a meeting with her head of compliance, Veselina Valkova, in order to 'discuss the online casinos'.

4 The date of October 2017 is specifically mentioned by Ivan Gershev, head of the Bulgarian Specialised Prosecutor's Office (a division of the Prosecutor's Office). Gershev became the State Prosecutor soon afterwards. 'Неутрализираха международна група за пране на пари чрез уанкойн' (YouTube, 19 January 2018): https://www.youtube.com/watch?v=-ou3lKge_wY

Chapter 27: The Day After

1 RavenR had been charging a monthly fee to 'One Network Services Limited' to cover the costs of the RavenR office.

2 Frank Ricketts agreed to rejoin OneCoin in a more senior role while he was in Pattaya, Thailand, in September 2017, with his OneCoin downline called 'OneWorld'. (Surprisingly, Juha Parhiala even turned up briefly.)

Chapter 28: The Raid

1 Interview with former employee of OneCoin who was working there during the raid and asked to remain anonymous.

2 McGarry, Dan, 'The Companies We Keep' (*Daily Post*, 5 May 2018): https://www.dailypost.vu/opinion/the-companies-we-keep/article_07616bfb-0705-5dbf-a89e-a75919c4c367.html

Chapter 29: Monkeys

1 RISG Limited certificate of incumbency (author's copy).

2 It may of course have listed one of her trusted associates, lawyers or family members (I have not seen the document).

3 Ruja had set RavenR up as a family office in Dubai, to 'focus on wealth accumulation and long-term capital appreciation through investments in high-quality businesses from around the globe', with herself as sole shareholder and director.

4 RavenR Capital Limited company filings are available at Companies House: https://find-and-update.company-information. service.gov.uk/company/10178932

Chapter 30: Arrests

1 Young, Kristen, 'Prosecutors Argue Over Evidence in Barnstable Man's OneCoin Case' (*Cape Cod Times*, October 2019)

2 *United States v. Mark S. Scott*, S10 17 Cr. 630 (ER), Document 318

3 *United States v. Mark S. Scott*, S10 17 Cr. 630 (ER), Document 19, 13 September 2019

Chapter 34: Co-operation

1 Konstantin Ignatov bail application letter, *United States v. Konstantin Ignatov*, S7 17 Cr. 630 (ER), Document 91, 28 June 2019

Chapter 35: The Missing Cryptoqueen

1 'OneCoin/OneLife leader King Jayms shoots: "pretending I see the OneLife haters"' (YouTube, 5 October 2019): https://www.youtube.com/watch?v=g6SuUfUiwzU

Chapter 36: The Dubai Mansion

1 'Amendment to the Memorandum & Articles of OneCoin Limited'. Dated 28 February 2017, stamped 1 March 2017. This case is also explained in the transcript of case number 724 (of 2020) at the Dubai Commerical Court. The court

filings explicitly mentions that Ruja received 230,000 bitcoin from al Qassimi as part of the Sale Agreement.

2 At the time of writing, the most recent hearing took place on 26 May 2021. Ruja Ignatova was plaintiff, and al Qassimi the respondent. Lawyers apparently acting for Ruja argued that the sale contract of 28 February 2017 (in which al Qassimi became sole shareholder of OneCoin Limited) should be annulled. At the time of writing the three cheques totalling AED 210 million Ruja handed over as part of the Sale Agreement had still not been cashed: and whoever the court ultimately determines in the rightful owner of OneCoin Limited may be able to access those funds. It is not clear whether Ruja herself is personally involved in this case.

Afterword: Trials

1 Details about the case are available from Court Listener: https://www.courtlistener.com/docket/7829201/434/united-states-v-scott/

2 Hennebert, Jean-Michel, 'Frank Schneider pas encore prêt à être extradé' (*Luxembourg Times*, 23 September 2021): https://www.wort.lu/fr/granderegion/frank-schneider-pas-encore-pret-a-etre-extrade-614c5027de135b9236015c24; Kaiser, Guy, 'Een Dag aus dem Liewen vum Frank Schneider' (GKOnline, 4 October 2021): https://guykaiser.lu/een-dag-aus-dem-liewen-vum-frank-schneider-2/

ACKNOWLEDGEMENTS

There are many people who helped me enormously in writing this book, but for several reasons most might prefer not to be named at this point. Needless to say a lot of people were very generous with their time and insights: they know who they are. None of this would have been possible without Georgia Catt from the BBC, who first told me about OneCoin and whose talents meant millions of people became interested in this story. There are plenty of other BBC people who made the original podcast a success, notably Rob Byrne, Philip Sellars, Rachel Simpson and Jason Phipps. My agent Caroline Michel is always on call, no matter what time or how small the problem. Andrew Goodfellow and Suzanne Connelly at Penguin Random House were a delight to work with and Vanessa Milton made the legal reads almost enjoyable. My family and friends, as ever, were a constant source of comfort, advice and calm and I'd name them all if I could.

I would like to pay special tribute to BehindMLM and the dozens of people who contributed to it through the years. At times it might have felt like a thankless task, but you never know who else is reading your late night posts.

Finally, to the people who invested in Ruja's promise of financial freedom: I'm sorry for your loss. It's a sign of strength, not weakness, to admit you were wrong. For those brave enough to speak out – thank you from all of us.